Chelsea School Research Centre Edition
Volume 9

Marc Keech/Graham McFee (eds.)

Issues and Values in Sport and Leisure Cultures

Meyer & Meyer Sport

British Library Cataloguing in Publication Data
A catalogue record for this book is available from the British Library

Issues and Values in Sport and Leisure Cultures /
Marc Keech/Graham McFee (eds.).
– Oxford : Meyer & Meyer Sport (UK) Ltd., 2000
(Chelsea School Research Centre Edition ; Vol. 9)
ISBN 1-84126-055-X

© 2000 by Meyer & Meyer Sport (UK) Ltd.
Oxford, Aachen, Olten (CH), Vienna,
Québec, Lansing/ Michigan, Adelaide, Auckland, Johannesburg
Member of the world
Sportpublishers' Association (WSA)
Cover design: Walter J. Neumann, N&N Design-Studio, Aachen
Cover exposure: frw, Reiner Wahlen, Aachen
Typesetting: Myrene L. McFee
Printed and bound in Germany by
Mennicken, Aachen
e-mail: verlag@meyer-meyer-sports.com
ISBN 1-84126-055-X

Chelsea School Research Cent
Volume 9

Issues and Values in Sport and Lei

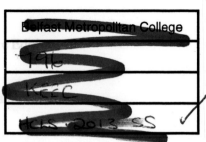

CONTENTS

Locating Issues and Values in Sport and Leisure Cultures
Marc Keech and Graham McFee 1

Sport and Nationalism
Claudio Tamburrini 25

Money, Morality or the Morgue? Educational Considerations
in the Politics of Anti-doping Policies for Sport
Marc Keech 55

Excellence and Expedience? Olympism, Power
and Contemporary Sports Policy in England
Ian McDonald 83

"Money can't drag you through another six tackles":
Amateurism, Professionalism and Rugby
Robert Ackerman, Mike McNamee
and Scott Fleming 101

'Going All The Way': Female Football Fans and
'Ladette' Culture in the UK
Joyce Sherlock and Nicola Elsden 123

The Media Spectacle of Women at the Olympics:
Dissimulation, Legitimation and Issues
of Patriarchy
Gill Lines 141

Teaching Moral Values Through Physical Education
and Sport
Andrew Theodoulides 167

Sport and Values: The Political Value of Sport in Germany
Udo Merkel 187

From the Field: Sydney 2000 and an
      Olympics Research Agenda
      Alan Tomlinson 207

Sport as Theatrical Event
      Rebecca Scollen 229

The Persistence of Value: An Olympic Case-study
      Graham McFee 255

Index   279

ABOUT THE AUTHORS

Robert Ackerman is rugby master at Glanalmond School in Scotland. He previously taught Physical Education in New Zealand, played international Rugby League for Wales and was a British Lion in Rugby Union in 1983. Robert was assistant coach to the Welsh Rugby League World Cup team 1996–6, and currently coaches the West of Scotland club in the Scottish first division.

Nicola Elsden is Young Woman's Co-Ordinator for Watford Area Youth Service (Herts County Council and Watford Borough Council). Currently she is working to establish a support group for teenage mothers and young women's groups. She graduated from De Montfort University Bedford in Sport & Leisure Studies in 1999 and continues to support Watford Football Club fanatically. The empirical research for the paper was conducted under the supervision of Dr. Joyce Sherlock.

Scott Fleming has been with the School of Sport at Cheltenham and Gloucester College of Higher Education since February 1999. Formerly with the University of Brighton and the University of Wales Institute, Cardiff, he has written in different places and presented to a variety of audiences on racism and ethnicity, methodological matters, and 'Fair Play'. He is the author of *'Home and Away': Sport and South Asian Male Youth*, (Avebury, 1995).

Marc Keech is a lecturer in sport and leisure studies in the Chelsea School at the University of Brighton. He graduated in Sport and Recreation Studies, holds a PGCE in Further and Higher Education and gained his PhD from Staffordshire University. Marc has worked in both Further and Higher Education and acted as consultant to Local Authorities and Colleges of Further Education. His research interests are in the politics and history of domestic and international sports policy. Recently, he has written a number of articles on the history and politics of sport in South Africa and is currently engaged in projects examining the utility of sport development policies.

Gill Lines is Senior Lecturer in Socio-cultural aspects of Physical Education in the Chelsea School at the University of Brighton. Formerly a Physical Education teacher with eighteen years experience in comprehensive schools in London and Essex, Gill gained her MA and PhD from the University of Brighton. Her research interests focus on the role of the media in the production and consumption of young people's identities, gender issues in sport and PE and the management and development of the PE curriculum. She was co-editor (with Udo Merkel and Ian McDonald) of *The Production and Consumption of Sport Cultures: Leisure, Culture and Commerce* (Leisure Studies Association, 1998).

Ian McDonald is a Senior Lecturer in the Chelsea School at the University of Brighton. He was formerly Co-Director of the Centre for Sport Development Research at Roehampton Institute and was also centrally involved in the campaign *Hit Racism for Six* in cricket. His research interests are in sport, racism and national identity and the politics of sports policy. He has written a number of articles on the politics of Hindu Nationalism in sport in modern India and is co-editor (with Ben Carrington) of *'Race', Sport and British Society*, to be published by Routledge in May 2001.

Graham McFee is Professor of Philosophy at the University of Brighton, and a member of the Chelsea School. His research interests include the philosophy of Wittgenstein, the aesthetics of dance, the nature of research (qualitative research/ action research), and the cultural study of sport. His publications include *Understanding Dance* (Routledge, 1992), *The Concept of Dance Education* (Routledge, 1994), *Free Will* (Acumen, 2000); and, as well as edited other collections, he edited *Dance, Education and Philosophy* (Meyer & Meyer, 1999)

Mike McNamee is Reader in applied philosophy in the Leisure and Sport Research Unit at Cheltenham and Gloucester College of Higher Education. His main research interests lie in philosophy of education, leisure and sport, and in applied ethics. He is co-editor of *Ethics and Sport* (Routledge, 1998) and of a series of the same name (also Routledge). He is currently president of the International Association for the Philosophy of Sport.

Udo Merkel is Senior Lecturer in the Chelsea School at the University of Brighton. He holds degrees in the Social Sciences and Sport Sciences from the University of Cologne and in the Sociology of Sport from the University of Leicester, as well as a PhD from the University of Oldenburg. Before he joined the University of Brighton in 1994, he was in charge of a research centre for comparative European Sport and Leisure Studies at the German Sport University in Cologne. During this time, he successfully completed an EU-funded research project on racism and xenophobia in European Sport in which six European countries were involved. The results were published in *Racism and Xenophobia in European Football* (co-edited by Walter Tokarski) (Meyer & Meyer, 1996). His research and academic interests are in the Politics and Sociology of Sport and Leisure, comparative European Studies and Football Cultures. He has published widely in these areas and is currently preparing a monograph *Sport in Divided Germany*. Most recently, he has investigated the hidden social and political history of the German Football Association, published in *Soccer and Society*.

Rebecca Scollen works as an arts industry consultant and academic. Rebecca is a Theatre Studies PhD candidate in her final year at the Queensland University of Technology in Brisbane, Australia. Her thesis, Building New Audiences: Post Performance Audience Reception in Action, presents a model for developing new audiences for the theatre, using a combination of post performance reception methods. She has a keen interest in sport and all other artforms. Rebecca believes that the Australian theatre industry should look to the sporting industry for ideas to improve audience numbers for the future.

Joyce Sherlock is Principal Lecturer at De Montfort University. A member of the School of Education in the newly founded Faculty of Education and Sports Science, based in Bedford, Joyce is Senior Tutor and teaches Social and Cultural Studies. Other research interests include women's sports culture and triathlon, and identity, wilderness trekking and offshore cruising. She is also Treasurer of the UK Leisure Studies Association.

Claudio Tamburrini is a Senior Researcher at the Department of Philosophy, Gothenburg University. He has published "Crime and Punishment?" (his PhD dissertation) and articles on penal philosophy and philosophy of sports, with some of the latter essays collected in *The 'Hand of God'?* (Actus Universitatis Gothenburgensis, 2000). He has recently co-edited *Values in Sport* (Routledge, 2000) with Torbjörn Tännsjö and has played professional soccer in Argentina.

Andrew Theodoulides is a lecturer in Physical Education in the Chelsea School at the University of Brighton, and pathway leader for the PGCE PE/Dance Courses. He is currently completing his doctoral studies in the area of children's personal, social and moral development within physical education. The main focus of his work concerns the practical and pedagogical challenges faced by teachers in promoting these dimensions of pupils learning.

Alan Tomlinson is Professor/Reader in Sport and Leisure Studies in the University of Brighton, and Course Leader of the University's Certificate in Research Methodology. His areas of primary research interest include the application of cultural studies to the analysis of sport, the study of sport as part of a critical sociology of consumption, challenges of investigative sociology, and the contribution of FIFA to the development of world soccer. Alan is internationally renowned as a lecturer, and has published widely, including *The Game's Up: Essays in the Cultural Analysis of Sport, Leisure and Popular Culture* (Arena/ Ashgate, 1999), and (with John Sugden) both *FIFA and the Contest for World Football* (Polity, 1998) and *Great Balls of Fire: How Big Money is Hijacking World Football* (Mainstream, 1999). He is also editor of many collections, including *Gender, Sport and Leisure* (Meyer & Meyer, 1995).

LOCATING ISSUES AND VALUES IN SPORT AND LEISURE CULTURES

Marc Keech and Graham McFee
Chelsea School, University of Brighton

Introduction

As the euphoria surrounding the Sydney Olympics recedes, it seems appropriate to reconsider the 'state of play'; and, in particular moral purge that 'sport' in general appears to be attempting recently. The Olympic movement has, historically, sought to promote values which are encapsulated in the 'Olympic Spirit'. However, the reality seems to be that sport is riddled with corruption (of various sorts), and subject to political mishandling. Scandal is now commonplace in the commodified, global sports marketplace. One only has to look at the excesses of the International Olympic Committee during the 1990s (Jennings, 1996; Jennings and Sambrook, 2000), consider the Tour De France (Waddington, 2000), or view the 'Cronjegate' affair and the Indian police's investigation into match-fixing in cricket to realise the extent to which sport has been appropriated. But, as Katwala (2000: p. 4) points out, "we don't expect an effective response to it. Those at the apex of governance are often at the centre of sporting controversies". Should it be a surprise, therefore, that governments are taking an increasingly active approach over sport, looking to establish a consensus over what value sport holds for contemporary society? The issue for those involved with any form of governance in sport is to ensure that sport is run effectively emphasising the values ascribed to it.

The value of sport is a central issue in local, regional, national and global dimensions of sport and leisure cultures, for from this derives a broad-based research agenda for the plethora of 'issues' that investigate the 'value' of and the 'values' attached to sport. As we will see, De Coubertin concluded that the cure for the social ills of the late nineteenth century was educational reform (Hoberman, 1993) and that sport only provided the means through which to address his concerns (Kidd, 1996: p. 84). As Bruce Kidd (1996: p. 86) further asserts, participation in Olympic sports does not encourage a concern for social issues, nor enhance the ability to address them. Thus, the image of Olympic sport in the mass media often clashes with the ideals that the movement purports to aspire to. One contention explored briefly here is that the uncritical pursuit of sporting excellence by the Olympic movement has permeated the practice of sport at local levels — that is to say, policies and programmes which have explicit social-policy objectives, are often fundamentally flawed. There needs to be a clearer demonstration as to how sport does address social problems in order for stronger and more substantive value to be identified in programmes attached to it. As Tony Skillen (1998) suggests:

> To those who think that sport ... should be in the core of an educational curriculum, it must be axiomatic that the practice of sport itself is good and that it is and of itself an education ... That sport may reach such an ideal is surely possible precisely through the central fact that blinds some people to its value: its being 'only play' its abstraction from the serious business of life, its pointlessness. (Skillen, 1998: p. 169)

The implication herein is the inherent paradox of sport — a forum for activity that can seem to have no intrinsic value whilst being held up as a beacon of virtue. More pragmatically Skillen (1998) goes on to demonstrate how sport actually inculcates 'values' that have little positive application.

Such ideas might seem to support a unitary conception of appropriate topics for study: we have written about *the* such-and-such. Instead, our argument, explicitly in this chapter but implicitly throughout the book, is one which recognises thematic continuities within varied kinds of difference. Thus we consider the diversity within the text as indicative both of diversities of interest, methodology, etc., appropriately located in the field and of what one might expect from shared thematic concerns.

Thus, the 'issues' for sport and leisure cultures explored in this volume are issues which derive from the differential social importance that sport (along with other leisure activities) may enjoy. Such issues (not all explored here) might include the application to sporting contexts and practices of the following: violence, 'fair play', gender equity, doping, child abuse, sexual harassment, disability, environmental concerns. Thus, while they may not all be *strictly* characterised as concerning *values*, this would not be too far wide of the mark: for all pose questions, in some way or other, concerning what we ought or ought not to do in certain situation, what it would be right or wrong to do in those situations, or what can be learned about the importance ascribed (by us or more generally) to particular activities.

Many believe that the opportunity to engage in sport is a fundamental human right, a belief highlighted in a powerful speech made by Nelson Mandela, the former President of South Africa, when he insisted that every child in South Africa had three fundamental rights: to health, to education, and to sport. At the least, this is a rhetoric commonly deployed by governments: but what is its basis? If we are to consider the value of sport, it would appear essential to explore the extent to which participants accept that they must conform with accepted practice in sport. Sport is inherently competitive, and most of us lucky enough to enjoy sport marvel at the competition between opponents whether it be in local league football, or in the hyper-glare of the world's media at the Olympic Games. Yet competition means one winner and one (though often many more) loser. When the former American football coach Vince Lombardi told us that in sport 'Winning wasn't everything' then we could have considered about what else individuals may take from sport. But Lombardi added the caveat that winning was actually the 'only thing'. Is that the reality of sport for most participants or spectators? We doubt it. Yet the experience of sport is rarely unmixed. For example, the pain incurred by athletes as a consequence of playing an excessive amount of sport when younger can be debilitating, but they (we!) accept the pain because they have consented to follies of the past — the past in which they were strong, fit and healthy. Any time we play a sport, we consent to the possible harms that may be caused by playing that game, within its rules. Because most sports require physical exertion, they carry some risk of harm; and in contact sports that harm may be caused by the legitimate and permissible actions of an opponent. Generally, acts which are within the rules of the game concerned are morally acceptable, even if they end-up causing harm. Indeed, as formalists[1] rightly note, if we move too far from the rules, we are no longer engaged in that sporting activity. This might suggest a 'high seriousness' to sport.

But sport has always had its 'flip-side' — the value that it brings to its participants, the enjoyment, the fun, the education, the vehicle through which so much else can be achieved or addressed. So one candidate set of values for sport might lie in its instantiation of ideals. Thus, for instance, the concept of 'Sport for All' not *just* as an egalitarian ideology since, if sport is available to, and (potentially) beneficial for, all, we can begin to articulate some of the values it might promote. So that one might think that, in the context of 'Sport for All' (when realised), sport promotes values of equity, inclusiveness, fairness, and respect. And one might see how these flow from the idea of 'for all'.

One of the issues becoming increasingly prevalent in discussions of sport concerns what value sport holds for contemporary societies. In contrast, the value of sport is often affected not just by economics, but by the extent to which issues deform ways in which sport is viewed by the public. Douglas Booth (1993: p. 1) argued that "modern social thought [has] idealised and consecrated sport" and in consequence, one might suggest, sport became lost, shrouded in a fog of amoral universalism. Yet, as Booth (1993) noted, there is little reason to take sport to be acultural, ahistorical, and apolitical. As Booth stressed, sport is inherently competitive and can inculcate values of superiority, thereby minimising other value-based judgements. Yet Booth convincingly makes the case that the dominant conception of sport identifies socially-generated interests and beliefs that are diverse and constantly changing, whether they be true or false (Booth, 1993: pp. 15–16).

If one is to believe Brohm (1978) or Rigauer (1982), sport had lost all its inherent value some time ago; but sport continues its permeation into global consciousness today. The issue is how to get value out of sport, not in the narrow sense of sport as an end in itself. Rather, by accepting that sport's moral purity rests in a bygone age and that those involved in all levels of sport maintain its integrity as a social institution, not as a social problem. For, as Eric Dunning (1999) has told us, "sport matters", whilst Lincoln Allison (1998) and Peter Donnelly (1997) have both urged the importance of "taking sport seriously". Views that reaffirm the positive moral and social qualities of sport have been consistently challenged but governments around the world continue to develop increasingly sensitive political strategies that utilise the profile of sport as a mechanism to address aspects of social policy, a topic to which we will return.

Here, then, we will first say something about the unity of the area of enquiry, as a way of explaining some of the unities we see within this volume. Then we will sketch some of the context for discussions of the value of sport, including the idealism often associated with such a project, and explore (briefly) one central idea with a policy dimension: namely, the idea of 'sport for all'. Further, we will outline some more specific themes from this text, before turning to a crucial epistemological issue which — although of great importance — is only be broached here. In doing so, we will begin to instantiate an argument about the nature of this area of academic study. For our concerns with issues and values in sport and leisure cultures are also concerns with the methods of enquiry (and their underlying assumptions) appropriate to the investigation of such matters.

It is a mistake to imagine that some simple account can capture the relationship between (say) sport and society. As Clement Greenberg (1993 p. 94) put the corresponding point for art:

> Society contains and throws light on art, receiving light in return, but this reciprocity does not completely explain either art or society.

So we should not expect some simply-put relation here: not as some uni-dimensional process of 'mirroring' or 'representing', nor as just the development of a cultural practice. Rather, complex sets of interconnections are to be expected, some normative, some descriptive. Here, therefore, we will include some abstract discussion of the context of such issues and analyses.

Unity in the study of sport and leisure?

If this picture of diversity were correct, should we expect that a single methodology (or small set of them) amounted to *the* way to interrogate sport and leisure activities? Clearly not: but then what forms might discussions take? One form, implicitly endorsed here, begins from a kind of inclusive pluralism: that various author pursue *their* interests, the issues that vex *them*, with their own methodological tools.

But might some more unified position be hoped for? Or might the pluralism itself be given a theoretical footing? There are reasons to doubt the likelihood of either outcome. First, the connections between issues and methods makes it seem unlikely that a single framework would unify all the issues: in a language recently fashionable, there seems little hope for a "grand narrative" (Lyotard, 1984 p. xxiv). To offer a simple model, we would not expect the concerns about my sports-activity of my doctor and my friend to have the same basic structure: the friend is interested in what I can do — say, can I play soccer on Saturday? But, while the question here *might* be better put as asking whether or not I *can* play soccer (full-stop), it is more likely that the range of answers will draw on something like: do I have the time? (Am I going to another friend's party?) Do I have the money to get to the venue, or the requisite kit? And so on. Of course, on that list will be a question the doctor might have asked: have I recovered from the hamstring injury? Yet the other range does not address anything the doctor's methodologies give him access to. In this way, what seemed like *one* request (whether I could play soccer on Saturday) becomes visible as potentially *numerous* requests, each implying a methodological solution. So we cannot expect one unified set of (candidate) answers to questions about whether so-and-so can play *soccer* (let alone *sport*) on Saturday: that form of words can embrace numerous different questions, each with its own (implicit) methodology. In this vein, then, we cannot expect a single 'over-arching' theory to incorporate *all* the soccer-playing-on-Saturday issues, for there is no *all* here, no finite totality of issues (McFee, 2000b: pp. 121–123). Once we recognise this point for one such topic, we can hardly hope for more from a general consideration of sport, or of leisure.

Perhaps, then, the hope should be for a *justified* pluralism: many methods are required, since many questions (or issues) are possible; but some basis might be sought which allows us to reject candidate perspectives — as we might feel that, say, the reading of horoscopes was not an appropriate technique to employ here. The difficulty, though, is to produce a principled basis for rejecting theoretical stances which is both plausible and robust enough to be helpful. For example, we might say that it is important that any methodological stances lead to the *truth* about the social world. The trouble here is that, while admirable, this seems too strong a constraint — we may never get to the truth about the social world, but if we are actively seeking it, that seems enough. The difficulty, then, is that this is just what is contentious: the advocates of horoscopes will argue that they too are searchers after truth! (We defer until later discussions which suggest that *truth* is not to be had: that the notion makes no sense in this context.) Again, we might urge that only *reputable* disciplines should be included, or only those that treat of *social phenomena*. Yet neither contrast is robust enough to distinguish (in a wholly general way) the suitable from the bogus; for the idea of a *social* phenomenon is contentious, while we also recognise that *having* high repute is not the same as *deserving* it!

Bewildering as it may seem, these considerations speak for a pragmatic pluralism: if a methodology looks fruitful (say, if some theorist wishes to employ it), and if it seems a candidate for making a contribution within more general constraints of reasonableness and rationality (hallmarks for academic enquiry), it should at least be considered. And, when addressing the notion of what is *reasonable* here, we should again prefer an inclusive position. In this vein, Stuart Hampshire has recently suggested that — for many cases — a model of rationality based on, roughly, *court-room practice* would be revealing, especially when contrasted with a (mistaken?) view of the linearity of logic or scientific reasoning. He asks:

> What is gained by representing the concept of rationality as having its origins in the adversary reasoning typical of legal and moral disputes about evidence, rather than in the formal deductions and proofs of logic and mathematics? (Hampshire, 2000: pp. 13–14)

And his reply identifies that, as one advantage of such a move:

> … an account can be given of how a common norm of rationality develops naturally from the necessities of social life; that is, from the inevitably recurrent conflicts which must be resolved if communities are to survive. On the other hand, the notion of pure reason, the eternal and governing part of the soul, is a theory without explanatory value. (Hampshire, 2000: p. 14)

Thus, this conception ties rational discussion to human practice; and also indicates how discussion might move forward that view of what follows from what, or what is implied by what — for these might themselves be debated topics.

Whatever such a view might offer to the consideration of issues in sport and leisure, it will tend away from a narrow conception of what is permissible. And such breadth is, in turn, what we might hope for when faced with the complexity of the social world, and of sport's place(s) within it.

The value of sport — an idealisation?

The idealism implicit in claims to the intrinsic value of sport is curious. Historically, sport has emerged as a breeding ground for the inculcation of 'appropriate' social and moral values (cf. Horne *et. al.*, 1999: pp. 3–21). The influence of the English public school system on De Coubertin's vision of Olympic values has been well documented (Biddiss, 1997; Kidd, 1996). From these beginnings, sport began to benefit from the 'presumption of innocence' — an innocence that was rapidly replaced during the latter half of the twentieth century. For the most part, the supposed relationship between sport and value is clearly located within the claims of the International Olympic Committee. The International Olympic Committee (IOC), the most significant non-governmental international actor within sport, has always projected sport as a vehicle for promoting world peace. In turn, the Olympic Games are the most powerful expression of international sport. Sport in general benefits from the presumption of innocence and Olympic officials are quick to promote 'Olympism' as a form of moral hygiene which can be applied efficiently to large numbers of people. The Olympic movement is therefore projected as being based on principles of universal opportunity and equality (Hoberman, 1986: p. 29). The Olympic Charter sets out the principles of modern Olympic sport:

> The goal of Olympism is to place sport everywhere at the service of the harmonious development of man, with a view to encouraging the establishing of a peaceful society concerned with the preservation of human dignity ... The Olympic Movement led by the IOC stems from Modern Olympism ... The goal of the Olympic Movement is to contribute to building a peaceful and better world by educating youth through sport practised without discrimination of any kind and in the

Olympic Spirit, which requires mutual understanding with a spirit of friendship, solidarity and fair play. (IOC, 1991: p. 7)

The underpinning philosophy known as Olympism had its roots in the idealism of the ancient Greeks and the late nineteenth century. As Jobling (1992) pointed out, the IOC's original mandate was "... to make the Olympic Games increasingly perfect, more and more worthy of their glorious past and in keeping with the high ideals that inspired those that revived them" (Jobling, 1992: p. 265). An exhaustive definition of Olympism is extremely difficult to find: thus, with typical fluency, IOC President Juan Antonio Samaranch claims:

Olympism is a state. A state of balance between body and the mind, spirit and matter, impulse and conscience; a state of grace in the search for self-transcendence. It is difficult to give a strict definition. Is this a shortcoming? I do not think so since it allows everyone to embrace it without difficulty or resistance. (cited in Francisco, 1993: p. 2)

Similar rhetoric based on the fundamental principles in the Olympic Charter is employed elsewhere. For example:

Olympism is an overall philosophy of life, exalting and combining in a balanced whole the qualities of body, will and mind. Olympism sets out to create a way of life based on the joy of effort, the educational values of good example and a respect for universal fundamental ethical principles. It has, as a goal, to place sport at the service of the harmonious development of humankind, with the object of creating a peaceful society concerned with the preservation of human dignity. (*Toward a Definition of Olympism* in Canada, 1985; cited in Segrave, 1988: p. 151)

No other sporting event has sought to spread its ideals to every corner of the globe as the Olympic Games has. The hope of promoting peace and international understanding is evident in numerous Olympic traditions including the Opening and Closing Ceremonies and the Olympic Village. Furthermore the aspirations for peace are symbolically represented in the

Olympic flag, the Olympic flame and the inclusion of doves, as a symbol of peace, into the Olympic movement. Sport's reputation as a guardian of moral values and moral authority is frequently asserted by the IOC and by the many state and non-state organisations that it comes into contact with. The Olympic motto of *Citius, Altius, Fortius* (faster, higher, stronger) is apparently something that all Olympic athletes aspire to (Jobling, 1993: p. 18). But contemporary sporting practices are often far removed from the high-minded principles espoused within the concept of Olympism.

The principles of Olympism have created a strand of international ideology through sport. Although many may not have been aware of it, The International Year for A Culture of Peace was 'celebrated' in 2000. In preparation for this celebration, the IOC and the United Nations Educational, Scientific and Cultural Organization (UNESCO) organised a World Conference on Education and Sport for a Culture of Peace from 5 to 7 July 1999 in Paris, at the UNESCO headquarters. The aim of the conference was to bring together representatives of the sports movement, governments and inter- and non-governmental organizations in order to identify and focus on the various aspects of the contribution that sport makes to promoting a culture of peace, based on respect for cultural diversity, fostering tolerance, solidarity, cooperation, dialogue and reconciliation.[2]

Despite the lack of evidence, the view that sport engenders social links is still prominent in contemporary society (Booth, 1993: pp. 1–4). It is easy to see why sport can be viewed so idealistically even in contemporary international society. The Olympic movement clings to beliefs, values and morals that were established a century ago and these themes pervade the ideology of modern sport. At the recent conference, grandly entitled 'The World Conference on Education and Sport for a Culture of Peace', Doll-Tepper (1999) indicated that the last decades have brought enormous social and political changes to our world; two major trends can currently be identified towards globalisation and towards individualisation. In this process, 'education' and 'sport' are playing key roles. Facing exclusion, racism, discrimination of individuals and groups from different cultural, religious, political, economical backgrounds, people with disabilities and women, sport can speak a universal language, and serve as a role model for development in societies in general. Thus through sport it is important to educate the individuals participating in sport, be it as an athlete, as a coach, as a referee, or as an administrator by emphasising ethical values and using sport as a strong instrument for introducing a behaviour of respect.

If one were to uncritically accept this view, then we should believe what Doll-Tepper (1999) believes: that sport offers a number of important benefits which relate to fundamental human rights: an opportunity to enhance overall health and well-being; a way to teach important values such as fair play, teamwork, respect, tolerance, and co-operation; a method to unify and integrate people from a variety of social, ethnic, and economic backgrounds; and a means to providing equity and access initiatives for underrepresented participants such as girls and women. However, we should remember that international non-governmental organisations have at their heart, utopian themes, which predicate their rhetoric, and to a certain extent their actions. UNESCO is one such organisation:

> UNESCO has a constitutional mission to construct the defences of peace 'in the minds of (all) and to promote the ideals of dignity, equality and mutual respect of (all)', together with the 'democratic principles' whereby those ideals may be put into practise. Its mission is therefore essentially of an ethical order. It also has a mandate to strive for justice and observance of human rights through education, science, culture and communication. It is in this connection that UNESCO helps to enhance the action of all those endeavouring to ensure that sport, ever faithful to its values and its humanist mission, becomes an integral part of the process of continuing education and function as a factor in unity and fulfilment, and a means of attaining peace, development, solidarity, respect for human rights and international understanding. (UNESCO, 1999: p. 2)

It is easy to fault international organisations for their failure to bring about harmonious global order, which is their promise, implicit or explicit (Hoberman, 1986: p. 126). As Paddick (1990: p. 6) outlines, the Olympic Games have grown and the pressures of commercialism, nationalism and politics have so modified the view of sport that the philosophy has been overwhelmed. That the Olympic Games cannot aspire to their idealistic principles is an indictment of the development of the practice of sport through the Twentieth Century and the failure of the Olympic movement to acknowledge this.

As La Costa (1991: p. 6) pointed out, there is a mistaken idea that sports organisations are independent from the external social environment. That sport benefits from this belief in equality and access to opportunity has become increasingly difficult to accept in a highly professionalised era. Historically, it is evident that the IOC and many international sports federations saw sport as upholding traditional values of equality and fair play, with politics and economics in particular having no bearing on the structure of sport.

Donnelly (1996) identifies Olympism as one of the two dominant sport ideologies of the Twentieth Century. The second dominant ideology is professionalism. He suggests that the modern Olympics have enshrined utilitarian values of sport within most forms of sport played on a mass participation basis. The participation of the Jamaican bobsleigh team at the 1988 Winter Olympics and the much heralded swim of Eric 'the Eel' Moussambani, from Equatorial Guinea, during the Sydney Olympics were two examples of amateurs participating in a professional world where the right to play badly was exercised. But such examples are few-and far-between. There is little evidence of Olympic ideals in contemporary sport and the erosion of the Olympic ideal can be attributed to forces of television and commercialism (Donnelly, 1996: pp. 26–32). In its place, has a global sports culture, with no 'cult of the amateur' (Prolympism), emerged? This theme is taken up later in the text.

Policy: the idea of 'Sport for All'

Moreover, the idealism implicit (when not explicit) in the claims made for sport can have a policy dimension, which will return us to the supposed virtues of 'Sport for All', mentioned earlier. The sports policy of the Council of Europe is "… to promote sport and the social and health benefits it brings to individuals and society, through policies based on the same principles throughout Europe". On 20 March 1975, the 'European Sport for All Charter' was launched prior to its endorsement and official adoption on 24 September 1976. Both dates are milestones in the Council of Europe's work in sport, as the Charter meant that, thereafter, sports policies in Europe might be thought to have a common programme based on the fundamental belief of the Council of Europe in the values of sport. Recent pronouncements that sport "reaps dividends in cross-cutting areas" such as public health, community safety and social inclusion, to name but three (from Sport England, 1999), may be seen to symbolise the culmination of a post-war era in which British sport has struggled to establish itself as politically viable. It is somewhat paradoxical that sport, often seen as one of the most visible manifestations of society's social ills, finds itself as a tool for the social reinvigoration of society.

It is not only in Britain where value of this sort is placed upon sport. Ogle (1997) succinctly summarises policy initiatives in Scotland, Northern Ireland, South Africa, Australia and New Zealand, all of which prioritised addressing the needs of young people. He suggests:

> ... the shift in focus to young people by government organisations is a partial recognition of the failure of the ideal or shibboleth of 'Sport for All'. This policy shift has its most explicit expression in the change from largely remedial or curative policies, designed to put right previous wrongs, towards preventive strategies which encourage a healthy and active (and, one might add, socially constructive) lifestyle from an early age. (Ogle, 1997: p. 213)

In Northern Ireland and South Africa, two of the world's most historically troubled countries, programmes and policies for sport have explicitly recognised underpinning social objectives (Sports Council for Northern Ireland, 1996; Department of Sport and Recreation, RSA, 1995, 1997). Moreover, sport at local and national levels has been utilised as a vehicle for enhancing cross-community relations in both these countries (Sugden, 1991; Sugden and Harvie 1995; Bose, 1994; Waldmeir, 1997), albeit to varying degrees of success. A concern now is to measure the impact of such projects (cf. Burnett and Hollander, 1999; Burnett *et. al.* 1999) insofar as policy shifts to prevention from cure demand returns on investment not only financially, but in terms of social and community regeneration.

Whilst 'Sport for All' has become the dominant global ideology for policy initiatives, it is clear that the ideal has not been realised. But we must remember from where such idealism originated, for it was De Coubertin who first attached explicitly a broader agenda to modern sport. For De Coubertin, the Olympic movement provided a means in which to promote education through the provision of and participation in organised sport — in essence, he believed that Olympism could promote 'Sport for All'. As De Coubertin put it:

> Let us work to facilitate the daily practice of sport, to multiply favourable opportunities which attract the individual, to destroy useless barriers, to simplify complicated regulations. Let us place the engine of sport everywhere to hand, let us continue to perfect it and to cheapen its manufacture, let us try to bring the different forms of sport closer together to exalt them through pleasure in their contrasts or through harmony in their similarities. (cited in Chalip, 1991: p. 66)

Whether challenging fellow academics or indeed, our students, most respondents agree that 'Sport for All' is a worthwhile aspiration — it provides policy makers at all levels with something to work towards, and much ammunition for critical analysts to highlight shortcomings of sport (in fields of policy making, as a chapter here exemplifies).

Themes from the text

Here, the diversity of issues, methods, concerns and values referred to earlier is reflected both in the themes explored in the various chapters of this work and in the theoretical commitments (implicit and explicit) deployed. For instance, to continue with our regular example, one central set of issues for 'sport and values' concern Olympism. Thus, De Coubertin writes, provocatively, that:

> [w]ise and peaceful internationalism ... will penetrate the new stadium and preserve within it the cult of disinterestedness and honour which will enable athletics to help in the tasks of moral education and social peace... (MacAloon 1981: pp. 188–189)

This seems, at best, a brave *hope*: but could it be more than that? Here, some of the many questions considered include: what values do we find embodied in opening ceremonies of the modern Olympic Games? How do these conform to or conflict with the 'official' values claimed for the Olympic movement, or with its contemporary rhetoric? Coming to a more specific question, how does the movement's avowed antipathy to performance-enhancing drugs relate both to its practices and its rhetoric? And should we think of one set of values for (modern) Olympism, persisting since (say) 1896, or treat successive 'incarnations' of an Olympic Ideal as a value-change?

Olympism also raises questions about the nature of the media-concern with sport, about nationalism, and (relatedly) about the audience for sport. So, here, there is a specific discussion of the claims of *nationalism*, and a case-study of the (distinctive?) role of sport in *Germany*, focusing on three key moments. Yet the manner in which 'identification' with sporting figures, teams and nations develops value-commitments is also important when we turn to the construction of gender-identities, once more traditional versions (for example, Victorian versions of 'femininity') have been given up. And such a topic bears both on how the audience for sport constructs itself and on how it is constructed more widely; for example, through the media.

One issue crucial here concerns the notion of *fairness*, which is central to any value-related matter, but especially pertinent in the context of sport. As Ronald Dworkin (1985 p. 219) put it:

> … the practice of worrying about what justice really is… [is] the single most important social practice we have. [our order]

And that concern with just action or implementation is here: it drove, for example, De Coubertin's decidedly *odd* conception of amateurism, for the point was to have sport done 'for its own sake' (which might them be morally uplifting) rather than (simply) for reward. As the history of the Olympic movement has illustrated, there was something right here. First, it *is* possible to be diverted from a concern with sport 'for its sake' by an over-emphasis on the financial — inducing a 'win at all costs' attitude (as when the USA 'Dream Team' in basketball at the 1992 Olympics declined to stay at the Olympic village because that would have meant them associating with their competitors — a laughable move, given their superiority on court!). But, second, a commitment to winning (and payment for playing) is compatible with the highest levels of sportsmanship, and does not undermine the 'level-playing-field' (McFee, 2000a: pp. 175–176) conception of fairness — the discussion here turns on the two codes within Rugby football, but similar considerations might be expected elsewhere.

Still, the Olympic Games are a large 'media circus': to what extent might that image — of sport as presentation — be revealing? Here, a consideration of parallels (as well as differences) between sport and theatre suggest some of the revelatory aspects of such a trope.

Moreover, a further richness of this text is its methodological diversity: for, once we grant that a variety of issues are to be considered, a variety of methodological perspectives seem implicated. And that is certainly true of this text: it reports the results of participant-observation studies and 'insider' interviews, as well as employing (and endorsing) certain conceptions of the comparative study of sports cultures; it includes introductions to hegemony theory, in the context of suggesting a specific use for such ideas, alongside contributions to the cultural politics or political economy of sport, and examples of philosophical analysis.

Origins of the text

Some of the impetus for this text came from within the Sport and Leisure Cultures Area in the Chelsea School, University of Brighton: in discussions with colleagues, it became clear that a number of us had ideas which, if not strictly overlapping, nevertheless clustered around a number of key themes: and that we had developed statements, in varying degrees of completeness, of our research findings in respect of these ideas. Further, members of our 'networks' were in a similar position — they too had 'results' which would benefit from dissemination in the context of the other, similar results. But it was never the intention to attempt the kind of unification that would have been required to justify our thinking of these as constituting a book with just one theme. Furthermore, we felt that the spirit of debate would be as clear in pieces of 'work in progress' as in the results of completed research projects: so we have included examples of both. Hence the title, in stressing 'issues and values', reflects how we thought of the book from the beginning.

The decision to locate these issues and values as within 'sport and leisure cultures' was a little more difficult: immediately in favour of this title was the name of the Area with the Chelsea School but, against it, most of the chapters were in fact to do with sport. In the end, we concluded that some difficulties might be avoided by adopting the more inclusive title: for example, some of the engagement with sport was as a spectator, even a television viewer — was it really right to call this an investigation of *sport*? Further, wasn't this at least mostly the sociology of sport? Why not include that fact in the title? Since we recognised that these sorts of issues were not central to the thinking *within* the body of the text, we simply put them aside: 'sport and leisure cultures' it was!

One sporting world?

Earlier, we broached the question of whether or not it was right to think of theoretical claims about sport as ever (in principle) *true*: we took for granted that it was, but that claim is worth defending briefly. The two central thoughts here are, first, that we should dispense with some grandiose view of truth (truth with a capital "T", conceived of as timeless and omnipresent) and, second, that the recognition of truths here is compatible with the diversity (especially the diversity of interests, concerns and perspectives) noted earlier. On the first of these matters, there are three points to make, if we are to recognise that claims in social theory (for example, in respect of sport or leisure) might be *true*:

- This is a thesis about what is *possible*. So we are not urging that any such claims are (or are not) true: merely that they are candidates for truth — that the possibility of truth here cannot be ruled-out prior to actual investigation;

- The sorts of truths here are equivalent to, say, the claim that so-and-so has an over-draft: there is no over-arching 'grand theory' being imported. Thus, we could agree when Richard Rorty (1989: p. xiii) disputes the idea of some fundamental truth by saying: "...socialisation, and thus human circumstance, goes all the way down ... there is nothing 'beneath' socialisation or prior to history which is definitory of the human".

  For we are only urging that, say, it is *true* (or part of the truth) that "[a] species of internationalism constitutes a chief rationale of the Olympic movement ..." (Hargreaves, 2000: p. 113). Or, if it is not true (something we might discover by detailed analysis), that is because it is false!

- Central to such an 'everyday' conception of truth (and falsity) are ideas of showing, or of finding out, that such-and-such was true (or part of the truth), where these are not simply made so by our wanting (or wishing for) it.

If this view of what it is for something to be true were adopted (and, clearly, a great deal more elaboration would be required), we could conclude that the notion of truth here is unthreatening.

We might then augment our discussion by recognising the diversity it tolerates: what is rejected here is both the position that 'anything goes' (that any view is as good as any other) — on the contrary, the true will generally be preferable to the false, and for that reason — and the position that 'the truth' here is unitary. As a comparison, consider some multiple-figure from psychology, such as the duck-rabbit or the 'old woman/young woman': here, the features of the design constrain what you can see it depicting (it is, say, old woman or young woman, but not 'anything goes'). If someone needed convincing that the design did indeed depict the young woman, we could point to features of the design that sustain that reading: say, that this line is her jaw, this a band around her neck. And then if someone else urges some other 'reading' (other than young woman or old woman) for the design, we expect that 'reading' to be similarly answerable to the features of the design. Here, then, we have a model for diversity, answerability to features of the case, and a rejection of 'anything goes'. And this is how we conceive of the operation of explanations of, say, sporting events.

Thus, for example, we might conclude that such-and-such (say, power conceived in class-based terms) was crucial to the understanding of sport in so-and-so context (say, Britain during the last century and a half: see Hargreaves, 1986 p. 209): have we thereby precluded other explanations? No, and in two dimensions. First, in locating *this* as an explanation in this case, we are not insisting that it be explanatory in all cases — it might, but it might not. So that other contexts might require reference to power-relations conceptualised in terms of gender, ethnicity, etc., in ways not simply reducible to social class. We have not even concluded that the explanatory tool will *always* be power (however much we might think this).

Second, in taking this to be the answer to *our* question, we have not precluded other questions being asked (even in the same, or similar forms of words): so that different preoccupations might lead to a (slightly) different question, and hence a different form of answer, even when discussing (say) Britain in the last century and a half.

One way to summarise this discussion would be as saying that there is one world; more specifically, one sporting world — that the diversities within our analysis of that world, within the concerns we might have for it, the values we might locate in it, speak directly to the idea of a single locus of attention: as Virginia Woolf is supposed to have remarked, "one of the bloody things is enough"! But we can also see why the metaphor of 'many worlds' might seem attractive, as a way to recognise diversity. Here, we have recognised the diversity of the disparate voices within the analysis of sport and leisure cultures by reflecting (some of) those voices.

Conclusion

In this chapter, we have sought to suggest that the pursuit of 'issues and values in sport and leisure cultures' might itself be valuable, but without prescribing just one kind of approach, either theoretical or methodological. Instead, we have aimed to defend a kind of pluralism (of issues) that the rest of the volume exemplifies. Further, we have suggested some of the factors which moderate idealism about the value of sport, together with some of the considerations (especially in policy terms) which might lead to a guarded optimism about the future of 'the sporting world'. Nothing in our argument here makes the actual value of sport *certain*; and we have highlighted reasons to doubt that sport's potential value is always realised. But if we have given reason to view that value less narrowly, and to grant its potential realisation, we have done enough here.

Finally, we would like to acknowledge contribution of Chelsea School, University of Brighton, to this project: in particular, to thank for their support the Head of School, Paul McNaught-Davis, and the Co-ordinator of the School's Research, Alan Tomlinson.

Notes

[1] D'Agostino (1995) invented the term, although he is taken beyond simple formalism by his reference to an 'ethos' as: "...that set of unofficial, implicit conventions which determine how the rules of that game are to be applied in concrete circumstances" (pp. 48–49).

For discussion, see Morgan (1995). Interestingly, then, the objection to arch-formalists [such as Meier (1995)] is not that their account of rules leaves out non-rule-based conditions on games/sport, but that they misunderstand the nature of rules, whether constituitive, regulative or whatever.

2   See http://www.olympic.org/ioc/e/news/worldconf/worldconf_intro_e.html

References

Allison, L. (1998) (ed) *Taking sport seriously*. Aachen: Meyer and Meyer.

Biddiss, M. (1997) 'Faster, higher, stronger: The birth of the modern Olympics', *The Sports Historian* Vol. 11, No. 1: pp. 1–11.

Booth, D. (1993) 'The consecration of sport: Idealism in social science theory', *The International Journal of the History of Sport* Vol. 10, No. 1: pp. 1–19.

Bose, M. (1994) *Sporting colours: Sport and politics in South Africa*. London: Robson.

Brohm, J-M. (1978) *Sport: A prison of measured time*, London: Ink Links.

Burnett, C. and Hollander, W. (1999) 'Sport development and the United Kingdom-South Africa sports initiative: A pre-evaluation report', *Journal of Sport Management* Vol. 13: pp. 237–251.

Burnett, C., Hollander, W., Uys, J. M., De Bruin, G. P. and Lombard, A. J. (1999) *The Australia-South Africa sport development programme: An impact study of the junior sport component*. Research Report, Johannesburg: Department of Sport and Movement Studies, Rand Afrikaans University.

Chalip, L. (1991) 'The revival of the modern Olympic games and Pierre de Coubertin's thoughts on Sport for All', Proceedings of the 31st session of the International Olympic Academy, Ancient Olympia, Greece, 16–31 July, pp. 66–72.

D'Agostino, F. (1995) 'The ethos of games', in W. J. Morgan and K. V. Meier (eds) *Philosophic inquiry in sport* (second edition). Champaign, IL: Human Kinetics, pp. 42–49.

Department of Sport and Recreation (1995) *Getting people to play: White paper on Sport and Recreation*. Pretoria: Department of Sport and Recreation

———— (1997) *Annual report of the Department of sport and recreation*. Pretoria: Department of Sport and Recreation.

Doll-Tepper, G. (1999) 'Sport as an instrument to fight against racism and peace', Paper presented to the World Conference on Education and Sport for a Culture of Peace, Paris, 5–7 July 1999. Summary retrieved on 12 August 2000 from http://www.olympic.org/ioc/e/news/worldconf/worldconf_them2_e.html

Donnelly, P. (1996) 'Prolympism: Sport monoculture as crisis and opportunity', *Quest* Vol. 48: pp. 25–42.

———— (1997) (ed) *Taking sport seriously: Social issues in Canadian sport.* Toronto: Thompson publishing.

Dunning, E. (1999) *Sport matters: Sociological studies of sport, violence and civilisation.* London: Routledge.

Dworkin, R. (1985) *A matter of principle.* Cambridge, MA: Harvard University Press.

Francisco, M. (1993) 'The Olympic spirit and its influence on African culture: Identity, cultural minorities, traditions and customs, racism' Paper presented to the 33rd International Session for Young Participants, International Olympic Academy, Ancient Olympia, Greece, 7–22 July.

Greenberg, C. (1993) 'Review of *The social history of art*, by Arnold Hauser' [1951], in his *Collected essays and criticism* Vol. 3. Chicago: University of Chicago Press, pp. 94–98.

Hampshire, S. (2000) *Justice is conflict.* Princeton, NJ: Princeton University Press.

Hargreaves, J. (1986) *Sport, power and culture.* Cambridge: Polity Press.

———— (2000) *Freedom for Catalonia?: Catalan nationalism, Spanish identity and the Barcelona Olympic Games.* Cambridge: Cambridge University Press.

Hoberman, J. (1986) *The Olympic crisis: Sport, politics and the moral order.* New Rochelle, NY: Aristide D. Caratzas

———— (1993) 'Sport and ideology in the post-communist age' in L. Allison (ed) *The changing politics of sport.* Manchester: Manchester University Press, pp. 15–36.

Horne, J. Tomlinson, A. and Whannel, G. (1999) *Understanding sport: An introduction to the sociological and cultural analysis of sport.* London: E. & F. N. Spon.

Jennings, A. (1996) *The new lords of the rings: How to buy gold medals.* London: Pocket Books.

Jennings, A. and Sambrook, C. (2000) *The great Olympic swindle: When the world wanted its Games back.* London: Simon and Schuster.

Jobling, I. (1992) 'Olympic games', in W. Vamplew, K. Moore, I. O'Hara, R. Cashman and I. Jobling (eds) *The Oxford companion to Australian sport.* Melbourne: Oxford University Press.

Jobling, I. F. (1993) 'The Olympic movement as an expression of the world's power system: An analysis of 'motives', attitudes and values.' Paper presented to the 33rd International Session for Young Participants, International Olympic Academy, Ancient Olympia, Greece, 7–22 July.

Katwala, S. (2000) *Democratising global sport*. London: The Foreign Policy Centre.

Kidd, B. (1996) 'Taking the rhetoric seriously: Proposals for Olympic education', *Quest* Vol. 48: pp. 82–92.

La Costa, L. (1991). 'How can the Olympic movement promote Sport for All?' Paper presented to the 31st Session of the International Olympic Academy, 16–31 July, 1991. Ancient Olympia, Greece.

Lyotard, J-F. (1984) *The postmodern condition*. Manchester: Manchester University Press.

MacAloon, J. (1981) *This great symbol: Pierre de Coubertin and the origins of the modern Olympic games*. Chicago: University of Chicago Press.

McFee, G. (2000a) 'Spoiling: an indirect reflection of sport's moral imperative?', in T. Tannsjo and C. Tamburrini (eds) *Values in sport*. London: Routledge, pp. 172–182.

McFee, G. (2000b) *Free will*. Teddington: Acumen.

Meier, K. (1995) 'Triad trickery: playing with games and sports', in W. J. Morgan and K. V. Meier (eds) *Philosophic inquiry in sport* (second edition). Champaign, IL: Human Kinetics, pp. 23–41.

Morgan, W. J. (1995) 'The logical incompatibility thesis and rules: a reconsideration of formalism as an account of games', in W. J. Morgan and K. V. Meier (eds) *Philosophic inquiry in sport* (second edition). Champaign, IL: Human Kinetics, pp. 50–63.

Ogle, S. (1997) 'International perspectives on public policy and the development of sport for young people', in J. Kremer, K. Trew and S. Ogle (eds) *Young people's involvement in sport*. London: Routledge, pp. 211–231.

Paddick, R. (1990) 'The Olympic philosophy — hypertrophy or atrophy?' Paper presented at the XII Commonwealth and International Conference on Physical Education, Sport, Health, Dance, Recreation and Leisure. Auckland, New Zealand.

Rigauer, B. (1982) *Sport and work*. New York, Columbia University Press.

Rorty, R. (1989) *Contingency, irony and solidarity*. Cambridge: Cambridge University Press.

Segrave, J. O. (1988) 'Towards a definition of Olympism', in J. O. Segrave and D. Chu (eds) *The Olympic Games in transition*. Champaign, IL: Human Kinetics, pp. 149–158.

Skillen, A. (1998) 'Sport is for losers', in M. McNamee and J. Parry (eds) *Ethics and sport*. London: E & FN Spon, pp. 169–181.

Sport England (1999) *Best value through sport: The value of sport to local authorities*. London: Sport England.

Sports Council for Northern Ireland (1996) *Sports development in the community*, Belfast: SCNI.

Sugden, J. (1991) 'Belfast United: Encouraging cross-community relations through sport in Northern Ireland', *Journal of Sport and Social Issues* Vol. 15, No. 4: pp. 59–80.

Sugden, J. and Harvie, S. (1995) *Sport and community relations in Northern Ireland*. Coleraine: Centre for the Study of Conflict, University of Ulster.

UNESCO (1999) 'Major issues in physical education and sport', Retrieved on 20 August 2000 from http://www.unesco.org/education/educprog/eps/EPSanglais/ MINEPS_ANG/major_issues_in_physicql_educati.htm

Waldmeir, P. (1997) *Anatomy of a miracle*. New York: Viking.

SPORT AND NATIONALISM[1]

Claudio Tamburrini
Gothenburg University

Introduction: What is sports nationalism?

Intellectuals have always had an antagonistic relation to sports. Behind their critical remarks, one can often trace a (more or less well concealed) snobbish disdain for massive, physical activities. However, some of the criticisms advanced by opponents of elite, professional sports are indeed troublesome and cannot be neglected. One of these objections, indeed a classical one, is that sports events inculcate undesirable nationalistic attitudes. As early as 1978, Christopher Lasch wrote, when accounting for current objections to sports:

> The violence and partisanship of modern sports lead some critics to insist that athletics impart militaristic values to the young, irrationally inculcate local and national pride in the spectator, and serve as one of the strongest bastions of male chauvinism. (Lasch, 1978: p. 103)

Nationalism is a form of particularist morality, as opposed to universalist moral theories. It consists of the identification with and a special concern for the promotion of the interests and well-being of our country and compatriots, even when this only can be obtained at the expense of other countries.

Moral universalism requires that our actions be governed by principles expressing equal concern for all sentient beings affected by our actions, independently of their relation to us. Nationalism tells us instead to favour the interests of 'our' people, that is, that we act in defence of our fellow-citizens and compatriots, even to the detriment of other nations. Thus, while moral universalism demands impartiality, nationalism demands undivided concern for our compatriots, unbound by any moral regard to outsiders[2].

25

In the context of sport, nationalism implies favouring one nation's athletes. Critics of sport believe that this favouritism can easily develop into hostile behaviour towards other countries' sports practitioners and fans. This hostility may manifest itself in various ways, ranging from violent behaviour against rival athletes and fans in the proximity of a sports event, to aggressive wars and genocide. Thus Lasch's argument reappears at present, although in a somewhat modified form, reformulated by contemporary critics of sport. The main point here is that sports nationalism contributes to the infliction of damage to other nations.

There is, however, another aspect of the present objection that has not been sufficiently highlighted in the current debate. It says that sports nationalism damages our own nation and our own compatriots, by diverting attention from more urgent social and political concerns. According to this line of reasoning, sports spectatorship, particularly when reinforced by nationalistic sentiments, induces apathy and distracts energy from political engagement. The most extreme case would be a country ruled by a dictator, that excels in some sports competition. In that situation, detractors of sport would argue, sports nationalism consolidates dictatorship, as the public's celebration of sporting victories detracts from common democratic efforts. To paraphrase Marx, then, for these critics, sports are the most recent opiate of the masses.

What is then wrong with nationalism as manifested in the realm of sports? More precisely, it might be damaging in three different ways. First, political nationalism gives rise to bad sporting practices. For instance, a common criticism of sports, and of professional sports in particular, is that they promote exaggerated competitiveness and even aggression towards other athletes. According to these critics, nationalistic feelings play a major role in furthering these processes.

Second, sports nationalism promotes political nationalism, which, in its turn, is considered, if not bad in itself, at least derivatively bad. Some critics believe that sports nationalism enhances dangerous manifestations of national chauvinism. Thus, Paul Gomberg (2000: p. 87) has argued that sports nationalism can be used in the service of aggressive bellicose enterprises. Further, in the view of Torbjörn Tännsjö (2000: p. 11), sports nationalism sustains a military ideology that justifies using individuals as 'canon-fodder' for the sake of the collective. Finally, Nicholas Dixon (2000: p. 75) believes that sports nationalism lies at the basis of what he calls jingoism, that is, aggressive sport cultures based not only on national identification, but also on group pressure, the most known example of which is hooliganism.

Third, sport gives rise to negative phenomena in combination with nationalism. These negative effects can affect both other people and our own compatriots. Thus, giving priority to our own national athletes might (i) reinforce the subordination of peripheral to central countries (the argument on neo-colonialism); and (ii) distract efforts from essential democratic activities in our own country (the argument on distraction).

In this chapter, I intend to discuss these objections to sports nationalism in that order.

Before setting about this task, however, two questions need to be clarified. First, we have the issue of for whom 'sports' nationalism is supposed to be bad. Is it bad for people? For nations? For states? In my view, a practice is bad when it yields negative consequences for people. Actions that affect nations or states negatively may be bad, but only derivatively, and to the extent they affect actual people. The damage that can be inflicted on abstract or collective entities is morally relevant only provided the welfare (interests, happiness, etc.) of their particular members is also affected negatively.

The second question has to do with what is judged to be negative for people when we say that nationalism is bad. Is it the sentiment we embrace for our nation (for instance, when we say "I love my country"), or the value judgement (expressed, for instance, in the statement "I believe we are superior to other nations") or the disposition to act ("I am ready to do whatever is required to benefit my people") that is of moral relevance here? As long as our nationalistic feelings and value judgements are not actualised in concrete behaviour, we should be left free to feel and think as we wish. Rather, it is the disposition to act that matters morally. The evaluation of sports nationalism focuses therefore on the concrete actions it gives rise to, not on the feelings or value judgements through which it is expressed.

Bad sports

Does the kind of nationalistic enthusiasm supporters show at the sports stadium really affect other people negatively? Before embarking on this discussion, it might be helpful to place current criticism of elite sports in the ideological context in which it originates. Therefore, let us first take a look at the orthodox Marxian criticism of sport. According to it, nationalism contributes to create bad sport practices contaminated by exaggerated competitiveness and aggressive behaviour.

An orthodox, Marxist-inspired criticism of sports focuses on the notion of competitiveness. This objection, indeed a common place in the ideological arsenal levelled against sport professionalism in the sixties, had a great influence on the theoretical discourse on sports. According to the revolutionary intellectuals enrolled in the 1968 movement, sport incarnates the harshness of capitalist competition. As such, sport was incapable of contributing to social change, as it limited itself to reflect — sometimes even to slavishly reproduce — current social values in a uncritical manner.

This criticism became even stronger when the issue was professional, elite sports. According to these voices, sports — once a recreational activity — evolved into a crude and wayward instantiation of the struggle for survival that characterises class society, where fame, money and success are the loot one sets out to appropriate, and competitors are seen as rivals to be defeated by whatever means deemed fit.

Within this critical approach to sports, and elite sports in particular, the issue of nationalism appears to be particularly troublesome. National antagonism might be expected to increase competitiveness in sport tournaments. Does this spoil sports? Or does nationalism result in better sports competitions instead?

Before saying anything on that question, we need first to dispose of a response that will not serve to meet the present objection. Sport enthusiasts might point to the fact that, in other professional fields, we seem to accept comparison of our working performances with others', and remuneration based on what we produce. Why should it be different in professional sport? Why worry about the inherent competitiveness embedded in elite sports?

Negative as it might be, the context in which elite sport practitioners act does not greatly differ from the one applying to other categories of workers. It is perhaps regrettable that labour (including professional sports) has evolved as it has. Many people are indeed working to change that reality. Even so, we are not prepared to see that as a good reason for abolishing work, because we consider it to be unbearable for human life. Something similar might be said to apply to sports. In spite of their shortcomings and imperfections, sports still have a central role in developing a sense of community and co-operation among people.

Thus, these sport enthusiasts might say, sport critics still owe us an explanation of what it is that turns emulation and competitiveness in sports into problematic aspects, while they are not merely accepted, but even encouraged in other professions. And until that explanation is provided, they might add, warnings and pessimistic forecasts about the future of sports can only be perceived as expressions of moral panic.

The problem with this line of defence is that it puts professional sports on a pair with recreational sports, or even with physical activity as a whole. There can be no doubt that if human beings are to thrive a certain amount of physical activity is required. Perhaps it could also be maintained that this physical activity is best provided by sporting activities, as, unlike for instance physically demanding labour, they allow for a playful approach that work often lacks. But this is not the issue here. What the present criticism calls into question is whether *elite professional* sports is at all necessary to provide the amount of physical activity needed for a fully developed life. So, if the present criticism is to be countered, it must be argued that nationalism does not spoil sport practices. Can this claim be substantiated?

I think it can. Far from spoiling sports competitions, enhanced antagonism contributes to making them more exciting. This makes higher demands of athletic performance. More sacrifices and efforts will be required from the athletes. But this is compensated for by the fact that spectators will enjoy the tension of combative competitions more. Increased competitiveness might also lead to improvements in the technical level of sports. So, not only the hedonistic experiences of the public, but also the very quality of the game itself might be enhanced by more combative confrontations on the sports field.

Currently, however, critics of sport have become more sophisticated. They now focus on the aggressive, chauvinistic feelings that international sports competitions supposedly enhance, and the manifestations of violence that take place at sports arenas. Some authors even believe in the existence of a more or less direct relation between nationalistic sports euphoria and aggressive, bellicose enterprises directed against other countries.

Besides, and parallel to this wider political analysis of the practice of sport, a new form of criticism of competitive sports has been advanced lately, which concentrates on the values that sports fans, rather than sports practitioners, seem to be expressing when they extol their heroes. This criticism says that the fascination people feel for sport stars will enhance militaristic and fascistoid values in the public, values that go with chauvinistic, antidemocratic ideologies. To sum up, critics see elite sports as responsible for: (a) aggressive wars and genocide; (b) the submission of individuals to the collective; (c) the promotion of violence at sports arenas and their environments; and (d) the reinforcement of fascistoid, elitist values. In the remaining sections of this chapter, I will scrutinise these different objections.

Bad nationalism

Sports nationalism has also been accused of promoting political chauvinism. This charge has been advanced in a variety of ways, but its central tenet is always that chauvinism affects people, often in other nations but even in our own country, negatively. Let us see if this criticism is tenable.

In the recent international debate on sports and nationalism, Paul Gomberg and Torbjörn Tännsjö have entered the scene as two powerful representatives of the new Leftist criticism of elite sports. Gomberg believes that competitive elite sports enhance aggressive nationalism and genocide. Tännsjö, instead, concentrates on the admiration the public feel for sport heroes, which he sees as expressing militaristic, fascistoid values. Are they right in what they claim, or should their arguments be dismissed as alarming statements, with no correspondence in reality of sports?

Sports have since long been accused of promoting unsound nationalistic feelings. Not only the physical aggression of rival fans and athletes, which finds most conspicuous manifestation in the phenomenon of hooliganism, but even exacerbated chauvinism leading to war between countries and genocide has been attributed to sports. This is the accusation directed by Paul Gomberg (2000: p. 87) to sports:

> Does nationalism in sports, epitomised in the nationalism at Olympic Games, contribute to the mobilisation of mass populations for popular wars and genocide? I will argue that it does.

The core of Gomberg's position can be summed up as follows. Patriotism, even of the moderate kind expressed in sports nationalism, implies:

> an identification with one's country and special duties entailed by that identification ... [among them] ... the duty of patriotic service in wartime. (Gomberg, 2000: p. 97)

Gomberg grounds his argument on a prediction he makes on the development of world politics in the near future. In his view:

> ... wars, including world wars, are far from being at an end. To wage these wars the belligerents will rely on religious and moral appeals, and ultimately on patriotism. Patriotism makes its adherents easy to control; as soldiers and civilians, they will be used in these contests between the capitalists (Gomberg, 2000: p. 96)

Now, without adopting a standpoint to Gomberg's prediction, what does all this have to do with sports? Admittedly, Gomberg (2000: p. 98) tells us that:

> moderate patriotism, even as cultivated in sports, gives way in these situations to the most barbaric, fascist attacks on others, all in the service of the capitalist ruling groups who initiate this process.

But the argumentation he delivers for such a statement is, to put it mildly, rather weak. Even if we can agree with him that "embracing patriotism has had terrible effects, and that we have good reason to reject identification with 'our governments' and 'our nations'" (Gomberg 2000: p. 94), he seems to be unwarrantedly equating the identification with one's government on the one hand with identification with one's nation and national sports teams on the other. Political history provides us with plenty of examples in which a community, although displaying internal cohesion and unity in support of common symbols of national identity, nonetheless repudiates its government. And, more pertinently from the point of view of the present argument, sports arenas are often utilised by popular sectors, not only to support common symbols of national identity, but even to manifest political opposition to the ruling political regime. In that regard, Gomberg seems to be unwarrantedly conflating sociological processes with political realities. First, he fails to distinguish between a country's government and a nation. And, further, he also confuses support for a national sports team (which, arguably, constitutes a part of a nation's identity) with support of its government.

What is needed to substantiate Gomberg's argument is historical evidence showing that sports nationalism has consistently been made to serve militaristic enterprises. The war between Honduras and Guatemala in the 1970s is often quoted as an argument supporting this thesis. This is meagre support, however. Many more cases of popular, antidictatorial sport manifestations might be quoted to neutralise the force of that isolated example[3]. Sports, and the fascination they evoke in the masses, can be used to support assertions of the popular will. There is no reason to leave such a powerful media instrument in the hands of antidemocratic forces.

Torbjörn Tännsjö also belongs to the group of people who feel troubled by what's going on in the field of elite sports at present. According to him, the public's (often exaggerated) enthusiasm for sport heroes is morally dubious. As a matter of fact, he expresses his worries in far more alarming terms than that. His thesis, in his own words, is that

> our admiration for the achievements of the great sports heroes, such as the athletes who triumph at the Olympics, reflects a fascistoid ideology. While nationalism may be dangerous, and has often been associated with fascism, what is going on in our enthusiasm for individual athletic heroes is even worse. Our enthusiasm springs from the very core of fascist ideology: admiration for strength and contempt for weakness. (Tännsjö, 2000: p. 10)

Tännsjö's attack is comprehensive: it is directed against all kinds of sports — individual or in team form — carried out on an elite level. However, he is not aiming to stigmatise the motives that lead top athletes to compete. Nor is he condemning promoters or coaches who motivate young people to become top sportsmen. Rather, his objections to elite sports concentrate exclusively on 'what goes on within the enormous, worldwide public, watching sports, usually through television'. The target of his criticism is "the values entertained by you and me, we who tend, over and over again, to get carried away by such events as the Olympic Games". Thus, what turns elite sports into a morally problematic matter is the kind of reaction it seems to evoke in us, the spectators. These reactions can be summed up in the following manner:

1)   Elite sports events reinforce undesirable nationalistic sentiments in the public that justify the sacrifice of individuals for the sake of collective, abstract entities.

2)   Our — the public's — admiration for winners in elite sports competitions is an expression of our contempt for weakness (which, according to Tännsjö, is an essential element of Nazi ideology).

Both of Tännsjö's objections to elite sports deserve consideration. However, the argument based on our admiration for winners deserves its own discussion, and so will be pursued elsewhere[4]. In the next section, therefore, I will concentrate on his first argument.

Sports nationalism turns individuals into canon-fodder

One could begin by asking why we should worry about the reinforcement of nationalism by competitive sports. After all, nationalist feelings in sports do not necessarily have to lead to political chauvinism. It has even been argued that sports nationalism is not only a rather innocent sort of patriotism, but even a substitute for more dubious versions of political nationalism as well. Tännsjö is well aware of this fact, but he thinks otherwise. According to him, political and sports nationalism reinforce each other:

> The nationalism fostered by our interest for our 'own' national team, and the nationalism we exhibit in the political arena, tend to reinforce each other. In particular, in periods where political nationalism is strong, what happens on the sports arenas tend to become politically important. (Tännsjö, 2000: p. 12)

This 'mutual reinforcement' thesis is a strong one indeed. However, the only support Tännsjö provides for it is the assertion that "[t]here is only a small step from being a soccer hooligan to joining a fascist organisation modelled on the Hitler Youth" (Tännsjö, 2000: p. 12) The example is clearly biased, however. If you are a hooligan, you already are a violent person. It would then not be surprising if you are inclined to join any organisation that will enable you to manifest your violent character. The relevant example here would be to show that it is a small step from being an ordinary soccer fan to joining a (politically undesirable) nationalistic organisation. Correctly formulated, this mutual reinforcement thesis seems false.

So if we have to worry about nationalism in sports, this worry would have to depend on negative consequences of the activity, rather than on its presumed connection with less desirable expressions of national feelings. Tännsjö indicates one such consequence: sports nationalism orientates people towards abstract symbols, such as "the flag, the team (seen as an emblem); yes, even the abstractly conceived nation" (Tännsjö, 2000: p. 11), and this is why we should reject it. According to him, celebrating abstract symbols is wrong because:

> abstract entities as such are of no value. What matters, ultimately, from a moral point of view, is what happens to individuals, capable (at least) of feeling pleasure and pain ... This means that if someone claims that the strength of his or her nation is of value in itself, he or she makes a value mistake. (Tännsjö, 2000: p. 11)

As a metaethical statement, this latter claim is uncontroversial. However, as an objection to our interest in sports, the argument is flawed on two grounds. First, it could be asked, what does it mean to see the team "as an emblem", or the nation or the flag, as "abstract symbols"? In the context of sports, these symbols stands for thousands and thousands of people who share the dream of seeing their team succeed. A sports team, for instance, is in part driven to win by the encouragement provided by its supporters. Victorious teams often acknowledge this support by dedicating the victory to their supporters. A particular kind of discourse is thus established between the team members and the public. This seems to me to be the sense to be ascribed to the traditional ritual — indeed a popular, large-scale celebration — in which a crowd receives its local team in a public place after a meritorious performance abroad. And even in those cases in which the victory is offered to more abstract entities than a exhilarating crowd, the symbol thus honoured (the flag, the City house, etc.) might reasonably be seen as representing the people who identify themselves with it[5]. We should not forget that, in the context of sports, abstract symbols refer to people of flesh and bone.

Secondly, there is no reason to suppose that if a sports fan cares about the strength of her team or her nation, she must necessarily be considering it as being valuable in itself. She might reasonably see this strength as instrumental to sentiments of pride, joy or whatever pleasurable state of mind the feeling of belonging to a team or a nation might bring about.

Therefore, it seems to me that the problem here, if there is a problem, cannot be the abstractness of the entities celebrated: after all, symbols usually are implemented in real life arrangements and affect actual people. The relevant issue here is what these symbols stand for. Being generally accepted as natural, historical symbols of a community, a flag, a City house, even a religious figure, can hardly be said to represent in themselves fascist ideals as soon as they are advocated in the context of sports events.

Another reason why Tännsjö finds spectator orientation on abstract symbols morally problematic is due to the priority given to group interests over those of individuals. Thus, he says that "[w]hen such entities are celebrated, the individual tends to become replaceable. ... When our football or soccer heroes are successful, we cheer for them. When they fail 'us', we despise them" (Tännsjö, 2000: p. 11). Thus, according to Tännsjö, when all we care about is the strength of a nation, a team or a flag, individuals are sacrificed for the sake of the collective. This ideology, he argues, accords with a view which is common in the military force: there, "young women are treated as potential instruments that shall safeguard the strength and survival of the nation, and young men are viewed merely as potential soldiers" (Tännsjö, 2000: p. 11).

Now, it can hardly be denied that there is something morally problematic, to put it mildly, about a practice that, first, raises a person to the level of a hero, and then discards her as soon as she fails to fulfil our expectations of victory. Such an attitude might reasonably be said to violate the Kantian principle that we should always treat other human beings as ends in themselves, and never merely as means. So perhaps Tännsjö is right after all in exhorting us to reflect upon our attitudes towards top athletes, and the kind of values we might be expressing through them. However, his account of what's going on when we express such disappointment misses the mark.

First, Tännsjö's description of the esteem in which spectators hold top athletes is simply inaccurate. The Swedish boxer Ingemar "Ingo" Johansson and football player Diego Maradona are examples of such sports heroes. Both "Ingo" and Maradona reached the pinnacles of athletic success and attracted adoring fans. In 1959, Johansson defeated the American boxer Floyd Paterson in a fight for the heavy-weight world championship, thereby giving Sweden its first (and hitherto only) world championship title in boxing. In 1986, Maradona led the Argentinean football team to an outstanding victory in the International Association of Federated Football (FIFA) World Cup in Mexico. In the matches that led to the final game against West Germany, Maradona scored a couple of goals (against England and Belgium) of such quality that more than fourteen years later they still are shown on TV-sport shows from time to time. (The goal scored against England has even been recorded with both classic music and tango tunes in the background with the intention of emphasising the plasticity of its conception.) In both cases, however, the outstanding sports performances were followed by defeats. "Ingo" clearly lost two return matches against Paterson and Maradona has never again reached the top level he showed at the Mexico tournament in 1986. In Maradona's case, rather than mere sports defeats, one could even talk of disappointing the wider expectations of the public by having been penalised twice by the FIFA's disciplinary committee for using performance-enhancing drugs. Both "Ingo" and Maradona, perhaps to different degrees and in different manners, can be said to have disappointed their supporters' expectations of victory. This notwithstanding, they still enjoy what is almost unconditional love and admiration from their numerous fans. Although no generally valid and definitive conclusions can be drawn from only two cases, I believe that they exemplify something typical about the relationship between sports heroes and the public. In that sense, the particular personal bond between them created by victory seems to be more resistant to defeat and disappointment than Tännsjö's argument assumes.

But what about ordinary athletes, those who have not been blessed (if it is a blessing) by the public's unconditional devotion? Standard performers are often strongly questioned by supporters. The recognition and admiration they might come to enjoy on favourable occasions is rapidly withdrawn in defeat. Would it not then be warranted to say that these athletes are loved and admired in victory, but criticised and slandered by the public when failing to live up to its demands? And would this not be tantamount to using those athletes simply as means of expressing our (rapidly changing) states of mind?

To begin with, I do not think this particular criticism affects elite sports more than it affects any other profession. In our professional life, our work is expected to satisfy certain standards. If we do not live up to these demands, we are criticised. And when, in spite of criticism, we still fail to react appropriately (that is, if we do not improve our work), the confidence we may have enjoyed before from employers and work-mates is withdrawn, we are deprived of certain benefits and, in some cases, even fired. From a moral point of view, this situation is no worse than that depicted for ordinary athletes who do not live up to the expectations of the public. Far from being an essential trait of elite sports, responding negatively to shortcomings in performances is a factor of all kinds of professional activity.

To this it could be objected that, due to the loudness and vividness of the way in which they are rejected, criticism of not-up-to-the-mark athletes is much stronger than that normally experienced by other professional categories.

My answer to this argument is twofold. First, there is no necessary link between contempt and the loudness and vividness of a critical reaction. A person can loudly and vividly criticise her best friend's conduct, without this having to imply she despises her friend. And contempt can indeed be expressed in very subtle manners. Indifferent work-mates, for instance, can turn out to be much more cruel and contemptuous than a hilarious crowd at the sports arena.

Secondly, especially in the context of sports, the vividness of the situation, the emotions experienced in a competition, inspires a particularly intensive communication between the athletes and the crowd. Through it, the existing bond between performers and audience — the discourse that links them to the public — now reaches a higher level of directness and interaction. This bond becomes, in other words, more personalised and humanised, independent of the final result of the athletic performance[6]. A similar situation seems to occur in other emotionally charged professional activities such as the performing arts. But even when an unsatisfactory result hinders the development of such a bond, there is no reason to underestimate an athlete's capacity to handle that failure. In sports, as well as in other areas of life, we have to accept that human relationships sometimes simply do not work out as we would wish. This should not bother sports supporters any more than it does devotees, say, of opera.

So, concerning common athletes, I also believe that it would be an overstatement to characterise the public's reaction as one of scorn or contempt. Even when overtly showing disappointment at an athlete's performance, the interactive relation that is attained between sports audiences and the athletes contains elements of human communication that go far beyond (and are essentially different from) the expression of contempt.

Sports nationalism generates violence

Many critics of sport blame the kind of nationalism expressed in sports arenas for being responsible for the violence which often takes place in connection with sports events. Nicholas Dixon (2000: p. 75) summarises the noxious effects usually ascribed to unrestricted, aggressive sports nationalism (which he calls "jingoism") as follows:

> A tiny minority of English soccer fans sometimes rampages through foreign cities where the national team is playing, destroying property and attacking opposing fans. Even when no physical violence occurs, racial and ethnic abuse of players for rival national teams is an all-too-common excess of nationalism. And chauvinistic fans can deliberately or inadvertently interfere with the performance of athletes from other countries, for instance by yelling as a player is about to serve a tennis ball or hit a putt, or — as happened during the 1996 Olympics in Atlanta — inappropriately chanting support for the United States team during the routines of foreign gymnasts. ... Finally, the patriotic fervour of athletes and their coaches may lead them to overstep acceptable boundaries in their pursuit of victory. The widespread use of illegal drugs in international athletics tournaments, often fully sanctioned in private by coaches, is a familiar example. What all of these instances of inappropriate, excessive patriotism have in common is a simple lack of moral regard for athletes, coaches and other people from rival countries. (Dixon, 2000: p. 75)

Now, a question that might be posed at the beginning is why this xenophobic violence should bother us at all. Nationalism — we have seen — demands that we disregard the interests of other nations. For a nationalist, the claims advanced by other national communities lack moral strength simply because they are not her own. According to MacIntyre (1984), for instance, patriotism tells us to act on our own society's conception of the good life, even if that implies "invading and raiding other nations" (Dixon, 2000: p. 79). For this reason, patriotism has been rejected by some authors as an ideology comparable to racism (Gomberg, 1990). However, far from seeing this statement as a problem for his theory, MacIntyre defends patriotism as a virtue that has a rightful place in a morality situated in the social life of a community. In his view, there is simply no external, universal moral point of view from which to judge this practice (see Dixon, 2000: p. 79).

Some authors have tried to temperate these counterintuitive implications of the patriotic stance without falling back into moral universalism totally. Stephen Nathanson (1989), for instance, advances what he calls "moderate patriotism". In his view, when a conflictive situation arises, a moderate patriot will evaluate the claims made by both sides and will strive to accommodate both sides' legitimate interests. However, when this is not possible, she will be allowed to choose her own side, and enter into the struggle, although with regret, as she is painfully aware of the moral remainders. In Nathanson's opinion:

> [t]he fact that the defence of their [moderate patriots'] own community would be undertaken with deep regret points to the moral superiority of their position. In contrast, extreme patriots, as MacIntyre describes their view, need not care in the least about the well-being of members of the opposing community. The choice to fight for survival would be made with ease and need not be preceded by any search for alternatives. (Nathanson, 1989: p. 541)

The reason why Macintyrean patriotism is deplorable is simply that it condones courses of action that are harmful to others on irrelevant grounds. The fact that a group of people do not belong to our community can hardly be considered as a reason that can justify hurting them. This criticism affects Nathanson's moderate patriotic position as well. As Paul Gomberg (2000: p. 90) stated it, this:

> would be little comfort ... to the Vietnamese whose homes were bombed, or the Iraqis whose children died because water treatment plants were bombed by moderately patriotic bomber pilots, or to residents of the Chorrillo neighbourhood in Panama City whose homes were destroyed and relatives killed by moderately patriotic soldiers in the United States invasion of December 1989. ... what is so moderate about this patriotism?

A further objection to the picture of sports delivered by Dixon above — indeed a "demonization" of sports nationalism — is that it is simply not warranted to ascribe all evils on earth to the public's enthusiasm for their national team jersey.

As he himself observes, these excesses are not necessarily connected with sport nationalism. Property destruction, racial and ethnic abuse, disturbing rival players' performance by yelling and cheating (through the use of forbidden drugs or other illicit means) might depend on nationalistic euphoria in some cases, but need not do so. The same kind of abuses can also take place when, for instance, Manchester United meets Newcastle in the English football league.

Besides, it could be argued in favour of elite sports, the undesirable phenomena listed above are probably caused by deeper social factors than nationalistic or team euphoria, in the form it takes at the stadium. The stadium simply happens to be the site where this underlying violence, generated by other factors than sport feelings, is expressed.

So, elite sports might be defended against the present objection by arguing that (a) hooliganism is also present in national sports competitions; and (b) sports nationalism does not generate the violence of hooligans; rather, international sports competitions are the occasions where that latent violence is manifested. Are these arguments sufficiently strong to neutralise the charge of hooliganism raised against sports nationalism?

In my opinion, they are not. A sports detractor will argue that, even if phenomena such as hooliganism and vandalism are present in national sports competitions, sports nationalism nonetheless augments these manifestations of violence. Further, she might say that, although hooliganism is not generated at sports arenas, the stadium constitutes an appropriate venue for its manifestation. So, though not the cause of spectator violence, sports are equally to blame for facilitating its occurrence and even increasing its magnitude.

But perhaps we are being unfair to sports. Is it not preferable that those manifestations of latent social violence take place in connection with sports events, rather than occurring spontaneously and unexpectedly? At least, at the stadium, police and other repressive forces are on the spot, prepared to confront outbursts of violence. This might be expected to reduce property destruction and personal injuries. The damage in connection with sporting events is probably less than it would, if the violence occurred in other contexts.

This line of reasoning assumes that sports vandalism takes the place of ordinary vandalism. However, there is no empirical evidence to suggest that this is the case. For explosions of violence to take place as they do in connection with sports competitions, some requirements must be met. A proper venue is needed (the sporting event), together with the identification of a target group distinct from the one to which we belong (supporters of the rival team) and the feeling that it will be relatively easy to get away with violence (for instance, because of the large amount of people present at the stadium). It is not at all obvious that these conditions are equally met in non-sporting contexts. Thus, far from replacing other manifestations of violence, it might instead be the case that sports vandalism augments these manifestations of vandalism. There are therefore good reasons to believe that the substitution phenomenon referred to by sport defenders has no correspondence in reality. Hooliganism is a problem for sports, and the national feelings associated with international sports competitions contribute to increase the number and magnitude of manifestations of hooligan violence.

I will not discuss these expressions of violence further, as Dixon considers them to be related to a kind of aggressive, unrestricted nationalism that has no place in the realm of sports. Rather, in what follows, I will concentrate my discussion on Dixon's own version of moderate sports nationalism, as he develops it in his article. Contrary to his opinion, I will affirm that sports patriotism, even in his moderate version, ends up by harming emergent nations in a morally relevant manner.

Starting from Stephen Nathanson's notion of moderate patriotism, Dixon tries to meet the objection that sports nationalism harms other nations. As moderate patriots, he writes, "we temper our preference for our own country by refusing to act immorally in furthering its interests" (Dixon, 2000: p. 76). That excludes, for instance, bombing other nations when this is not required by reasons of self-defence, or invading other countries simply to impose our political will or further our interests. In spite of name similarity, there is then a fundamental difference between Nathanson's and Dixon's moderate patriotism. According to the former, we should try to settle conflicts without resorting to violence against other nations. But if this is the only way out, we are in Nathanson's view justified in injuring other people, though with regret. Instead, Dixon tells us to refrain from hurting other nations, even in situations in which conflicts cannot be settled by peaceful means.

Unlike jingoistic sports patriots, Dixon's moderate sports nationalists do not treat other countries' athletes, coaches and other people as if they lacked moral status. Instead, they consider them worthy competitors they are not allowed to "harm" in any other sense than doing the best they can to deprive them of a sporting victory. This deprivation, however, does not violate the demand for impartiality that characterises morality, according to Dixon. The reason is that "[i]mpartiality demands that we respect the negative rights of all people, whether or not they belong to our favoured group" (Dixon, 2000 pp. 76–77). But it does not require that we benefit strangers. "When it comes to benefits that I choose to bestow on a person or group of people", he says, "I am morally free to follow my whim, as long as the cause that I support is not itself immoral" (Dixon, 2000: p. 77). In the context of sports, Dixon's nationalistic stance might be summed up by saying that, although strangers have a right not to be harmed by our conduct, we have no obligation to benefit them by withdrawing our support for our national sports teams. Thus, in Dixon's opinion, although sports nationalism implies a certain form of partiality, it is an innocuous form of patriotism, "because athletes' attempts to win and fans' preference for their own country's athletes in international sporting contests inflict no significant harm on people in other countries" (Dixon, 2000: p. 82).

Dixon's position rests on the argument — which he does not substantiate — that there exists a morally relevant distinction between harming (for instance, by violating someone's negative rights), and not benefiting (for instance, by not honouring someone's positive right to be helped if in need). On the grounds of this distinction, Dixon then presents his moderate sports nationalism as morally permissible, because, in his opinion, it does not harm other nations in such a way that it would amount to a violation of their negative rights.

That very distinction is blurred, however. As Paul Gomberg has argued, preference for compatriots in hiring, in philanthropic donations to the hungry, and in consumer purchases by those in relatively wealthy countries is "like racism, helping a relatively advantaged group in preference to a group that was already disadvantaged, adding to their disadvantage" (Gomberg, 2000: p. 88).

Besides, it might reasonably be argued that emergent, poor countries have a positive right to help from developed countries, not only for reasons of international solidarity, but also because their poverty facilitates — as a matter of fact, it might even be causally related to — the high level of welfare of the central nations. Often, nationalism, even of the moderate kind, hinders us from giving developing countries their due.

According to Dixon, however, this should not worry partisans of sports nationalism. In his view, favouritism of our national sports teams does not affect other nations, emergent countries included, in any morally relevant manner. For instance, our desire for sporting success is compatible with other nations' right not to have their socio-economic development or their political order adjusted to the particular interests of our country.

But is sport nationalism indeed so innocent as Dixon suggests? There is at least one argument that seems to advocate the contrary. According to some critics, international sports competitions reproduce the historical subordination of the former colonies to the central countries. I shall now address that argument.

Nationalism with sport is bad

Finally, we have the objection that sports, together with nationalism, gives rise to practices that are bad. First, it is argued that, albeit indirectly, the combination of sport and nationalism affects other nations negatively by denying them the possibility of obtaining international recognition. Second, sport and nationalism are said to affect the citizens of our own country as well by distracting them from more valuable activities. Let us see now if these objections find their mark.

Some critics of elite sports affirm that, due to their ongoing commercialisation, they are reinforcing the subordination of peripheral countries to international economic power. And, indeed, it has to be acknowledged that leading sports federations are almost without exception run by representatives of central countries, often with links to the interests of major multinational enterprises.

William J. Morgan has nonetheless argued to the contrary. He advances an account of sports as a special kind of a people's narrative that unfolds their idiosyncratic social and moral character. His argument is that the creative character of this process, and its appropriation by new nations, has allowed emergent countries, not only to beat colonialists at their own game, but also to transform the original emulation into a self-affirming practice. Thus, in his view, international sports competitions provide an excellent opportunity for emergent nations to gain recognition in the international scene, improve their self-esteem and, thereby, reinforce their national identity. He substantiates his assertion with some examples gathered from reality. After referring to the sporting successes of some African countries following the decolonization process in the 60s, he says:

I could, of course, have just as easily cited Cuba's triumphs over the
United States in baseball, or Brazil's victories in the World Cup, or West
Indian successes in cricket. For this 'beating them at their own game'
phenomenon, and the vertiginous narrative outpouring it induces, is a
widespread one indeed, and, at least with respect to the dominated
nations involved, a dialogical coup of sorts. (Morgan, 2000: pp. 67–68)

In football, Nigeria and Cameroon are further examples of emergent nations
whose national pride has been empowered by sporting prowess.

Against Morgan, it could be argued that his argument justifies, at best, sports
nationalism in emergent nations. For them, the defence of their national symbols
in sports contexts is needed to secure national identification and international
recognition. However, that is not the case with already established national
communities. How can we justify the sports nationalism of, say, German and
English people? These are countries that are rather homogenous internally, and
also well established on the international scene. Do German and English sports
supporters, then, act wrongly when they cheer for their team?

Not at all. When they meet a national team of another well established
country, German and English sport fans are allowed to support their own team,
as this has not direct bearing on the international recognition enjoyed by the other
nation. And when they meet emergent nations, they are not only allowed, but
even required to cheer for their team. Otherwise, the victory eventually obtained
by the opposing team would have no value. To feel pride in your achievements
in a competitive enterprise you must be sure that your competitors have done
everything in their power to beat you. Otherwise, you will experience no sense
of prowess. Victory over condescending rivals does not enhance self-esteem,
even less external recognition from others.

Morgan's argument, however, does not fully strikes at the heart of the present
objection. Even if sporting victories have led to international recognition for
emergent nations, and thereby helped to reinforce their self-esteem, it is
nonetheless true that competitive sports also have reinforced the subordination
of these countries to international economic power. In that sense, the recognition
is not authentic, and the self-esteem illusory, as they are simply symbolic gestures
with no correspondence in practical politics. Morgan's argument, then, even if

right, does not neutralise the present objection, which focuses, let us recall, on economic and political subordination.

Seen in that perspective, sports nationalism can actually be said to harm developing nations, albeit in an indirect manner. Admittedly genuine recognition requires opposition. Central countries should therefore try to defeat emergent nations. But this is separate from the question of supporting emergent nations' sporting activities (for instance, by building training facilities for them or by giving financial aid to their promising athletic figures). Doing so would increase the possibility of emergent nations to achieve sporting success and, with it, increased international recognition and self-esteem. However, such support is blocked by the sports nationalism of the central countries. They prefer to use their resources to encourage their own athletes. That means that, after all, the sports nationalism of the central countries is harmful for emergent nations, as it makes it more difficult for them to affirm themselves in the world sports arena. The only nationalism that is unproblematic is therefore the nationalism of the emergent nations. From the point of view of the central countries, the right policy to adopt is to manifest nationalistic fervour when sports competition take place, but to combine this with an internationalist stance which supports the development of sports in peripheral countries. The conclusion then is that sports nationalism in central countries is not as innocuous as Morgan and Dixon argue: if implemented consistently, it does deprive emergent nations from things or goods of essential value.

To those who dislike emergent nations adopting this way of achieving international recognition and national identity, there always remain the possibility of exhorting people, both in central and in peripheral countries, not to overestimate the importance of sporting successes and to try, instead, to go for what (in their view) are more important national achievements. In doing so, they should find comfort in current trends towards the increased commercialism of sports, which may also reduce concern about many other problematic aspects of contemporary sport. This commercialisation will mean that athletes, even those from emergent nations, will give more priority to their professional careers and show less interest in participating in their national teams. Seen over a long time perspective, this trend can only lead to the reduction of public interest in international sports competitions. This may result in sports nationalistic sentiments being tempered, and thus allow for more substantial ways of achieving international recognition and self-respect as a nation, than victory in a mere sports contest.

Harm to our own nation: diverting social efforts

So far, we have been discussing the noxious effects of sports nationalism on other nations, according to sports critics. An exaggerated involvement in sport matters, however, might also be damaging for members of our own nation and our own people. By focusing our attention on the achievements of our national sports teams, we might be diverting efforts from more urgent social and political issues.

In this respect, two different situations can be distinguished. The first one is concerned with involvement in sports nationalism under normal political conditions. An example of this would be the football euphoria that overwhelmed Sweden in connection with its national team's successes in the World Football Cup in the United States, in 1994.

But, second, sports nationalism might also be present in a situation of political and/or socio-economic crisis. Argentina won its first football world championship in 1978, under military rule. Football fans cheered their team to victory while thousands of their fellow-citizens were being tortured and murdered by the military. In Brazil (for many, the most outstanding football superpower of the past century), sporting achievements have always been celebrated in a context of massive poverty and total absence of social and economic rights for large segments of the population. Should not all that nationalistic enthusiasm be used instead to get rid of dictatorship and to secure appropriate living conditions for the masses? In the rest of this chapter, I will discuss the morality of engaging in sports nationalism in the different situations outlined above.

(a)   Sports nationalism under normal political conditions

Did Swedes act morally wrongly when they cheered for their team in the US football championship in 1994? In general terms, Sweden is a well-functioning democracy, free from urgent social and economic problems of the magnitude that we witness in developing countries. Thus, at first sight, there seems to be no moral wrong in the overwhelming enthusiasm of Swedes for their team: there are simply no other enterprises to which all that enthusiasm might be channelled and used for.

However, this is a wrong intuition. The corollary of the argument that Swedes did not do wrong at that time because they did not have any urgent problems to solve, is that people in poorer nations, in which such problems still are unsolved, are acting wrongly, if they celebrate their sporting triumphs. This is indeed a rather unpalatable conclusion. It means that poverty not only deprives people of appropriate dwelling, education and health care: it also deprives them of their right to cheer! That adds sadness to misery for developing nations. Seen in that light, it becomes evident that, arguing that the poor should commit themselves to dealing with more urgent problems than celebrating sporting victories is a dominant-nation perspective. It justifies, in a paternalistic way, depriving them of joy, in the name of their own interests. Seen like this, celebration by the poor becomes an expression of an alienated conscience. They should not celebrate, but should instead deal with their problems. And the very fact that they do cheer, it is argued, shows they are incapable of understanding what should be done. So stated, however, this stance is marked by such an elitist tinge that it becomes evident it should be rejected.

Further, it is also incorrect that, in 1994 as well as after that, there were no other enterprises to which Swedes could usefully have diverted all their sporting enthusiasm. There may well be no urgent issues within Sweden's boundaries. Personally, I doubt it. Nevertheless, there is still a great deal of poverty in the world. Why limit our efforts to palliate misery to the territory of our own nation-state? In that sense, Swedes had less right to celebrate than, for instance, Nigerians, when their Olympic football team beat Argentina in the final match at Atlanta 1996. Because of their wealth, Swedes — unlike Nigerians — can alleviate much of the misery still affecting the world. So, though not negative (at least not directly) for the own nation, the Swedish football celebration of 1994 can be called to account, not so much for diverting efforts from urgent social issues in their own country, but rather for not having been followed by active international aid overseas.

(b)   *Sports nationalism in a situation of crisis*

Since the sixties, a certain ideological mistrust over the exultation manifested by Brazilians in their public celebrations has been a recurrent theme in the political discourse of many Latin American Leftist intellectuals. Carnival, as well as the vivid enthusiasm provoked by football victories (by far the most popular sport in the country), have been interpreted by sociologists, philosophers and political analysts as a kind of unconscious strategy to escape a sad social and economic reality, instead of dealing with it in order to change the situation. According to this criticism, then, Brazilians — in particular, the lower classes — possess a false social conscience that creates obstacles to their social emancipation and keeps them in chains, politically speaking.

I remain unconvinced of the relevance of this argument. Not only does it deprive the poor of the right to cheer; it also sets up a political agenda for the disadvantaged in a paternalistic manner, an agenda that is not supported by any known facts about personal or political action. Has it really been established that concentrating efforts exclusively on political and social issues is the most efficient way to cope with poverty and inappropriate living conditions? It might equally well be argued that joy (deriving, for instance, from sporting achievements or large-scale popular celebrations such as Carnival rituals) not only helps people to endure their harsh social situation, but even gives them strength to continue the fight against injustice and for the implementation of social changes. The supposed link between abstaining from celebration and the achievement of social and political improvements is, to put it mildly, indirect and difficult to substantiate. In fact, there are certain empirical data suggesting that watching sports events may on the whole raise participation in other activities as well. Different studies from Austria, Canada, Denmark, East and West Germany and Switzerland have concluded that athletically active persons are more likely to engage in other activities (including politics) than non-active individuals[7]. Another empirical investigation revealed a correlation, not only between practising sports and engaging in other kinds of activity, but even between sports spectatorship and increased social involvement[8]. Of course, these findings are not conclusive. But they are enough to cast doubt on the supposed diversion of efforts caused by involvement in sports and other activities, including celebrations. In that sense, there is an element of uncertainty of outcome in the Brazilian scenario that exonerates large-scale public celebrations from any accusation of stifling political consciences.

What about the Argentinean example? Argentina is a typical football country. Football is the dominant subject when friends talk at cafeterias and bars. Sunday family lunches — a deeply rooted tradition probably originating from European immigration — are regularly deprived of some members of the family who leave the table early to get into the stadium in time. It is not therefore surprising that, during the period of military rule that led to the assassination of thousands of people between 1976 and 1983, the concept "Argentina 78" became a slogan repeatedly heard in the pro-government media. That was the year when the country would be hosting the Football World Cup, and its military rulers were hoping to better their international reputation by trying to convince the world that the international community's accusations of violations of human rights were unfounded. Argentina won the championship, and the victory over the Dutch national team in the final was followed by massive celebrations in the streets. A concentration camp was located beneath one of the largest avenues of Buenos Aires, and in it political opponents were kept captive under barbaric conditions. Years later, survivors of that camp have described how they understood that Argentina had become the new football world champion when, in their cells, they heard the noise made by the crowds marching and cheering over their heads. In such a political context, was it right to celebrate the sporting victory?

It is, of course, impossible to reach consensus on this matter. Opinions will probably differ, depending on how those asked value sporting triumphs. Different political preferences add also to the difficulty of reaching a common agreement on the subject. However, unlike the Brazilian case, I would tend to conclude that Argentineans acted wrongly in endorsing the celebration promoted by the regime, provided they knew about the abductions and the killing. I base this intuition on the direct, almost concretely ascertainable effect that a massive boycott to the celebration would have had on the political stability of the military government. It is not far fetched to say that such an action would probably have accelerated the political disintegration of the regime, and thereby saved the lives of people who were killed during the final years of military rule. When dictatorship starts to kill people, it must be eliminated immediately. In that regard, the situation does not seem to differ much from the Brazilian scenario. Poverty also kills people, albeit more indirectly and over a longer period of time. But in the Argentinean case, the link that we must presuppose existed between not celebrating a sporting victory and the saving of human lives is much more direct than in the Brazilian example. It is more than likely that a politically enfeebled dictatorship will not dare to keep on executing those who oppose it. But a government might still remain passive in the face of social and economic injustices, even if confronted with popular indifference for a national sporting victory.

It should be noted that this conclusion applies even if the empirical data cited in connection with the Brazilian case proved to be accurate. Sports spectatorship might indirectly enhance participation in other activities, included political engagement. But what the Argentinean situation demanded, as is the case with other similar dictatorial regimes, at that time was immediate, direct action to stop the killing. And a boycott at that moment would probably have inflicted more damage to the military rulers than the damage caused to them by the ulterior (and indirectly enhanced) political activity of the cheering crowd.

To sum up: When the factual consequences of sports spectatorship and popular celebrations are not easily ascertainable, we should feel free to express our enthusiasm for sporting victories. The motto here is: "When in doubt, cheer!" That might enhance, albeit indirectly, your will to change the social and political reality. But when there is no reasonable doubt that a boycott of sporting events can save lives in a rather direct manner, we should not give away to our enthusiasm for sport.

Conclusions

In this chapter, I tried to establish whether the supposed menace from nationalism in sports can be substantiated.

The upshot of the previous discussion seems to leave us with mixed results. On the one hand, neither the traditional nor the newly formulated Marxian criticism of competitive elite sports appears to hit its target. There is not enough evidence to confirm that sports nationalism enhances war and aggression between countries. On the contrary, the entry of business interests in the world of sports makes it more difficult to exacerbate national sentiments and use them to promote nationalistic wars and genocide. Today, athletes are often perceived as bearers of a commercial brand, rather than representatives of a supposedly superior race or nationality. This process cannot but weaken nationalistic bigotry and aggression. The history of mankind is a living testimony to how individuals in all times have been disposed to kill for their own tribe, kin or national community. To my knowledge, however, nobody has yet been ready to lay down her life for Adidas.

On the contrary, it is in connection with hooliganism and vandalism that sports nationalism becomes problematic. National chauvinism lies behind many violent episodes between supporters of different national teams. In that sense, it could be argued that sports nationalism adds to the already existent violence and animosities between different group of supporters within one and the same country.

Nor were things less troublesome when moderate patriotism was scrutinised. According to Nicholas Dixon, for instance, we do not deprive other people from valuable assets when we cheer for our nation. I was not convinced of the validity of this statement, however. As a matter of fact, I believe that a certain kind of sports nationalism (namely, the chauvinistic sporting fervour of the central countries) causes considerable damage to emerging, peripheral countries. Misguided by nationalistic sentiments, former colonial metropolises fail to contribute to the development of sports in peripheral countries (for instance, through international aid). They disregard the need of these nations for sporting accomplishments, as one step in the process of strengthening sentiments of dignity and national identity. Sporting victories improve self-confidence and pride in a community.

Finally, exaggerated sports nationalism might also be damaging for the nation which practices it, at least under regimes that persecute and kill their people. But when these exceptional political conditions are not fulfilled, it is legitimate for the deprived masses to cheer for their national team. The right to feel joy should not be made dependent on the level of material betterment that has been achieved.

The final accounting, then, is negative for sports nationalism. Without it, there would probably be fewer victims of the violence of hooligans, and emergent nations and nations ruled by dictatorial regimes would be better off than they are at present. If my arguments above were correct, there can be only one conclusion: sport would be better rid of its nationalistic character.

Notes

1   Another, similar version of this material appears as a chapter in Tamburrini, 2000: the reprinting of passages from which is authorised by the University of Gothenburg.

2   As Gomberg (2000: p. 98 note 1) notes, the word "compatriots" suggests the
        idea of "patriotism", which could be said to stand for something different from
        "nationalism". The former refers to partiality for one's state and its citizens
        (compatriots); the latter, for one's co-nationals, with whom one may or may not
        share a state, but perhaps instead the same ethnic origin, a language or a
        religion. In this chapter, the terms "patriotism" and "nationalism" will be used
        interchangeably.

3   The latest example of the utilisation of sports to further a just political cause is
        the marathon held in Rome on January 8th 2000. The competition was named
        after the only Argentine federate athlete, Miguel Sanchez, who is still missing
        after being abducted by the military regime in the 70s. The runners bear a T-
        shirt with a picture of the missing athlete.

4   This topic is pursued in a chapter in Tamburrini, 2000.

5   In the city of Barcelona, for instance, according to an ancient custom, city
        teams dedicate their victories to the patron saint of the village by placing a
        flower arrangement depicting the coat of arms of Catalunya. Such practices
        might be related to the tradition of armies paying tribute to the city by
        dedicating to it the victory in a public ceremony. The example of Barcelona is
        not an isolated one. Unlike ancient communities, we no longer make soldiers
        the object of our admiration in our societies. Their place has been taken by
        athletes. The hero worship of athletes might in that sense be seen as a sign of
        higher culture.

6   We often see the public honour a failing athlete who, though not victorious, has
        at least 'done his or her best'.

7   See here the studies on this topic cited and discussed in Guttmann, 1986 pp.
        150–154.

8   See, for example, the quotation from Hanhart in Guttmann, 1986: p. 154.

References

Dixon, N. (2000) "A justification of a moderate patriotism in sport", in T. Tännsjö
        and C. Tamburrini (eds.) *Values in sport: Elitism, nationalism, gender equality
        and the scientific manufacture of winners*. London: E & FN Spon (Routledge),
        pp. 74–86.

Gomberg, P. (1990) "Patriotism is like racism", *Ethics* Vol. 101: pp. 144–150.

———— (2000) "Patriotism in sports and in war", in T. Tännsjö and C. Tamburrini
        (eds) *Values in sport: Elitism, nationalism, gender equality and the scientific
        manufacture of winners*. London: E & FN Spon (Routledge), pp. 87–98.

Guttmann, A. (1986) *Sports spectators*, New York: Columbia University Press.

Lasch, C. (1978) *The Culture of narcissism*, W.W. Norton & Company Inc.: New York.

MacIntyre, A (1984) "Is patriotism a virtue?" Lindley Lecture, Philosophy Department, University of Kansas.

Morgan, W. J. (2000) "Sports as the moral discourse of nations", in T. Tännsjö and C. Tamburrini (eds.) *Values in sport: Elitism, nationalism, gender equality and the scientific manufacture of winners*. London: E & FN Spon (Routledge), pp. 59–73.

Nathanson, S. (1989) "In defence of moderate patriotism", *Ethics* Vol. 99, pp. 535–52.

Tamburrini, C. (2000) *The 'hand of God'?*. Gothenburg, Sweden: Acta Universitatis Gothoburgensis.

Tännsjö, T. (2000) " Is it fascistoid to admire sports heroes?" in T. Tännsjö and C. Tamburrini (eds.) *Values in sport: Elitism, nationalism, gender equality and the scientific manufacture of winners*. London: E & FN Spon (Routledge), pp. 9–23.

MONEY, MORALITY OR THE MORGUE? EDUCATIONAL CONSIDERATIONS IN THE POLITICS OF ANTI-DOPING POLICIES FOR SPORT

Marc Keech
Chelsea School, University of Brighton

Introduction

I need the money; it's the only reason I'm here. We change into our strip. There are five of us in the room. I sit on the bed, wishing the others to get ready, waiting for the moment. I know it has to happen. I'm waiting for it to happen. The pressure … I can't take this pressure. It happens — the smiles … the bag is produced. In it small white ampoules of amphetamines and a handful of short syringes. A glance is thrown in my direction. My "chastity" is well known throughout the team but it is only polite to offer. I scratch my head and breathe in deeply. If I walk out the door with only the hotel lunch in my system I will crack mentally … I can't face the humiliation. The pressure. I need the money. I nod in acceptance.

My syringe is prepared. As it's my first time it is decided that 7cc will be enough. Ten to fifteen is the average dose but the real hard men use double or treble this. Amphetamines work strongly for about two to three hours and then the effects diminish. The criterium will last two hours which means we can take them in the privacy of our hotel before going out to start. I roll up the sleeve of my jersey. No turning back now. The needle is slipped under the skin of my left shoulder. I'm charged. One of my ambitions has been to leave the sport without taking anything. I got a certain satisfaction as casting myself as the pure white hero in an evil black world. But that was over now. To hell with the past! (Kimmage, 1998: p. 143)

Imagine standing in my shoe when one of our top athletes comes up to me and says 'I have the best equipment, nutrition programme, my coach is great, I have money to get to races and I know I'm fast. But there is no way I can break into the top 15 at the Worlds — these other guys are juiced. I want to stay clean — but don't expect me to win.' (Milburn, 1999: p. 1)

The Irish cyclist Paul Kimmage rode in cycling's Tour de France three times during the 1980s. His emotive admission of finally succumbing to using amphetamines in order to perform on an equal footing with his contemporaries is one of sport's most painful, cynical, but also compelling stories. When his book *Rough Ride* was initially published in 1990 Kimmage was vilified for breaking the 'veil of silence' that surrounded the doping culture in cycling. Eight years later, the furore that accompanied the 1998 Tour De France illustrated that doping was still as much a part of cycling as it was when English cyclist Tom Simpson died on the climb of Mont Venteux in 1967. The autopsy on Simpson revealed his heart had collapsed and traces of two forms of amphetamines were found in his blood stream.

Philip Milburn, Chief Operating Officer for USA Cycling, exemplifies the realisation by other cyclists that 'non-doping' is a measure of the possible achievements of an athlete. The use of blood and urine tests for EPO at the Sydney Olympics exemplifies that the techniques utilised by international sports organisations to combat doping in sport have advanced significantly since the 1960s. Conversely, it should also be recognised that international sports organisations have consistently refused to acknowledge that doping cultures are prevalent in many sports, particularly where individual performances predominate. Just as a method for detecting the use of EPO has been established a replacement product could already be in highly used. Perflurocarbon (PFC) is a substance with remarkable oxygen carrying capacity and, according to Milburn (1999: p. 7), was allegedly used in speed-skating and cross-country skiing in the late 1990s.

The profile of anti-doping policies

As the Sydney Olympics drew to a close, the general euphoria that accompanied the success of the event made it easy to forget that there was intense media examination of anti-doping measures in the two years prior to the Games. In response to the 1998 Tour de France, the International Olympic Committee (IOC) convened the World Conference on Doping in Sport, held in Lausanne in February 1999. One of the consequences of the conference was a revised Olympic Movement Anti-Doping Code, which affirmed the IOC's (1999: p. 3) commitment to "completely eliminate doping from sport" and "intended to ensure respect for the ethical concepts implicit in Fair Play and the Olympic Spirit". In contrast, the previous year had seen the Prince Alexandre de Merode, chair of the IOC's Medical Commission, comment that "We will never eliminate doping from sport" (BBC News online, August 20, 1998).

Anti-doping policies are easily criticised, particularly because of the unevenness of responses from different organisations. National sports federations in countries with traditionally more interventionist governments, such as in Scandanavia, have sought to lead the establishment of a global anti-doping framework. The IOC has followed lamely, belatedly announcing itself at the 'forefront' of anti-doping policies. IOC President Juan Antonio Samaranch has often commented on his organisation's 'leadership' of anti-doping policies, but in doing so has only exemplified the indifference of sports administrators to doping. Prior to the 1994 Asian Games in Shanghai, Samaranch commented that "Chinese sport (was) very clean." A week later he proclaimed that "... doping is really declining and there are very few problems in the main competitions" (Jennings, 1996: p. 233). Significantly of the 23 swimming gold medals won by Chinese athletes at those 1994 games, nine had to be returned following positive drug tests (BBC News online, January 1, 2000).

With the collapse of apartheid in South Africa, and the end of the Cold War, doping emerged as the most significant issue in international sports politics during the 1990s. Ten years on from the publication of Kimmage's book, this chapter examines why it is not enough to just develop and seek to harmonise anti-doping policies. Instead it seeks to build on Ljungvist's (1999: p. 4) proposal that a complete anti-doping programme "should include not only dope testing but also information, education and research." The chapter traces the inability of policy makers to acknowledge that the constitutive[1] demands of sport are often the primary reason for athletes using illegal methods to compete in their sport. The recent educational initiatives proposed for comprehensive anti-doping policies are reviewed and it is questioned whether such initiatives seek to provide justification for the ban on doping in sport. Consequently, the rationale for any harmonisation of anti-doping policies is questioned unless policy makers can educate and inform all those who are involved in the production, construction and consumption of sports about the consequences of incorrectly combating doping in sport.

Doped or duped, what is the 'problem'?

For many, sport arouses passions that are born of a deep-rooted desire to see one's team, favourite athlete or international representative succeed. Yet doping remains one of the most complex problems facing modern sport and a number of authors have attempted to tease out a variety of discourses which underpin the integrity of anti-doping policies, but concomitantly, threaten the validity of these very same policies. The issue of 'fairness' is not at the heart of discussion here. Instead when one analyses the implementation of anti-doping policies, what's wrong with doping is that sports administrators have refused to acknowledge the suspicion that many sports are constituted in part by a culture of doping. Yet nobody can say for certain to what extent each sport is 'doped'. Until the 'veil of secrecy' is replaced by a more open and honest approach then the practice of modern sport will remain to some degree concealed from the watching public.

The issue of doping in sport continues to affect perceptions of sporting performance and the moral credibility of elite sport particularly when viewed through linkages with media discourses and the politics of identity. The revelation that a sports star has been implicated in contravening doping rules is often an unpalatable truism. Denham (1997) discusses how the herofication of athletes lead public audiences in America to dismiss the attribution of rumours surrounding the untimely death of Florence Griffith Joiner to her immediate retirement after the 1988 Olympics and consistent steroid abuse. He also cites the case of baseball star Mark McGuire's revelation that he was using an over-the-counter testosterone substance, one banned by the IOC. In contrast Jackson (1998) explored the reaction to Ben Johnson's positive test at the 1988 Seoul

Olympics and noted that many Canadians disassociated themselves from the national and international significance of the affair. The reaction to sports stars in the media concerning their (alleged) use of doping substances neglects to address that doping is an integral component of modern sporting practice. Regardless of the nationality of an athlete, doping has permeated sport to the extent that governments have been forced to take action. In considering how sport can stop 'duping' the public three issues can be considered: first, the need to accurately define doping; second, the extent to which doping is an acknowledged element of sporting culture or whether a form of repression exists in the self-contained world of modern sports; and third, why there is an argument to remove the ban on doping in sport.

Defining the 'problem'

For something that is simplistically viewed as a question of being in the 'right' or in the 'wrong', defining doping is not that simple. As Houlihan (1998: p. 28) points out:

> Many would agree with Sir Arthur Gold's observation that providing a definition of doping may well prove impossible yet everyone who takes part in sport knows exactly what it means. The definition lies not in the words but in integrity of character.

Wadler (1999) analysed three definitions by different institutions. In 1963 the Council of Europe defined doping as:

> The administration of or use by a competing athlete of any substance foreign to the body or any physiologic substance taken in abnormal quantity or taken by an abnormal route of entry with the sole intention of increasing in an artificial and unfair manner his/her performance in competition. (quoted in Wadler, 1999: p. 4)

The IOC Medical Code views doping as:

> The use of certain substances and methods intended to enhance and/or having the effect of enhancing athletic performance, such practices being contrary to medical ethics. (quoted in Wadler, 1999: p. 4)

A third definition was provided in the Olympic Movement Anti-Doping Code wherein doping is:

> the use of an artifice, whether substance or method, potentially dangerous to an athlete's health and/or capable of enhancing performances, or the presence in the athletes' body of a substance, or the ascertainment of a method on the list annexed to the Olympic Movement Anti-Doping Code. (quoted in Wadler, 1999: p. 5)

All of the definitions are highly problematic and vary according to the changing nature of doping practices. The measurement of intent is impossible and, after an athlete protests their innocence, often subject to legal challenge, with litigation often forcing sports federations to reconsider an athlete's intent beyond all doubt.

Acutely aware of the problems of anti-doping policies, Houlihan (1999: p. 107) correctly asserts that, until a satisfactory answer is given as to why doping should be opposed, it will not be possible to define with sufficient clarity the problem that sporting and governmental authorities are trying to tackle, nor will it be possible to defend anti-doping policies with any confidence. Perhaps one should add that international sports administrators should stop bemoaning the difficulty of the task, as they are the chief architects in the construction of modern sporting practice and keen to seek the commercial rewards available for 'entertaining' sport.

Houlihan (1999: p. 108) surmises that anti-doping strategies are justified in three ways. First, that doping is potentially injurious to an athlete's health; second, that doping is unfair; and third that doping undermines the credibility of sport in the eyes of external bodies or interests, including governments, multi-national corporations and the general public[2].

Tamburrini (2000: p. 202) persuasively argues against the ban on doping but concurs with Houlihan and adds that doping is objected to because if permitted, the practice would proliferate amongst young or amateur participants. Furthermore, "doping is said to run counter to the competitive ideal as it makes the outcome of competition depend upon artificial and irrelevant factors" and that "sport should not be a competition between technical products" (Tamburrini, 2000; p. 202).

Acknowledging the 'problem'?

Traditional concepts of sport purview doping as an externally attributed plague of modern sport. Yet, as Paul Kimmage demonstrated, doping practices have been syonymous with characteristics of the growth of sport in the latter half of the twentieth century. According to König (1995: p. 248), critiques of doping characterised by moral conviction make it appear that doping represented a general threat, jeopardising the very nature of sport. However, one must question whether the consecrated notions of sport can repel notions of doping. König (1995: p. 257) provocatively argues that doping is part of the constitutive demands of sport (see also note 1) and he dispels notions of doping being characterised as "an infringement of and treason to the idea of pure sport". He attributes the decline of sport to the moral indifference that has accompanied doping as a practice inherent in modern sport. Yet, whilst König's argument is highly persuasive, its discussion of doping occurs specifically in the context of sport ethics. In a more practical sense, sport concerns itself with how the issue of doping in modern sport must be addressed. To eliminate the practice may indeed be an additional, unobtainable ideal to preserve the value of sport, but that has not led to the abandonment of anti-doping policies. If one accepts König's view, then those concerned with the organisation of sport either intentionally neglect to understand what constitutes acceptable or unacceptable sporting practices, or they seek to unintentionally sanctify sport through a desire to blame external forces for moral crises that sport encounters. To eradicate doping from sport (as far as is possible) requires consideration about how to eliminate doping culture from sport.

It is difficult to disagree with Hoberman (1998) who contends that a form of social repression surrounds many sports which are vulnerable to significant doping practices. It would be profoundly misleading, he argues, to assert that athletics or weightlifting are two of the few sports that have a problem with doping, because of the advanced nature of their anti-doping programmes when compared to other sports. Hoberman (1998: p. 33) comments on the drug-dependent nature of cycling and states that "the logic of the dependency is the tour's [de France] open secret — a paradoxical expression that captures the ambivalence of a civilisation that demands such entertainments but is unwilling to acknowledge their physiological costs".

Waddington (2000) expands upon Hoberman's work in seeking to understand why professional cyclists have used various doping methods for a number of years, arguing that such an understanding provides a more secure basis for the formulation of policy in anti-doping strategies. Waddington (2000: pp. 160–163) identifies a 'culture of tolerance' in cycling's approach to doping in that a majority of riders may seek to compensate for the "extreme physical demands of professional cycling" simply in order to complete a race as gruelling as the Tour de France.

Doping therefore has become an inherent practice within the sport which is accepted, albeit reluctantly. The fact that the TVM and Festina teams were not banned from the sport following the 1998 Tour (and indeed, they were competing elsewhere almost immediately following their expulsions from the race) meant that it was difficult "to imagine that many people within cycling had no knowledge of the nature and extent of doping in sport. Perhaps most striking as an indication of the tolerance of doping, and of the associated hostility to outsiders who did not share this aspect of cycling culture, was the reaction of almost everyone involved in professional cycling to the police investigation during the 1998 Tour" (Waddington, 2000: p. 165). Thus, the paradox that Hoberman identified was, according to Waddington, exemplified by two key considerations.

> First, although we cannot be sure about precisely how many riders in the Tour were using drugs, the practice of doping was widespread. Second, despite routine dope tests after each stage of the tour, *not a single rider was excluded from the tour as a result of failing a doping control carried out by the Tour organisers* (original emphasis). All of the riders who tested positive did so rather as a result of tests which were conducted following the police action, rather than ... under the auspices of any authority within the world of professional cycling. (Waddington, 2000: p. 166)

Despite implementing non-absolutionist policies, international sport organisations still have not openly acknowledged the extent to which doping takes place. Consequently, such ambivalence creates a doubt in which 'clean' athletes who perform beyond their potential are tarred by suspicion. The mantra that athletes are innocent until proven guilty (i.e. caught doping) does little for the credibility of individuals and indeed, for the sport.

The 'problem' is no problem!

Black and Pape (1997: p. 84) suggest that the ban on doping in sport should be lifted. They argue that:

> Because of the ban, athletes are suspected of cheating. In the absence of the ban, neither coaches nor athletes would have cause to complain if competitors used drugs whilst (the former) remained drug free ... Perfection is not of this world, it is a choice between imperfect markets and imperfect regulation.

Black and Pape essentially argue that the removal of the ban would solve a number of ethical dilemmas with regard to the practice of doping in sport. In many respects, their suggestion would support König in that sport would be a practice in which a doping culture would be accepted. Tamburrini (2000: p. 202) puts forward three primary reasons why there may be some support for lifting the bans on doping in sport. First, the prohibition of on doping puts arbitrary restraints on the further development of sports, Second, the ban is responsible for the lack of knowledge on the eventual harmful effects of doping, which in spite of the ban does occur and will continue to occur. Lifting the prohibition would then allow supervised research aimed at harm provoked by (medically) unsupervised doping. Third, doping deprives professional elite sport from the transparency it so badly needs. In elite sports, it may be that spectators celebrate not the best, but the most sly athlete, the one who dopes best, and then gets away with it. The significance of this lack of transparency for the educational role of sports cannot be exaggerated.

However, the ban (on doping) remains and has the support of the majority of athletes, politicians, sports officials and spectators and for many, to remove the ban would destroy the consecrated notions of sport, and ironically, challenge its commercial viability, thus threatening the future development of sport. Doping is without question contrary to the fundamental principles of the Olympic movement, yet the *IOC* is guilty of malpractice and blatant hypocrisy with regard to the issue of doping in sport. The inability of the IOC and its member federations to accept the culture of doping in sport is a primary reason why Tamburrini (2000) and Black and Pape (1997) can rationalise the removal of the ban. Disconcertingly, the IOC has categorically failed to acknowledge that by encouraging a commercialised approach to sport, athletes would seek to establish natural or doped levels of performance that would reap the rewards on offer. The ban exists and remains but the IOC appears unable to fully justify why the ban should exist. For many sports administrators, the consideration that doping is simply 'wrong' remains the only way to justify the ban. Yet, nobody seems willing to accept that many in sport are committing acts of 'wrong'-doing, because the ban also serves to highlight that anti-doping policies have an effect only when someone gets caught. To explore why necessitates an examination of the idealistic origins of modern sport and the convergence of such notions with modern, commercially manipulated sporting concerns.

'Independence' and the credibility of anti-doping policies

The moral credibility of modern elite sport, from a traditional perspective, has only recently become a serious concern to international sports administrators. To acknowledge doping as a constitutive demand of sport would be an admission that sport is a distorted and even deformed practice, much removed from projected, traditional ideals espoused by sports organisations. One must question why athletes are not predisposed to such information and examine how sport still benefits from images of purity that are clearly not evident in practice. Furthermore, a brief historical overview would illustrate that it is becoming increasingly evident that if sport regulates its own practice anti-doping policies are likely to be less effective than if overseen by an independent non-sport organisation. The Olympic Games are established as the most powerful expression of global sporting practice, yet the International Olympic Committee has been strongly criticised for moulding sport into a highly commodified practice (see Simson and Jennings, 1992; Jennings, 1996; Senn, 1999) whilst refusing to acknowledge the hypocrisy of their approach (Zakus, 1992). Sport as a social practice benefits from a presumption of innocence, an innocence which has no justifiable rationale. Olympic officials still cling to the ideals of "Olympism" as a form of moral hygiene in sport which can be applied efficiently to large numbers of people in the form of gatherings precipitated by sport. The Olympic movement therefore projects itself as being based on principles of universal opportunity and equality. The IOC's definition of Olympism espouses the traditional moral integrity of sport:

Olympism is an overall philosophy of life exalting and combining in a balanced whole, the qualities of body, will and mind. Olympism sets out to create a way of life based on the joy of effort, the educational values of good example and a respect for universal, fundamental ethical principles. (cited in Segrave, 1988: p. 151)

Given the prominence of the Olympic Games, the influence of the IOC has penetrated the practices of modern global sport. The rhetoric that accompanies moral statements in sport tends to limit its effectiveness. The extreme prescriptiveness of idealistic notions of sport are indelible marks on the ideology and construction of modern sport yet the Olympic movement clings to values, beliefs and morals that were established over a century ago. Doping, the Olympic movement would contend, has been an external component of sport's image, not part of its constitutive elements. The idealised and consecrated notions of modern sport have been transcended by a highly professionalised, commodified notion of sport in which the rewards have inculcated an acute awareness of the competitiveness and inherent superiority that minimise other value-based judgements.

Whilst it has been evident that the IOC and many international sports federations (ISFs) have viewed sport and the notion of "Olympism" as an ideology designed to uphold traditional values, the reaction of the IOC to the issue in doping in sport has demonstrated that commercial influences have instilled a professionalised, commodified approach to the practice of sport. Yet whilst the IOC have reaped the commercial rewards associated with the Olympic Games, the organisation has ignored its responsibility to nurture a constructive social fabric within sport.

Donnelly (1996) contends that *Prolympism* has replaced Olympism as the dominant ideology in sport, where Prolympism inculcates values of Olympism/ idealism within a broadly commercialised and professionalised framework. That is to say, the traditional notions of sport have been appropriated within, and integrated into, a highly complex network in which a global sporting monoculture has emerged, characterised by remarkable financial rewards that reinforce differences between winners and losers. The IOC has embraced the immediate commercial benefits of Prolympism but neglected to inculcate the development of a framework that realises rewards are incentives to utilise doping methods. In doing so, the IOC has overlooked the process through which doping and rewards have become concomitant practices in global sport.

The manipulation of sport to replicate national identities and superiorities led nations to utilise doping programmes to improve their athletes' performance. As standards of performance improved during the latter half of the Twentieth Century, training methods developed concurrently, becoming more intense but also utilising 'legal' and 'illegal' scientific knowledge. Realising the rewards for successful performance, athletes in many sports have developed a culture that explores an almost limitless infatuation with doping practices.

Prolympism in the form of doping has manifested itself in a number of different ways. Political ambivalence to doping practices has been apparent in some of the most successful sporting nations in the world. The discovery of records in the Stasi files of the former East Germany demonstrated that the Honnecker regime was comfortable with a systematic state-run and co-ordinated doping programme for all their Olympic athletes bar those in yachting. In September 1999, Manfred Ewald and Manfred Hoeppner, respectively the former head of the East German Sports federation and the former chief medical officer of the same organisation were charged with complicity to cause bodily harm through administering banned hormones to young female athletes (BBC News Online, 9 September, 1999). In January 2000, the former chief doctor of the East German swimming team was jailed for fifteen months following his conviction for administering steroids to the swimmers in his charge. The women involved in the cases are now suffering from disturbed muscle growth, excessive body hair and deepened voices (BBC News Online, 12 January, 2000). Former communist states were not the only nations to engage in doping practices. For example, Lasse Viren, the Finnish distance runner used methods of blood doping to ensure his supremacy in the 1972 and 1976 Olympic Games. Even though Viren's methods were known in the sport, his actions were withheld from public consumption as the IOC did not ban blood doping until 1986. Kaarlo Maanika, the Finnish distance runner who won bronze in the 5000 metres at the Moscow Olympics, returned home to admit his shame about blood doping prior to the Games. He offered to return his medal but as there was no IOC rules against blood doping, the offer was not taken up. In Italy, information for a legal case to be held in November 2000 alleges that whilst those involved in sports medicine programmes with elite athletes were involved in a systematic programme of

Blood Doping, their work was being funded by the Italian Olympic Federation (CONI) and the IOC (Walsh and Follain, 2000: p. 11).

In 1968, doping controls in the form of immediate post-competition tests were first utilised at the Olympics. However, these developments were derided by many as a disguise through which the integrity of the Games themselves could be maintained as long as the occasional positive test was announced. The testing procedures of the time were not particularly sophisticated but were becoming more so. Despite initial progress the Moscow Olympics of 1980 was cited as a Drugs Olympics and the 1984 Los Angeles Olympics included a number positive track and field tests on the final day of competition that were never made public by the IOC. In 1990, the publication of the Dubin report on the inquiry into the use of drugs and banned practices intended to increase athletic performance in Canada, concluded that the practice of doping in sport was widespread not only among Canadian elite athletes but also amongst their international contemporaries. The International Amateur Athletic Federation (IAAF) responded to the report and the stain on athletics by intensifying its own anti-doping programmes to the extent that by 1993, athletics was the most thoroughly tested Olympic sport.

It may be comforting to believe that sport aspires to an idealistic moral purity, but it is universally apparent that participants in elite sport operate in a highly commercialised and commodified cultural practice where rewards for the successful few are often of unprecedented financial significance. Given this scenario, it is obvious that the challenge to anti-doping policy makers in each sport is an increasingly daunting one, made more difficult by the growth of commercial opportunity for the successful athlete in that sport. Governments are often ambivalent on the question of doping in sport and commercial interests conveniently ignore the issue, lest it tarnish the nature of an investment. Against this background agencies concerned with anti-doping policies in sport have to cope with forms of doping that are increasingly more difficult to detect, the continued growth in elite competition and the high level of geographic mobility inherently required by modern international sport (Houlihan, 1999: p. 32).

Professor Arnold Beckett was a deeply respected of the IOCs medical commission for many years. However, following numerous scandals, alleged doping infractions and the intransigency of the IOC, he departed to tell a rather different story. On the 1999 BBC television Panorama documentary 'Drug Runners', Beckett gave this commentary on the IOC:

It's like this — you can catch a few but don't catch too many. Just do enough to demonstrate to the world that we can combat the drug users.

Had the scandals inherent in major sporting events during 1998 not occurred then whether the IOC would have convened this conference is an issue of some contention. For the IOC, there is an inherent need to revitalise the moral integrity of modern sport. However, the IOC's reasons for doing this are to ensure public confidence, interest, spectatorship and television viewing in sport to ensure that sponsors continue to agree to multi-billion pound deals. Thus the dilemma for the IOC is how to demonstrate sport is not permeated by doping cultures whilst refusing to accept the permeation of doping within sports.

Quality control in anti-doping policies

The IOC's World Conference on Doping in Sport heralded one of the first attempts by the IOC to publicly address doping in sport. However, many commentators and delegates were distinctly unimpressed by Samaranch's latest soundbites that sport would become 'clean' as a result of the outcomes of the conference (see Jennings and Sambrook, 2000: p. 290–306). At the centre of attention was the decision to establish an independent anti-doping agency part funded by the IOC to the tune of $25 million. The final communique from the Lausanne conference stated that the IOC would be willing to work with governments to ensure a co-ordinated approach to anti-doping policies, but many governments, among them Britain, Italy, the United States and Germany, were openly critical of the IOC during and after the conference itself. The main focus for their criticism was that although the new World Anti-Doping Agency (WADA) was to be an independent body, it would be convened by the IOC President himself, Juan Antonio Samaranch, and it would have its headquarters in Lausanne, which is also the IOC's home city[3]. Given the reaction of cycling to the police investigation of the 1998 Tour De France, the prominence of the WADA, publicised through the IOC, would ensure that sport would regulate itself, rather than accepting an external body. The IOC was working frantically to form 'a self-preservation society' to protect the culture of tolerance within sport.

Although there was some discussion of how to ensure the new agency's independence, the over-riding impression was that the agency would obtain little credibility outside of sport, should the organisation be regulated by sport itself. A number of politicians such as Per Kristian Skulberg, Norway's Minister for Cultural Affairs, voiced their concerns that the new agency must be truly autonomous, free from the influence of the IOC and ISFs. General Barry McCaffrey, director of the White House drug policy commented:

> Let me sadly but respectfully note that recent examples of alleged corruption[4], lack of accountability and failure of leadership have challenged the legitimacy of this institution. (cited in Hoberman, 1999: p. 1)

However Samaranch, under fire following the revelations of bribery and corruption, refused to relinquish some form of influence commenting on the need for the IOC to do it all it could to eradicate doping. The implication was clear; for the IOC not to have some influence on anti-doping policies would be tantamount to an admission of failure and would further tar the reputation of the IOC and Samaranch. By the end of the conference it was clear that many delegates were extremely dissatisfied with the outcomes noting the pseudo-independence of the proposed anti-doping agency. A strong message was being sent to the IOC that to fail to eradicate doping would ruin future sport, yet the conference's final communique did not draw unanimity from all ISFs present, with football, cycling and tennis refusing to accept that all doping infractions should warrant the same punishments. Consequently the communique was refined to permit differential sanctions under exceptional circumstances. This loophole ensured that the Lausanne Conference did little more than highlight the continuing ineffectiveness of anti-doping policies. For Samaranch, it was a bitter blow and, following intense media criticism of his proposed role, the IOC President did not assume leadership of the new agency. Furthermore, the conference provoked consternation over the legitimacy of the new agency and demonstrated that the politics of those concerned with anti-doping policies seemed of more importance than the desire to tackle core educational and ethical concerns raised by doping cultures in modern sport.

As Houlihan (1998: p. 26) observes the primary challenge facing the WADA is the restoration of confidence in the doping control system. Athletes are sceptical of the reliability and validity of testing procedures whilst many governments question international sports organisations commitment to tackle doping. The WADA will have to front these two concerns and "the fact that there are no simple answers — reflects not indecision or a lack of commitment but rather the fundamental and complex issues of principles and implementation" (Houlihan, 1998: p. 26). However, a brief exploration of how the WADA was formed may lead many to doubt what the agency can achieve. Hoberman (1999: p. 6) believes that in the first instance, the WADA does not have credibility because of its origins but policy-makers within and outside of sport could act. He argues that effective doping control will require an organisation comparable to Interpol, purged of active and passive sympathisers with doping who have managed to neutralise most drug testing programmes so effectively up to this point.

Established on November 10 1999 the WADA held its first two meetings in January and March 2000. The minutes of the inaugural meeting begin thus:

> The Chairman [IOC Vice President, Dick Pound] welcomed participants … [and] introduced the IOC President (who commented that) the Day was an historic one for sport: a new dimension had been given to the fight against doping in sport with the collaboration of world sport organisations and governments. (Minutes of WADA inaugural meeting, 2000: p. 1)

Despite his failure to lead the WADA, Samaranch's presence at the meeting, albeit briefly was symbolic and would not be the form of independence required to police anti-doping policies. A brief glance at membership of the Executive Committee would not please many others. It includes the Prince de Merode, chair of the IOC Medical Commission, Hein Verbruggen, President of the UCI, the international cycling federation, and the President of the International Swimming Federation (FINA), Mustapha Larfoui. It is highly ironic that all of these administrators have been implicated (directly or indirectly) in poorly administered elements of anti-doping policies (1984 Olympics, 1998 Tour De France and 1998 World swimming Championships respectively) and yet they all claim to be committed to eradicating doping. In total, there are five IOC members on the Executive Committee, which numbers eleven in total. Conversely, some committee members have not been involved in doping controversies, notably those committee members from governments such as Senator Amanda Vanstone, Australian Minister for Justice and Customs — one of those at the centre of organising the 1999 International Drugs in Sport conference held in Sydney, November 1999. Results from the initial meetings were largely structural although Dick Pound commented that the WADA would have to rely on existing agencies to collect out-of competition samples and the accredited IOC laboratories to examine the samples prior to the Sydney Olympics (Minutes of WADA inaugural meeting, March, 2000: p. 28). With the next meeting of the WADA due to be at or after the Sydney Olympics, it is difficult to assess what impact the organisation may have, but it has approved an annual budget of $8 million for research and education.

A more credible alternative to the IOC's efforts may well be through the International Anti-Doping Arrangement (IADA), a government-to-government agreement that reflects the commitment of a number of nations to deal with doping in sport. The current signatories are Australia, Canada, New Zealand, Norway, the Netherlands, Sweden and the United Kingdom. The aim of the IADA is to influence the international sports community to implement more effective programmes through established benchmarks of best practice. Thus, whilst the IADA has a status that is distinct from national laws, the arrangement cannot dictate national law but can significantly influence a nation's policies. The demonstration of best practice has led to the development of the Quality Concept and Standard for Doping control. Such a quality management framework represents the most realistic chance for harmonising policies. The scope of the IADA quality concept is based on four elements — The IADA Standard for Doping Control; The ISO (International Organisation for Standardisation) certified Quality System for Doping Control (based on ISO 9002); guidelines for implementing ISO quality systems; and Common International Quality Documentation for doping control (Mendoza and Andersen, 1999: pp. 7–10). It is apparent that the collective knowledge and experience of the IADA provides a basis from which to combat doping in sport, although as Mendoza and Andersen (1999: p. 11) point out, the extent to which the IADA is influencing and being embraced by other agencies is open to question. Even so, whether the governments who support the IADA are willing to work with the IOC is a moot point and it could well be that because of its profile within sport the WADA will represent international sports organisations in attempting to 'police' international sport. As mentioned earlier, where prototype projects exist, this means an implicit acceptance that certain sports require a 'culture of tolerance' when addressing anti-doping policies.

Education — that's what you need!

If it is accepted that the WADA does not form a truly independent agency through which to implement anti-doping policies, one area to which quality control in doping procedures does not apply to at the present time is the area of ethical and educational considerations. Sport has long overlooked its obligations to provide a programme of education regarding doping in sport. Adopting ethical practices in sport requires all concerned to establish some common principles based on characteristics such as integrity, responsibility, competence, confidentiality, commitment, co-operation, and humanity. However, if a sport is to establish a code of practice based on these principles, qualifying the outreach of these principles, qualifying what constitutes an infraction and what to do when an athlete is found guilty of an infraction are essential questions that must be addressed.

Educating sports participants and administrators about what actually constitutes intent provides the first and possibly the only challenge for policy-makers in the foreseeable future. Former Olympic marathon champion Alberto Salazar (1999: pp. 1–2) believes that athletes fall into three groups: those that have no value conflicts with doing whatever it takes to succeed; those who who will not engage in any activity that would contravene the laws, and those who may have started out with high values, but through disillusionment have become frustrated either with their own performance, or the ease with which athletes can beat the system. Salazar believes this latter group is dismayed about the authorities' attempts at "merely making public relations efforts" to counteract doping in order to "protect the image of the respective sports and the money that flows from corporate sponsors" (Salazar 1999: p. 2). Hein Verbruggen has remarked that about 90% of doping cases are undetectable. Faced with these figures the athlete has a number of choices. Is it (the substance/method) banned? Will it adversely affect my performance? Is it safe? Does it work? How does it work? Can it be detected in out of competition testing as well as at the competition? (Wadler, 1999: p. 6) Thus, the challenge for educational concerns is to understand where athletes actually stand on the issues and to ascertain exactly the reasoning why doping infractions may be committed on an individual basis. There cannot be many organisations involved in anti–doping policy-making seeking to explore these issues.

Refreshingly some national sports organisations have challenged international counterparts to look on athletes not as characterless commodities but as the "prime asset in sport ... therefore through their individual and collective contribution and commitment against doping" would be essential to any anti-doping stance (Australian Olympic Committee, 1998: p. 2). The AOC argued that the ethical basis for an anti-doping policy is three-fold; first, any policy should protect athletes' health from doping; second the unethical nature of using performance-enhancing effects; or third the combination of the two aforementioned factors (AOC, 1998: p. 6). However, to simply ask for athletes' support achieves nothing. For such a policy to become effective, education of athletes must begin at an early stage of their development, preferably well before they reach national or international standards of representation. However, it is also clear that the events of recent years has irrevocably tarnished the IOC's moral stance in its "war against drugs" The Olympic movement has lost a good deal of credibility through its inability to deal with inherent corruption as well as for its anti-doping stance. Yet many castigate the movement for failing to have moved much more quickly to combat the problem. Athletes looking at the IOC may well wonder why, given the nature of corruption in sports administration, they should behave any differently.

The next challenge is to discover whether or not athletes actually view doping as cheating. There is much evidence to support the notion that doping is cheating (Sports Council, 1996), although athletes subscribe to the view in different ways. Mark Tout, the British bobsleigh driver who tested positive for anabolic steroids, acknowledged that his actions contravened the rules of his sport, despite his suspicions of others, and therefore labelled him a cheat. In contrast, Canadian sprinter Ben Johnson stated that he was not a cheat because many other athletes whom he competed against were engaged in doping practices ('Drug Runners', BBC television, 1999). Thus sports federations are also challenged with accepting doping as a constitutive element of their sport or abrogating responsibilities to their athletes and letting them enmesh themselves within such cultures, regardless of the future consequences to their health.

The preoccupation with doping in modern sport has created a remarkable level of interest in athletes about substances that might enhance performance. Indeed, recent years have seen anti-doping programmes conducted in a near clandestine manner, as elite athletes continue to operate in a culture that leads many to believe success will not arrive without doping support mechanism. Unless the culture of cynicism against outstanding performances in sport is addressed, then anti-drug programmes and the World Anti-Doping Agency will continue to be regarded with a strong degree of scepticism. Salazar (1999: p. 2) believes that it is

> ... currently difficult to be in the top five in the world of any (track and field) distance event without using EPO or Human Growth Hormone. While some athletes may be clean, so many athletes are running so fast that their performances are suspect. This compounded by the fact that the times ... happen to coincide with what top exercise physiologists have calculated EPO would produce.

Changing attitudes and cultures requires a widespread programme of education in younger athletes. In addition, there is a case for demonstrating a chasm between the incentives for not doping and speaking out against doping, as opposed to punishing those who are guilty of doping offences. Again, this is the responsibility of international sports organisations not the athletes.

Standards of education — can sports organisations be trusted?

It is evident that sports federations do not provide an example of why athletes should not commit doping infractions. Speaking at the Lausanne conference, Lauri Tarasti, a member of the Supreme Administrative court of Finland and also a member of the Sport and Law commission of the IOC, criticised the method by which substances used in doping practices are added to the list of prohibited substances (Tarasti, 1999). The committee of the German Athletic Federation (DLV) suspended Katrin Krabbe and Grit Breuer for one year and Silke Derr for eight months, as the athletes denied a doping offence, but did test positive for Clenbuterol. Although Clenbuterol was not at the time on the list of prohibited substances, the federation treated drug misuse in this instance as unsportsmanlike (sic) behaviour. The IAAF arbitration panel conformed this ruling, although whilst Derr and Krabbe retired, Breuer returned to competition and won the 1998 European 400 metres championship. The Court of Arbitration in Sport (CAS) exonerated the Russian athletes who used Bromantan at the Atlanta Olympics, as the substance was not on the IOC prohibited list. Whilst Clenbuterol and

Bromantan have been added to the IOC's list of prohibited substances, such loopholes predispose young athletes to seek further methods that will exploit opportunities for doping infractions because testing positive would not end their careers.

The Chinese Swimming team escaped a ban at the end of the 1998 World swimming Championships, despite four of the team failing tests. FINA, the sport's international governing body, said a technicality in the sport's rule book meant the team would escape an automatic ban. As it stood at the time, FINA was able to expel any nation if four of its athletes tested positive for steroids within a one-year period. However, the swimmers were found to have used Triamterene, a diuretic. Although another swimmer, Yuan Yuan, was deported after phials of Human Growth Hormone (HGH) were found in her luggage, FINA was still unable to act because of the technical definitions of doping it had drawn up. What the aforementioned examples demonstrate is that although international sports organisations are working toward more effective anti-doping policies, no sports organisation will actually admit that doping is a constitutive element in their sport.

In order to create a universal framework against doping offences, minimum standards must be applied. Minimum standards are used to harmonise testing procedures to protect the rights of the athlete and thereby increase confidence in doping programmes. In attempting to create such a framework, ethical considerations, particularly educational programmes must be prioritised. Anti-doping education needs to focus on the individual motivations for committing doping infractions. Thus the delivery of educational messages must have a broad base and should include government sponsored sports organisations as well as international federations, all of whom are organisations that have contact with athletes and who should stand credibly with those who are subject to anti-doping policies. It is ironic that whilst the Olympic movement is justifiably heavily criticised for its moral hypocrisy regarding value systems in sport, the movement still has the potential to provide a unique vehicle through which to educate athletes.

There is considerable debate over whether the WADA should be involved in the production of educational programmes. If the organisation was to demonstrate independence of the IOC that might imply the IOC was not central to the revised changes. The IOC's role in anti-doping education must be limited to symbolic functions until it acknowledges the doping cultures that pervade modern sporting practices. A working group from the Lausanne Conference, headed by Schmitt (1999), presented a number of immediate symbolic changes in the Olympic oath regarding ethical considerations in athletes' training methods. In addition, each athlete would be asked to take the oath in the form of a contract, with the oath also being extended to coaches and officials. What consequences would be should people contradict the code or oath, would be open to debate and clearly any punitive attachments to contravention of an oath may be subject to a legal challenge at best or purely dismissed.

The recommendations of the working group exemplify the weakness inherent in the IOC's approach to anti-doping policies. By projecting doping as a practice that has interfered with symbolic notions of the construction and production of sporting performances, the group and the IOC in general do not acknowledge doping as a constitutive element of elite sport. It is clear that symbolic actions or punishments related to codes of practice are not an effective form of doping control. It would also appear optimistic to hope that international sports organisations, given their recent past, are able to effectively initiate education programmes, given that their primary intentions appear to focus on the need to protect the sport, rather than the athlete.

Which way forward?

The International Drugs in Sport Summit, held in Sydney in November 1999, proposed the establishment of a comprehensive set of educational initiatives to combat doping in sport. The Summit convened an international meeting of government ministers responsible for sport and aimed to encourage governments to take a firmer line to doping in sport. The role which governments can take in the education process will vary although the Summit proposed that governments should undertake three policies. First, governments should incorporate anti-doping education initiatives within existing education systems and programs over which they have control. Second, governments would be asked to work with sports to ensure that anti-doping messages are incorporated into broader sport education programmes. Third, in co-operation with sports organisations, governments should make information available to elite athletes and other members of national teams (e.g. coaches, officials, team doctors) (International Drugs in Sport Summit theme paper 5).

Education alone could achieve some deterrent effect for a period of time, but the perceived risk involved with doping decreases eventually if education is not supported by harmonised testing procedures within sports whose individual anti-doping policies may differ. Longer-term education programmes for athletes (and their support personnel) to prevent the use of drugs in sport are essential if doping is to be eliminated as a constituent element in the practice of sport. The IOC-funded WADA will not address these issues unless it, the IOC and international sports federations come clean and demonstrate exactly what is going on in their sports. Governments appear unwilling to support sport's own attempts to create effective anti-doping policies yet also appear unable to produce a transparent picture of actual practices because of the 'veil of secrecy' that sport cloaks itself within.

Education programmes should be based on sound research and delivered at a range of levels. As a minimum standard, athletes need to be aware of their individual sport's anti-doping policies and their obligations under the drug testing programmes to which they are subject. As Waddington (2000) has argued, policies which aim to ensure health risks are minimised, whilst concomitantly reducing the punitive nature of many sanctions may be a first step to educating current and future athletes. It is essential that if education is considered as a priority in resource allocation by governments and the WADA It is important for responsible authorities to make information available about drugs in sport that is relevant, accessible and delivered in an appropriate manner to those who are involved in sport. An athlete has a right to know about his/her obligations under anti-doping policies and are entitled to receive information that assists them to abide by the policy. It is essential that preventive drugs in sport education programmes for athletes, coaches, administrators and officials be based on researched needs. (International Drugs in Sport Summit, theme paper 5). Attitudes to drug use and the issues that athletes encounter regarding doping in sport should be carefully considered. There needs to be overt recognition from sports administrators that anti-doping messages are most effective when based on current research and targeted at appropriate audiences. Once developed, anti-doping messages need to be tested through further research to ensure their effectiveness prior to implementation.

Conclusions

The quotations given initially from the sport of cycling illustrate that it is one of an increasingly large number of sports with a history of doping culture. Other sports involving power or endurance related-qualities have also been shown to exemplify inherent, but often, clandestine doping cultures tolerated by competitors, coaches, officials and administrators. Therefore the initial consideration for initiating effective anti-doping policies in sport is that until the IOC, International Sports Federations and the WADA acknowledge sport as a constitutive element of modern sporting practices.

The IOC has carefully remained unattached to the affairs of any nation state and its capacity to influence educational programmes is limited, although many might concede this is no bad thing. Thus one might readily challenge what the WADA can do except to be a forum wherein integral components of educational programmes can be agreed, not just by WADA committee but by sports federations, both international and domestic. The next challenge is to link spoirts federations into government actions in order to provide some form of legitimacy and accountability for an anti-doping policy. Governments who work with national sports organisations have the ability to influence a range of educational areas and can ensure that doping education is included in a variety of these areas. They may include:

- National education systems and curriculums.
- Sport education programmes (e.g. coach education) which operate within community level sport.
- Sports policies (such as junior sport policies) that may include messages to discourage drug use.
- State supported sport institute programmes.

(International Drugs in Sport Summit — Theme Paper 5: p. 7)

Independence is achieved by having the jurisdiction of anti-doping programmes made accountable to policies of governance, permitting a programme to operate independently of those who are subject to or involved in the programme. Independence is not an abrogation of responsibility but an exercise in authority and a trust in those who are responsible for implementing anti-doping systems. Preventive education programmes can concentrate on a number of aspects of doping in sport. The concept of fair competition and the ethical aspects associated with doping in sport remain redundant unless policy-makers regulate sport more forcefully and identify what actually is fair. The values of fair play and the ideals of equitable participation in sport can be raised but to young athletes these values mean little in the face of phenomenal commercial rewards for Olympic success. Preventive education programmes may also focus on the consequences associated with being caught such as sanctions, fines and the humiliation of being branded a drug cheat. However the historical development of the politics of anti-doping policies imply that to be branded a cheat may well be worth the risk, given that the punitive intentions of anti-doping policies have historically been ineffective at the very best. The health risks associated with the use of performance enhancing drugs may also be an element of preventative educational programmes. Indeed, it may well be that a 'shock' component could have a greater impact upon young people than simply explaining the health implications of doping. However, if doping continues to be an element of modern sporting practice, these policies have a diminishing effect on emerging performers seeking an extra edge. It is important that the effectiveness of education initiatives is regularly monitored and reviewed, as changes in environment and attitudes may alter the approach that is required for any form of long-term educational programmes.

There is no quick-fix solution to eradicating doping from sport and previous attempts to 'fix the problem' have provided numerous opportunities for critics of anti-doping policies to argue for the removal of the ban. The starting point for policy-makers is to rip the façade from sport, accept that doping is a constitutive element of sporting practices and confront those at the very top of sports administration with one simple question: can educational elements of anti-doping policies have any validity until the prevalence of doping in sport is acknowledged?

Notes

1   In this instance, the term 'constitutive' is taken to mean that the prevalence of (and lack of control of) doping, combined with the rewards it offers, are basic factors for athletes in deciding whether they should use doping methods, and also that members of the public might acknowledge that the competition they witness has doping methods as but one ingredient for performance.

2   In addition to those authors mentioned, more detailed discussions on why doping in sport should or should not be opposed can be found in Yesalis (1996), Voy (1991), Waddington (2000).

3   The WADA will take permanent residence at a new base at the beginning of 2002. Until then, it will work from its temporary base in Lausanne.

4   For a detailed account of corruption within the IOC, see Jennings and Sambrook (2000).

References

Australian Olympic Committee (1998). Submission by the Australian Olympic Committee to the World conference on doping in sport, 30 November. Retrieved 5 February, 1999 from http://www.nodoping.org/contributions_pdf/SubmissionAustralia_e.pdf

BBC News Online (20 August 1999), 'We will never eliminate doping', Retrieved on January 12, 2000, from http://news2.thls.bbc.co.uk/hi/english/sport/newsid%5F155000/155056.stm

———— (9 September 1999), 'Doping charges catch up with communist officials', Retrieved on January 12, 2000 from http://news.bbc.co.uk/hi/english/world/europe/newsid%5F443000/443257.stm

———— (6 January 2000), 'New tests for Chinese swimmers', Retrieved on January 12 2000 from news.bbc.co.uk/hi/englis h/sports/newsid_593000/593521

———— (12 January 2000) 'Sports doctor doped swimmers', Retrieved on January 12, 2000 from:
http://news.bbc.co.uk/hi/english/world/europe/newsid%5F599000/599971.stm

Black, T. and Pape, A. (1997). 'The ban on drugs in sports. The solution or the problem', *Journal of Sport and Social Issues* Vol. 21, No. 1, February: pp. 83–92.

Denham, B. E. (1999) 'On drugs in sports in the aftermath of Flo-Jo's death, Big Macs attack', *Journal of Sport and Social Issues* Vol. 23 No.3 August: pp. 362–367.

Donnelly, P. (1996) 'Prolympism: Sport monoculture as crisis and opportunity', *Quest*, 48: pp. 25–42.

Hoberman, J. (1998) 'The concept of doping and the future of Olympic sport, in L. Allison (ed) *Taking sport seriously*. Aachen: Meyer and Meyer.

Hoberman, J. (1999) 'Learning from the past: The need for independent doping control', Paper presented to the Duke conference on doping in sport, Duke University, May 7–8, 1999. Retrieved on March 12, 2000 from http://www.law.duke.edu/sportscenter/hoberman.an.pdf

Houlihan, B. (1998) 'The World Anti-Doping Agency and the campaign against doping in sport in Europe' in *Council of Europe Yearbook*. Strasbourg: Council of Europe.

Houlihan, B. (1999) *Dying to win: Doping in sport and the development of anti-doping policy*. Strasbourg: Council of Europe.

International Drugs in Sport Summit (1999) 'Summit theme paper 5 — Education'. Retrieved on March 12th 2000 from http://drugsinsport.isr.gov.au/section_3/EducationFINALnew.doc

International Olympic Committee (1999) 'Olympic Movement Anti-Doping Code', Retrieved on March 12th 2000 from http://www.nodoping.org/code_anti_doping/doping_code_e.doc

Jackson, S.J. (1998) 'Life in the (mediated) Faust lane: Ben Johnson, national affect and the 1988 crisis of Canadian identity', *International Review of the Sociology of Sport* Vol. 33, No. 3: pp. 227–238.

Jennings, A. (1996) *The new lords of the rings: Olympic corruption and how to buy a gold medal*. London: Pocket Books.

Konig, E. (1995) 'Criticism of doping: The nihilistic side of technological sport and the antiquated view of sport ethics', *International Review of the Sociology of Sport*. Vol. 30, No. 3/4: pp. 247–262.

Kimmage, P. (1998) *Rough ride: Behind the wheel with a pro cyclist* (2nd edition). London: Yellow Jersey Press.

Ljungvist, A. (1999) 'Out of Competition testing'. Paper presented at the World conference on doping in sport, February 2-4, Lausanne, Switzerland. Retrieved on February 5 from http://www.nodoping.org/contributions_pdf/Ljungqvist_e.pdf

Mendoza, J. and Andersen, R. (1999) 'Doping control in sport — Harmonising procedures and practices. *ISO Bulletin*, July: pp. 6–11.

Milburn, P. (1999) 'The form and substance of independence: An insider's view', Paper presented to the Duke conference on doping in sport, Duke University, May 7–8, 1999. Retrieved on March 12, 2000 from http://www.law.duke.edu/sportscenter/miller.pdf.

Salazar, A. (1999) 'Locating the line between acceptable performance enhancing and cheating', Paper presented to the Duke conference on doping in sport, Duke

University, May 7–8, 1999. Retrieved on March 12, 2000 from http://
www.law.duke.edu/sportscenter/salazar.pdf

Schmitt, P. (1999) 'Prevention, ethics, education and communication, Working group
presentation to the World conference on doping in sport, February 2–4,
Lausanne, Switzerland. Retrieved on February 5, 1999 from http://
www.nodoping.org/contributions_pdf/Summary_3feb_e.pdf

Segrave, J. O. (1988) 'Towards a definition of Olympism', in J. O. Segrave and D.
Chu (eds) *The Olympic Games in transition*. Champaign, IL: Human Kinetics:
pp. 149–158.

Senn, A. (1999) *Power, politics and the Olympic games*. Champaign, IL: Human
Kinetics.

Simson, V and Jennings, A. (1992) *The lords of the rings*. London: Simon and
Schuster.

Sports Council (1996) *Doping control in the UK: A survey of the experiences and
views of elite competitors, 1995*. London: Sports Council.

Tamburrini, C. (2000) 'What's wrong with doping?' in T. Tannsjo and C. Tamburrini
(eds) *Values in sport: Elitism, nationalism, gender equality and the scientific
manufacture of winners*. London: E& FN Spon, pp. 199–216.

Tarasti, L. (1999) 'When can an athlete be punished for a doping offence'. Paper
presented at the World conference on doping in sport, February 2–4, Lausanne,
Switzerland. Retrieved on February 5, 1999 from http://www.nodoping.org/
contributions_pdf/Tarasti.pdf

Voy, R. (1991) *Drugs, sport and politics*. Champaign, IL: Leisure Press.

Waddington, I. (2000) *Sport, health and drugs: A critical sociological perspective*.
London: E & FN Spon.

Wadler, G. (1999) 'Doping in sport: From strychnine to genetic enhancement, it's a
moving target', Paper presented to the Duke conference on doping in sport,
Duke University, May 7-8, 1999. Retrieved on March 12, 2000 from http://
www.law.duke.edu/sportscenter/wadler.pdf

Walsh, D. and Follain, J. (2000) 'Poison in the heart of sport', *Sunday Times*, 9th
January, p. 11.

Yesalis, C. and Cowart, V. (1996) *The steroids game*. Champaign, IL: Human
Kinetics.

Zakus, D. H. (1992) 'The International Olympic Committee: Tragedy, farce and
hypocrisy', *Sociology of Sport Journal* Vol. 9: pp. 340–353.

EXCELLENCE AND EXPEDIENCE? OLYMPISM, POWER AND CONTEMPORARY SPORTS POLICY IN ENGLAND

Ian McDonald
Chelsea School, University of Brighton

Introduction

For over twenty years from the mid 1970s to the mid 1990s, poorly funded piecemeal developments coupled with weak political leadership resulted in earnest but ultimately futile attempts by the GB Sports Council to meet the needs of a diverse sporting community. While elite-level athletes took the Sports Council to task for failing to support their efforts to compete with the world's best, lack of funds meant that community-based projects rarely lasted long enough to outlast their initiative status. By the late 1990s however, with an annual budget of over £200 million from the National Lottery, and with a revamped Sports Council enjoying high profile government support, there is a general sense of optimism in the sport policy community that both the sporting landscape and sporting fortunes of England will be transformed. The upbeat mood of many in the wake of this new found position was expressed by a leading figure in the Sports Council in an interview for the *Guardian* newspaper in 1996:

> I think in 40 years time people will say it must have been extraordinary to be around in the mid-1990s, when sport got a political profile, a new national stadium and a national academy. (*Guardian*, 21 March 1996: p. 25)

Although it is not likely to be before the year 2003 before the new national stadium at Wembley is built and maybe less time before a national academy structure is in operation, sport has certainly got a political profile. Given the historically unprecedented levels of funding available, such optimism may be well founded. And with the unexpected levels of success of British Olympians at the Sydney Games in 2000, cited by various media pundits as evidence of a properly funded sport policy, it is little wonder that an air of excitement and expectation continues to permeate the sport policy community. In "40 years time", people may comment on the 1990s as an "extraordinary" period, when it was possible to improve the sporting infrastructure to the benefit of all, and provide the necessary services to assist the elite.

However, there is another interpretation. For the critically informed policy analyst of 40 years hence, it may represent the moment when the pluralistic sporting culture of England finally succumbed, and acceded to the promethean logic of modern sport, and when sport policy was subjected to heavy influence by the government's political imperatives. It may be seen as the beginning of a process where the residues of creative and liberative possibilities in sporting practice were extinguished. In short, it may be seen as the period when a sport policy paved the way for a qualitative shift in the sports-participation culture away from the egalitarian and empowering aspirations of community-based sporting activity to an hierarchical and alienating culture of high-performance sport. Students of sport policy in 40 years time might consider that the extraordinary fact about the mid 1990s was the paucity of debate and critical reflection within the sporting world about this paradigmatic shifts in sports culture facilitated by an annual £200 million of public money.

Therefore, in an attempt to provide a least one dissenting voice from the wilderness, I want to take issue with the celebratory posturing of many within the sport policy community, and raise some important questions about the direction of policy. In particular, I will argue that the development of excellence is the main objective of Sport England policy and the improvement of Great Britain's status in the international sporting arena the main Government aspiration. Many people will want to dispute this assertion as a one-sided reading of sport policy that ignores the government's commitment to grassroots sport, to school sport, to sport in the community, to the use of sport to tackle aspects of social deprivation and what is referred to in New Labour speak as "social exclusion". They could also refer to the Sport England Lottery Fund Strategy for 1999–2009, to show that three-quarters of all lottery funding will go towards "community sport" with the remaining third devoted to the development of "excellence" (Sport England, 1999).

However, my argument does not depend on a denial of other policy object-ives other than the development of excellence. Rather it is to say that other ob-jectives are either peripheral, or exist to support this fundamental strategic objective. In other words it is the commitment to excellence that frames strategic thinking and specific policy objectives. For example, many of the most signi-ficant initiatives located within programmes that are designated as 'community sport' for example Sport Specialist Colleges, are actually geared towards the development of sporting excellence. In order to substantiate such an interpre-tative position about excellence defining the framework for the totality of sport policy, it is necessary to go beyond the policy text, and to examine the deeper ideological framework of sport policy. That is, it is necessary to substantively identify the ideological scaffolding within which sport policy is constructed.

I will argue that national sports policy is based on a particular discourse — I will call it "neo-Olympism" — which is predicated but not reducible to the adoption of achievement-oriented Olympic (*citius, altius, fortius*) sport, and that this discourse occupies a privileged position in relation to alternative sporting cultures. The second contention of this chapter is that this achievement-oriented model of sport, with its strategic emphasis on the development of 'excellence', is heavily influenced by political expediency — in particular, the quest for national patriotism via sporting success. A consequence of this influence is that the concept of excellence is neither absolute nor completely relativist, but contingently interpreted in accorzdance with government imperatives. My argument is that what is called "community sport" and "excellence" need to located with this politically contingent interpretation of excellence — thus positing an ideological framework that I am labelling "neo-Olympism", within which the substantive nature of sport policy can be examined as closer to excellence than community-based sport, and where the legitimacy and meaning of 'community sport' is derived from the push towards (politically contingent concept of) excellence. The point of such an argument is that it highlights the fact that policy commitments do not exist in a political and cultural vacuum, but emerge out of a deeper structure of norms, values and belief-systems, and it allows us to reveal the inherent power relations hidden within sport policy.

Conceptualising power in sport policy

To properly examine the power relations in sport, it is necessary first of all to problematise the dominant sporting culture within which sport policy is situated. The notion of a *sporting culture* is useful as it allows an understanding of the constructed nature of sports offered in particular times and spaces. Eichberg's paradigmatic insistence on the dissolution of the unitary concept of sport and the adoption of body culture as the frame for a critical study of sports is of use here in analysing types of sporting cultures. In proposing a 'trialectics' of body culture, Eichberg distinguishes, first, *achievement sport*, which is constituted on the basis of production of results, maximisation and hierarchisation; second, *fitness sport*, associated with physiological and social-psychological health and well-being, and the ideals of sport for all; and thirdly, *body experience* which is less tangible, but finds expression in the older forms of popular sport, in the sensuousness of dance, and in alternative holistic exercises (Eichberg, 1989: pp. 43–60). Clearly then, neo-Olympism is rooted in the culture of achievement-sport, which begs the question as to the extent that it necessarily marginalises, co-opts or excludes other cultures of sport identified by Eichberg.

A properly critical analysis of sport policy needs to operate at two levels. Firstly, it needs to be critical of the ideas which form the conventional wisdom about sport and sport policy, following in the 'debunking' tradition of humanistic sociology (Wright Mills, 1949; Berger, 1963). Secondly, it needs to be critical in the Bourdieuan sense of a theoretical argument that seeks to expose the more or less concealed relations of power in sport policy, which itself can potentially undermine the very relations of power it uncovers. According to Bourdieu, all theoretical works are constitutive elements of what he refers to as the 'intellectual field', which although has a degree of autonomy, is partly encompassed by the wider 'meta' field of power (Bourdieu, 1994: pp. 140–149). His reflexive sociology therefore contradicts claims that studies of power can remain politically neutral:

> By uncovering the social mechanisms which ensure the maintenance of
> the established order and whose proper efficacy rests on the
> misrecognition of their logic and effects, social science takes sides in
> political struggles. (Bourdieu, 1992: p. 51)

However, whilst Bourdieu's point about the inherently political nature of social
scientific theorising and research is pertinent, what if there is no "side" to take
because of the apparent absence of "struggle", such as the case in the study of
power within the national sport policy community? Fortunately, Lukes's (1974)
classic account of the exercise of power provides a solution to this dilemma.
He has argued that a proper understanding of the exercise of power goes beyond
the existence of visible conflict, where to cite the pluralist theorist Dahl from
his early writings, "A has power over B to the extent that he can get B to do
something that he wouldn't otherwise do" (Dahl, 1957: p. 203 in Hill, 1997:
p. 38). As Bachrach and Baratz (1970) have noted, Dahl's formulation is a
one-dimensional view of power that ignores the importance of 'non-decision
making' whereby conflicts are suppressed and prevented from entering the
political process. According to Lukes, however, this criticism, whilst valid, is
still based on grievances that are expressed, albeit covertly. The analysis needs
to be developed to challenge the conceptual conflation of expressed conflict
and power. Lukes important contribution was to introduce the possibility of
'latent conflict', which exists when there would be conflict over preferences
between those exercising power and those subject to it were the latter to become
aware of their interests. While this 'three-dimensional view' of power relations
may raise thorny ontological and epistemological issues concerning questions of
existence and objective interests (thorny at least for some Marxists), it does have
particular value in problematising views that equate consensus with an equal
distribution of power, or as where power is not being exercised at all. As
Lukes argues:

> Is it not the supreme and the most insidious exercise of power to prevent
> people, to whatever degree, from having grievances by shaping their
> perception, cognitions and preferences in such a way that they accept
> their role in the existing order of things, either because they can see or
> imagine no alternative to it, or because they value it as divinely ordained

and beneficial. To assume that the absence of grievance equals genuine consensus is simply to rule out the possibility of false or manipulated consensus by definitional fiat. (Lukes, 1974: p. 24)

For Lukes, it is the 'deep structures' of power that conditions the terms of the debate that require investigation, for it is these 'structuring' levels that frame the realms of possible action and thought, and therefore precludes alternative 'deviant' ways of acting and thinking. In short, an understanding that power is both multi-dimensional and hierarchically structured (that is, some dimensions of power are more powerful in their effect than others) provides a means of differentiating the politics underpinning the ideas and myths, images, symbols, and language; in short, the discourse of sport policy. To concur with Bourdieu then, a critical analysis of sport policy is, *sui generis*, a political task, because in the specific case of sport policy, structures of power are institutionally centralised around central government (and therefore heavily influenced by political imperatives), and go largely unchallenged by a largely supine policy community resulting in minimal dissent from government priorities. Without such a critical framework, the high degree of consensus over sport policy is then treated unproblematically, rather than raising alarm bells and turning the spotlight on the deep relations of power in the sport policy community and the politics of sport policy discourse. How and in what ways then are policy preferences constitutive of particular political values?

National sport policy: changes and continuities

Ushering in their new policy in the mid 1990s, the Conservative minister for sport, Iain Sproat, declared that "… the Sports Council will withdraw from the promotion of mass participation, informal recreation, leisure pursuits, and from health promotion … and shift its focus to services in support of excellence" (DNH, 1994: p. 4). The policy of 'Sport for All', chronically weakened after years of financial cuts, was finally laid to rest (McDonald, 1995). In his introduction to *Sport: Raising the Game*, which outlined the new sport policy, John Major declared that his government would "bring about a sea-change in the prospects of British sport — from the very first steps in primary school right through to the breaking of the tape in an Olympic final" (DNH, 1995: p. 1).

Undoubtedly, *Sport: Raising the Game* had a significant impact on sports policy-makers, administrators and practitioners. Local authorities, governing bodies, voluntary sector organisations, schools, further and higher education, and most significantly, the GB Sports Council were called upon to revisit and adapt their strategies and operations in the light of the government's new policy. In April 1996, the GB Sports Council was restructured into the English Sports Council (to take effect from January 1997 and, since February 1999, branded as "Sport England") with a brief to develop structured sporting opportunities for young people, develop excellence, and to distribute monies from the National Lottery Sports Fund that came on-stream in 1994. The UK Sports Council (also branded since February 1999 as "UK Sport") meanwhile was created to bring success to Britain's athletes in the international arena. The financial windfall from the bulging coffers of the National Lottery raised expectations that, at last, real progress could be realised. Ambitious projects were given the green light: over £100 million set aside for the construction of a 'British Academy of Sport' (though abandoned by the Labour Government in 1999 in favour of a regional network of academies); and £168 million set aside for a new National Stadium to replace Wembley Stadium in London (*London Sport*, 1995: p. 5). When the Conservative Party was swept from office in the general election of 1997, the sporting excellence baton was passed smoothly to the new Labour administration, which, notwithstanding some important additions and adjustments, faithfully pursued the vision set out by its predecessors.

The contemporary specificity of neo-Olympism

Since the mid 1990s, national sport policy itself has been framed by a set of ideas, images and a language, in short a discourse, based around four recurrent and interdependent themes: excellence, sport (the achievement-oriented [Olympic] conception), youth, and pedagogy. They are interdependent in that excellence is fed by developing a mass participatory base of specific sport activities for the nation's youth promoted in schools and justified by emphasising sports pedagogic utility. Of the four related themes, excellence is determinant. The political significance and ideological nature of this sports policy discourse is itself constituted via a process of complex articulation with three further interrelating factors. These are (a) the philosophical legacy of

De Coubertin's Olympism, (b) the political imperatives of the previous Conservative and the present Labour government, and (c) the influence of 'positivistic' attitudes to sport within the sports policy and development communities.

Neo-Olympism is the ideological 'product' arising out of the interweaving of the culture of *achievement-sport* (in Eichberg's terms) with all three elements just identified. It is ideological in the sense that a particular way of conceptualising sport, and promoting participation in sport, is presented as the only, or at least, the most productive way, and in so doing buttressing relations of dominance. Neo-Olympic ideology, as it is presented here, is based on a discourse where the concept of sport is denoted by organised, competitive achievement-oriented activities, and a policy for sport in which the creation of opportunities secure their legitimacy by reference to an educationalist and/or nationalistic instrumentalism. There is always scope for disjunctures and even opposition within neo-Olympic ideology (as with any ideologies), but the analytical advantages of examining current national sports policy as an expression of this ideology is that its covert political nature, which it depends on to maintain its power, can be made explicit and therefore, potentially, less powerful.

Neo-Olympism operates, first, by drawing on a particularly powerful tradition of Olympism: that is, the indivisibility of sporting excellence and mass participation. Second, because of political expedience, the meaning of excellence is subjected to a double conceptual slippage so as to be; a) conterminous with British champions, and b) more applicable to prescribed 'traditional' rather than 'minor' sports (an aspect that was far more pronounced under the previous Conservative administration than the present Government). Third, due to the absence of a tradition of critical confrontation within the sports policy and development communities, the politicised operationalisation of excellence goes unchallenged and is consolidated and so legitimised by the design and implementation of strategies and programmes, such as the proposal for a network of Sporting Academies, and the World Class Programmes (DCMS 2000). It is useful at this juncture to examine the philosophical legacy of De Coubertin's Olympism within sports policy, then analyse how this aspect of the policy is affected by government political imperatives, before finally commenting on the ways in which programmes and initiatives offered from the sports development communities operate to construct and consolidate the ideology of neo-Olympism.

Olympism: past and present

Identifying how De Coubertin's Olympism feeds into contemporary neo-Olympism ideology is problematic, because of the problematic nature of Olympism as a concept. As Segrave comments:

> Despite the ubiquitousness of the term Olympism, and the rhetorical uses to which it has been put, a clear, precise, and simple definition that goes beyond generality has yet to be formulated. (Segrave, 1988: p. 151)

Olympic historian John Lucas (1992: p. 14) has also noted the absence of a binding definition of what is understood by the Olympic idea. As well as the conceptual ambiguity of Olympism, one can add a temporal mystification. Part of the enduring power and appeal of the Olympic Games is the link with the Ancient Games. The nature, extent and ideological significance of this link has been extensively debated (MacAloon, 1981; Segrave and Chu, 1988). It is often assumed that Olympism, as the philosophical expression of the Olympiad, must have similarly existed in the classical period. Indeed, the December 1995 edition of the *Olympic* magazine (1995: pp. 4–8) previews a permanent exhibition called "Olympism in Antiquity" at the Olympic Museum in Lausanne. And yet it is well established, if not widely perceived, that Olympism is a modern construct. It is the philosophical expression of the modern Olympic Movement, and therefore to talk of "Olympism in Antiquity" is incorrect. To quote Lucas, Olympism is a "De Coubertin coinage" (Lucas, 1992: p. 6).

In founding the modern Olympic Movement, De Coubertin constructed its philosophical counterpart — Olympism. It stemmed from the anxiety a youthful De Coubertin felt as a member of the French aristocracy at his country's defeat in the Franco-Prussian war of 1871. De Coubertin identified education as the key arena for French revival, which led him to observe, admire and then adopt as the basis of his Olympic ideal, the 19th century English public school athleticist conception of sport. Bearing in mind the ideological potency of tracing a line of continuity with the Ancient Games, De Coubertin astutely fused the idea of sport as a vehicle for the construction of physical, moral and social sporting gentlemen, with a classical Greek philosophical concern with the attainment of fulfilment and excellence via the harmonious development of mind and body in order to benefit the soul (McIntosh, 1987). In packaging this fusion of muscular-christianity with the Greek quest for excellence in secularist wrapping, De Coubertin produced the basis for the philosophy of Olympism. However, in the process of fusion, the Greek idea of the equal importance of body, mind and spirit was given a 19th century aristocratic twist by De Coubertin. First, De Coubertin was selective in his references to the ancient Games. De Coubertin and the self-appointed International Olympic Committee subscribed to an idealised, romanticised, and largely apocryphal image of the Games in the 'peak years' of the Classical period (479–404 BC) (Metheny, 1981: p. 325). Second, Thomas Arnold's sporting pedagogy led De Coubertin to place supreme value on character training in sport, thus equating spiritual development with character building. For example, at the closing session of the 1894 Congress for the re-establishment of the Games, De Coubertin declares:

> Gentlemen, there are not two parts to a man — body and soul: there are three — body, mind and character; character is not formed by the mind, but primarily by the body. (De Coubertin, 1966: p. 7)

Olympism is a late 19th century construction, carved out by De Coubertin from a synthesising of his interpretations of classical Greek and English public school conceptions of sport. Its basis is a belief in the educational value of sport, but ultimately Coubertin was to internationalise Olympism; placing sport at the centre of a universal campaign for peace and international understanding, again drawing on the legacy of the truce and the symbol of peace associated with the Games in Antiquity.

Baron Pierre de Coubertin was a complex figure, a genuine patriot and believer in internationalism, simultaneously paternalistic towards the poor and chauvinistic towards women, thus displaying the contradictions of "a displaced aristocrat"(Tomlinson, 1984: p. 95). However, as Segrave (1988: p. 154) comments, De Coubertin's point of departure was a belief in the intrinsic benefits of sport:

Despite the elitism of the Olympic Games, where entrance and performance are typically reaffirmations of excellence, De Coubertin's ideology was towards a more egalitarian aspiration. Emerging from his vision for educational reform in France was a passionate desire to provide the underprivileged with a genuine access to culture.

This did not exclude a vision of excellence. For De Coubertin, the Olympic Games should be the showcase for the exaltation of excellence achieved by individual athletes. Both the Games and the individual elite athletes were to be role models, not necessarily to be emulated, but certainly to provide inspiration. The links between these aspects of Olympism and the role of elite athletes in current national sports policy are apparent. As with Olympism, current sport policy presents the essential unity of the educational utility of sport, the mass participatory base of youth sport, and the value of sporting excellence.

However, the similarity is more apparent than real, as a fundamental difference exists between the two approaches. For De Coubertin, the place of the Olympic Games was as a means to a higher end — the involvement of larger numbers of youth in sport. In current policy thinking, success in the international arena and the attendant swell of national prestige is the end. The promotion of youth participation is the means, a way of ensuring that from a conveyor belt of young talent, progress towards the creation of British champions is secured. Both approaches stress the unity rather than the contradiction of mass sport and elite performance, but differences over means and ends impacts upon their respective strategic approaches in crucially different ways. According to De Coubertin's formula:

In order for a hundred people to take part in physical culture, it is necessary for fifty to take part in sport; in order for fifty to take part in sport, twenty must specialise, five must be capable of astonishing feats of prowess. (De Coubertin, 1966: pp. 131–2)

Interestingly, De Coubertin's starting point here is not increasing involvement in sport, but in physical culture (although his conceptualisation of physical culture probably never developed far past sport) — however, sporting excellence is identified as a key means of maximising participation in sport. By contrast, in current national sports policy, mass participation is desired not as an end in itself, but as a means of improving the chances of creating champions. Two implications of this different starting point follow: first, it encourages a focus on Governing Body-structured sport rather than the athlete or the community; thus, a priori, narrowing the nature of sporting opportunities. Second, these opportunities are judged in terms of how well they act as a feeder to excellence rather than excellence acting as a feeder to involvement in sport. Hence, De Coubertin's formula is turned on its head.

The significance of the different, indeed opposite, starting point of current national sports policy to De Coubertin's Olympism, is that the former, in its concrete practices, produces a tendency to exclude conceptions of sport geared towards sensual and/or holistic body experiences, and fitness sport, based on the ideals of 'Sport for All'. By contrast, the ideals of Olympism (rather than De Coubertin's historically specific Olympism, or the actual sports practices supported by National Olympic Committees) are not inherently hostile to broader and different conceptions of sporting practice, but become so in practice when located within the political context of current sports policy. Therefore, the argument is not for a straightforward translation or mapping of the ideals of Olympism (excellence, sport, pedagogy and youth) to contemporary sports policy, but rather a mutated form, or neo-Olympism. Neo-Olympism is constructed out of the raw material of De Coubertin's original philosophy, but assumes its contemporary specificity by its location within the political and sport development arenas. The sport development community occupies an important position in the policy process, as they are responsible for disseminating and implementing national sport policy. They have proven to be extremely receptive to the neo-Olympic ideology of Government sport policy.

Since the early 1980s, the number of sport development officers has grown to approximately 2,000, principally employed by local authorities and national governing bodies in Great Britain (Collins, 1995: p. 20). But sports development, as a concept and as a 'profession' changed significantly from the mid-1990s. Although marked by a degree of ambivalence, the early work of sport development tended to be framed within a community recreation rationale, loosely drawing on Eichberg's definition of *fitness sport*. Perhaps the slogan 'Sport for All' best summed up the early ethos of sport development. However, as I have argued elsewhere, a numerical increase in the number of sport development officers does not mean that Sport for All has flourished (McDonald, 1995). On the contrary, in the mid-1990s antithesis, rather than symbiosis, characterised the conceptual relationship between sports development and Sport for All. A key element of this argument centred on the pivotal nature of the sports development continuum (SDC). The aim of the SDC was to locate mass participation within a broad, strategic approach to sports development. It identified four relatively discrete but incremental building blocks which classified levels from 'lower' stages, foundation and participation, to 'higher' stages, performance and excellence (Eady, 1993: pp. 11–15). Although the Sports Council originally conceived the SDC merely as an explanatory tool, in the political and financial context of the late 1980s and early 1990s, it underwent a process of reification to assume the status of the primary definer of 'proper' sports development (McDonald, 1995). So, unless the activity was located within the SDC it was deemed to be beyond the remit of 'proper' sports development, a clear case of the tail wagging the dog. And the activities that best fitted with the hierarchical and developmental nature of the SDC were not recreational or physical leisure activities, but governing-body sporting activities. As Lentell observed, this reinterpretation of sports development based on the SDC facilitated a conceptual slippage and practice of sport development "…away from community recreation, both towards a greater concern with the development of specific sports and sporting performance, and towards a greater dependence on market related factors" (Lentell, 1993: p. 44). Community recreation, if it was mentioned at all, existed as an emasculated concept. SDC-based sports development has reconceptualised and relabelled community recreation as 'community sport' and as 'foundation' and 'participation'; and these levels were defined in terms of sport-specific pathways for young people to progress from foundation to performance, and for some, excellence.

Concluding thoughts

In her discussion of the politics of sport and physical education, Talbot (1995: p. 21) concludes by saying that, "The shared task for researchers, policy makers and practitioners is not to ignore dominant ideologies, but to put them into perspective and to understand how they are formed, shaped and maintained." In this chapter, I have attempted to follow this advice by using Eichberg's trialectics of body culture as a methodological point of departure to distinguish the particular culture of sport underpinning the discourse of sport policy in the UK. By then applying the insights offered by Lukes on the need to understand the deep structures of power relations, I have analysed the specific ideological form of current sports policy, which I have called "neo-Olympism". Neo-Olympism, then, emerges out of the interweaving of interdependent processes occurring at different levels — social context, policy, strategy and programmes — in three discrete domains: the philosophy of Olympism, the politics of sport, and national programmes to develop opportunities and excellence in sport. Its structuring features can now be ordered and identified as:

- a paradigmatic conceptualisation of achievement-oriented Olympic sport;
- a belief in the interdependence of grass roots (that is, youth sport) and elite sport;
- a politicisation of sports policy based on the quest to raise national pride and patriotism;
- a determining role for excellence;
- a concept of excellence which is contingently interpreted based on the degree to which national pride and patriotism results.

My suggestion is that the resultant sports-participation culture likely to emerge from such a sports policy will be problematic, not least in the sense that intrinsic rationales and benefits of sports participation will exist only incidentally, if at all.

Neo-Olympism can be understood as a particular ideological formation that represents a shift in the range of "structured possibilities" (Gruneau, 1999: p. 106) in the culture of sports participation. In his seminal study *Class, Sport and Social Development*, Gruneau argued that, depending on how it was structured, sporting practice can be enabling by opening "pathways for various freedoms, pleasures, forms of disciplinary mastery, social bonding, and identity", or constraining by "directing practices and the meanings associated with them into social and cultural forms that sustain relations of domination" (Gruneau, 1999: p. 115). The argument presented here is that the aforementioned shift in sports policy promotes a culture of sports participation that is more constraining than enabling in its range of 'structured possibilities'.

I will finish by raising a broader philosophical point about the new sports-participation culture. The impetus behind the policy changes is clearly related to a political desire for sporting success in the international arenas. Therefore, what may have been perceived as essentially domestic or parochial concerns are now locked into and affected by the wider global Olympic sports culture. Hoberman (1992) has written a devastating account of the dehumanisation of this sports culture that has occurred as a result of a cult of high performance sport in a modern industrial and scientific age. The problem of doping and sport is given as an illustration of this process. Hoberman warns that as we enter a new era of unprecedented developments in genetic engineering and hormonal manipulation, the symbiosis of sport and science threatens to transform, to a qualitatively different level, the human body into a "mortal engine" and push back yet further the boundaries of 'human performance'. The Canadian physiologist Claude Bouchard has pointed out that high-tech societies place a premium on competition and success and will want to apply genetic engineering to an entire range of performers, including writers, musicians and scientists. For Hoberman, it is genetic engineering that:

> Promises to bring about the most profound biological transformations of the human body, and it is likely that this technology will be used to develop athletes before it is applied to the creation of other kinds of human performers. Athletes will serve as the most promising experimental subjects because it will be easier to identify correlations between the actions of particular genes and performance-related traits if the test performances are physical and quantifiable in a way that musical and scientific talent are not. (Hoberman, 1992: p. 286)

If this scenario is realised then the dehumanisation of sport will be complete, because genetic engineering raises issues that concern "nothing less than human identity itself" (Hoberman, 1992: p. 289). This, then, is the context and the ultimate logic of the new government sports policy. The rapid, seemingly uncontrollable and autonomised dynamism of sport modernisation, could perhaps be analysed as a symptomatic moment in the social order described by Beck (1992) as 'reflexive modernisation' which he argues is producing the "risk society". Elsewhere, Beck asserts that:

Industrial society, the civil social order and, particularly, the welfare state and the insurance state are subject to the demand to make human living situations controllable by instrumental rationality, manufacturable, available and (individually and legally) accountable. On the other hand, in risk society the unforeseeable side and after-effects of this demand for control, in turn, lead to what have been considered overcome, the realm of the uncertain, of ambivalence, in short, of alienation. (Beck, 1994: p. 10)

A comprehensive and systematic critique of sport as an increasingly uncertain, ambivalent and alienated aspect of "risk society" is clearly a greater task than the analysis attempted here. My brief has been more focused, but hopefully not irrelevant to these urgent philosophical issues confronting contemporary sport.

References

Bachrach, P. and Baratz, M. (1970) *Power and poverty: Theory and practice.* New York: Oxford University Press.

Beck, U. (1992) *Risk society: Towards a new modernity.* London: Sage.

———— (1994) 'The reinvention of politics: Towards a theory of reflexive modernisation' in U. Beck, A. Giddens and S. Lash (eds) *Reflexive modernisation: Politics, tradition and aesthetics in the modern social order.* Cambridge. Polity Press, pp. 1–55.

Berger, P. (1963) *Invitation to sociology: A humanistic perspective.* Harmondsworth: Penguin.

Bourdieu, P. (1994) *In other words: Essays towards a reflexive sociology.* Cambridge: Polity Press.

———— (1992) *An invitation to reflexive sociology.* (with L. Wacquant) Cambridge: Polity Press.

Collins, M. (1995) *Sports development, locally and regionally.* Reading: ILAM/ Sports Council.

De Coubertin, P. (1966) *The Olympic idea: Discourse and essays.* Cologne: Carl-Diem-Institut.

DCMS [Department of Culture, Media and Sport] (2000) *A sporting future for all.* London: DCMS.

DNH [Department of National Heritage] (1994), *Sport for 21st century.* London: HMSO.

——— (1995), *Sport: Raising the game.* London: Department of National Heritage.

Eady, J. (1993) *Practical sports development.* Harlow: Longman Group

Eichberg, H. (1989) 'Body culture as paradigm: the Danish sociology of sport', *International Review for the Sociology of Sport* Vol. 24, No. 1, pp. 43–60

Guardian, The (1996) 'Duo with walletful of clout', 21 March: p. 25.

Gruneau, R. (1999) (2nd edition) *Class, sport and social development.* Illinois: Human Kinetics.

Hill M. (ed) (1997). *The policy process — a reader.* London: Harvester/Wheatsheaf

Hoberman, J. (1992), *Mortal engines: The science of performance and the dehumanisation of sport.* New York: Free Press.

Lentell, B. (1993) 'Sports development: Goodbye to community recreation?', in C. Brackenridge (ed) *Body matters: Leisure images and lifestyles.* Eastbourne: Leisure Studies Association, pp. 141–149.

Lucas, J. (1992) *Future of the Olympic Games.* Illinois: Human Kinetics.

Lukes, S. (1974) *Power: A radical view.* London: Macmillan Press.

MacAloon, J. (1981) *This great symbol: Pierre de Coubertin and the origins of the modern Olympics.* Chicago: University of Chicago Press.

McDonald, I. (1995) 'Sport for all — RIP. A political critique of the relationship between national sport policy and Local Authority sports development in London', in S. Fleming, M. Talbot, and A. Tomlinson (eds), *Policy and politics in sport, physical education and leisure.* (LSA Publication No. 55) Eastbourne: Leisure Studies Association, pp. 71–94.

McIntosh, P. (1987) *Sport in society.* London: West London Press.

Metheny, E. (1981) 'Athletes, aesthetes, intellectuals, and the Olympic games: Then and now', in J. Segrave and D. Chu (eds), *Olympism.* Champaign, IL: Human Kinetics, pp. 317–328.

Olympic (magazine of the Olympic Museum Lausanne) (1995) No. 8, December.

Segrave, J. (1988) 'Towards a definition of Olympism', in J. Segrave and D. Chu (eds), *The Olympic games in transition.* Champaign, IL: Human Kinetics, pp. 149–161.

Segrave, J. and Chu, D. (eds) (1981) *Olympism*. Champaign, IL: Human Kinetics.

Sport (magazine of the GB Sports Council) (undated but issued in 1995) Issue 5: p. 9.

Sport England (1999) *Investing for our sporting future: Sport England lottery fund strategy 1999–2009*. London: Sport England.

Talbot, M. (1995), 'The politics of sport and physical education', in in S. Fleming, M. Talbot, and A. Tomlinson (eds), *Policy and politics in sport, physical education and leisure* (LSA Publication No. 55). Eastbourne: Leisure Studies Association, pp. 3–26.

Tomlinson, A. (1984) 'De Coubertin and the modern Olympics' in A. Tomlinson and G. Whannel (eds), *Five ring circus: Money, power and politics at the Olympic games*. London: Pluto Press, pp. 84–97.

Wright Mills. C. (1949) *The sociological imagination*. London and New York: Penguin Books.

"MONEY CAN'T DRAG YOU THROUGH ANOTHER SIX TACKLES": AMATEURISM, PROFESSIONALISM AND RUGBY

Robert Ackerman, Mike McNamee and Scott Fleming
Cheltenham and Gloucester College of Higher Education

Introduction

In Britain at least, the development of many sports has brought in its wake acrimonious discussions about the role of payment for performances. In this chapter particular attention is paid to the role that financial remuneration plays in the value-hierarchy of a group of elite rugby players in general, and their attitudes to their self-identification as professionals and how that was effected in their performances. The timing of the research, a combination of philosophical, historical and social commentary and data collection is crucial. The original data were collected during the 1995–6 season when the game of rugby union was undergoing a sea change in its own structures and values almost certainly due to the decline in performances of the respective national teams. Only part of those data has been incorporated here. As an historically amateur practice, rugby union was self-consciously to be distinguished from rugby league, its professional counterpart. The two 'codes' of rugby, as they are referred to, though similar in some technical and tactical respects, are worlds apart when considered from social and economic perspectives. Many of these differences were thought, mistakenly we argue, to rest upon an ideologically charged rhetoric about the moral superiority of playing the amateur game and preserving a pure and special ethos that would be corrupted by the presence of direct monetary reward. The data collected from seven international Welsh professional rugby league players, six of whom had also played rugby union at an international level, directly challenge the assumption that payment for performances in any way motivated their commitment to standards of excellence within rugby. After contextualising the amateur/professional debate historically, we set out a picture of sports as a particular kind of cultural practice with a range of goods that are not necessarily undermined merely by the presence of financial reward. We show how professional performers may indeed sustain the best traditions of a sporting practice hand in hand with a commitment toward excellence and a sense of pride in their own demonstration of sporting excellence.

Some historical remarks

Almost exactly one hundred years ago in England, the Rugby Football Union (RFU) expelled some northern rugby union players who wanted cash to supplement the time they took off work for playing. In reaction, the Rugby Football League was formed which generated the game of professional rugby league, and a split between the two codes came about. Any contact with those who played the game of rugby league, meant instant excommunication from rugby union; players became pariahs. The social and historical antecedents to this climactic rupture in the game are worthy of note.

The failure to attend to conceptual nuances in sportstalk and writing is something of a commonplace. The terms in need of clarificatory remarks, "amateur" and "professional", have however been the object of serious study in the recent past (see for example, Schneider and Butcher, 1993; Morgan, 1993). Part of the difficulty of distinguishing and unpacking these ambiguous terms lies in certain ways of viewing sport both socially and historically.

It will be clear to most students of sport that the Victorian era was one of profound importance for the creation of a certain way of sports and indeed of life. Most too will recognise, in the development of these modern phenomena, an ancient precursor (Sansone, 1988). Sports journalists and media commentators (as much as early sports historians) have been keen to deride the greed and corruption of modern sports while make passing references to halcyon days of Victorian England and Ancient Greece, to straight bats and olive wreaths. In our contextualisation of the values of professional rugby league players, some critical remarks here are necessary since the terms themselves have such historical baggage.

First, it should be clear that as far as elite sport goes, there is little if any evidence to suggest that there was ever so "pure" a time when external goods such as status or money rewarded sporting excellence. Young (1988), in a particularly damning set of essays, writes respectively of the two high priests of historical scholarship in classical sport who have contributed to such a view: Gardiner and Pleket. Having described the myth of the ancient amateur as a combination of a "misleading quote in Herodotus and a tongue in cheek joke in Lucian" (Young, 1988: p. 27) that was used by privileged Anglo-Americans to legitimate and restrict access to certain sports participation to a wealthy leisured class. He writes:

> The misconceptions which we have held about Greek athletics come from decades of misleading classical scholarship and false Historical analogies. (...) Imbued with notions of Greek exclusivist sport from all sides Pleket questioned the myth of Greek amateurism only at its outer surface. He never peered back into its almost hidden origins in the nineteenth century amateur movement. He apparently never imagined that the entire amateur thesis — including the aristocratic monopoly — could be quite groundless, a mere house of cards. Pleket's archaic gentleman will practice and accept prizes, but otherwise he shares most things with his Victorian counterpart; namely, upper class birth, inherited money, a contempt for money honestly earned. This tendency to fit ancient sport to nineteenth century molds sometimes leads Pleket to irrelevant distracting questions. He wonders why "there was never any movement in antiquity to ban monetary rewards and prizes completely from sport". The answer is embarrassingly simple: the concept of amateurism did not yet exist. (...) Until we throw away the wholly anachronistic concept of amateurism, we will continue to formulate ambiguous definitions, to tinker with the evidence or to use it selectively, and to pursue irrelevant issues which distract us from the truly important questions about the nature of Greek athletics. (Young, 1983: pp. 107–108)

Later he continues:

> When E. N. Gardiner (1910) argues that *idiotes* is the ancient Greek word for "amateur" he is wrong. *Idiotes* means "untrained" or "non-competitor," surely not what we mean by amateur athlete. And *idiotes*

athletes, a "non-competitor athlete" would be a contradiction in Greek terms; for the word *athletes* literally means "competitor for a prize". (1988 p. 27–28)

But the myth of amateur sport became as pervasive as the British Empire itself and indeed was a key rampart of the whole ideological baggage of imperialism (Holt, 1989: pp. 74–134; Mandell, 1984: pp. 132–57). It had enormous influence on the organisation and practise of British sports and therefore of sports played over much of the world. It is worth stepping back from this ideologically charged view of sports to consider an alternative account that attempts to capture them as inherently valuable and ethical enterprises in order to develop a dual focus of what sports can be in relation to how they may actually be instantiated in this or that time or place.

Sports as practices

The idea of cultural practices that have value in and of themselves as well as being vehicles to other things of worth has long been discussed in philosophy. More recently, philosophers of sport have begun to draw upon the work of Alisdair MacIntyre (1984) to illuminate a normative account of the possibilities they offer as part of living full and valuable lives. For MacIntyre, a practice is a social, co-operative endeavour, wherein people try to achieve the standards of excellence that are definitive of it in ways that extend them as human beings individually and collectively in respect of intellectual and/or physical attributes in a morally admirable manner

Such a characterisation of activities like banking, architecture and commerce may have all but disappeared from the modern world or, at best, exist only at the margins. Yet it is still recognisable in some forms of activity such as academic life, serious musicianship and, of course, some sports and games. All these, highly specific, practices are partially defined by internal goods that must be distinguished from external ones. External goods are those benefits that accrue from engagement in, say, basketball, lacrosse or track and field, but can be achieved in a number of other fields of endeavour. As we have noted above, these are the objects of instrumental valuing. The most obvious of these are prestige, status, medals and money. Characteristically these are the goods of the market.

By contrast, internal goods can only be secured by engaging in any given practice. The satisfaction felt at hitting a perfectly timed slice service can only be had in tennis; the exhilaration at wrong-footing an opponent by a deft change of direction or the precise co-ordination of power to achieve maximal elevation in a back somersault can only be had by the practitioner who dedicates him or herself to the practice. This is why they are called "internal". Of course there will be some family of resemblances between different sports as Brown (1990: p. 75) writes:

> Clearly a central place will have to be found for the skills and techniques whose acquisition, though a matter of degree, is a *sine qua non* for full mastery [sic] of the sport. I have in mind the rich complex of cognitive and neuromuscular repertoires that are the basis for athletic achievement. Different sports place different demands on participants in this respect but not uniquely. There are clear carryovers from one sport to another, especially the psychological skills of concentration, tactical imagination, and physical and intellectual toughness.

For practitioners to grasp these goods they must display a range of virtues such as justice, courage and honesty. The cheat may gain the prize, the wealth, the adoration but never the internal goods. The coward in boxing cannot understand the internal goods offered by that practice for his or her lack of courage. Individuals become enjoined to others in a practice; they seek a common good in athletic excellence. To achieve this they must display commitment to understanding its ways, rituals, skills, history and to see the good of the practice as partially definitive of their own good in leading a full and valuable life.

Sociologists of sport have characteristically been wary of this type of "ideal-typical" account of sport. Instead of recognising the kinds of virtues that sports both require and develop, they often point to sports excesses whether in terms of chauvinism, cheating, greed or violence. MacIntyre's account can withstand such claims because it invites us to view sports as separable from their institutionalisation. Practices like basketball, soccer and track and field must be distinguished from their institutionalisation under the NBA, FIFA or the IAAF. It is institutions that distribute external goods, justly or otherwise, while at the same time attempting to commodify, package, sell, shape and guide the practice in a market-driven world. MacIntyre seems to ask us to use our philosophical imagination heuristically. We can distinguish the activities from their particular orientation in an overly-bureaucratic and corruptive market-driven world and imagine how they could be shaped by virtuous sportsmen and women, officials, administrators and aficionados.

It is precisely this idealized conception of the practice that is the proper guide to professional conduct set out below. Where practices are sustained and invigorated by virtuous players, coaches, administrators, officials, the excesses of institutionalization can be kept at bay while the best traditions of the sport can develop and thrive whether payment for performance is prevalent or not. The point here is perhaps a relatively simple one. It is that the picture of the professional sportsperson ought not to be an egoistic one; payment for athletic excellence must not slide into voracious greed; pride must not lapse into subjective self-esteem. Rather performers must aspire to an objective understanding of the standards of excellence of the activity, and a proper recognition and evaluation of their performance in relation to them. This claim needs to be premised on the assertion that a practice demands that the practitioner gives himself/herself inferior importance, in a certain way, to the standards and exponents of the practice. As MacIntyre writes (1984: p. 191):

> Every practice requires a certain kind of relationship between those who participate in it... the virtues are those goods by reference to which, whether we like it or not, we define our relationships to those other people with whom we share the kind of purposes and standards which inform practices.
>
> Professional sport as a practice conveys a precise conception of sport as a vocation worthy of one's devotion, in which what is at stake is not just the playing of the game, but literally one's livelihood, and in which earning that livelihood is regarded as one of the ends, if not the primary end. Though that is to load a considerable baggage into the term professional such that it necessarily means more than a paid occupation but more akin to the commitment to a way of life.

Morgan (1993) argues correctly that the moral efficacy of professional sport cashes in on the moral inefficacy of amateur sport. The chief defect of amateurism is that is consigns sport to a non-paying vocation. This moral rendering of sport puts those athletes who wish to make sport their chief occupation in an impossible bind. This moral rendering requires that they forsake either their own conception of the meaning, and value of sport or those tenets of amateurism that forbid treating sport as a profession.

This point has often been ignored in the literature by a too sharp distinction between what is inside and what is outside of a given activity such as sport which is itself goal-oriented or instrumental in character. So when Morgan (1993: p. 485) writes that:

> ... professionalism inevitably fall[s] short in that the external goods that it emphasises, such as fame, and money stand only in contingent, whereas the internal goods stand in a constitutive relation to sporting practices ...

he is presupposing an analytical conception of MacIntyre's account. The analysis presented has ignored the historical relationship between certain external goods, such as status and wealth, with elite sports (as we noted above). We might think instead that professionalism removes the dual prohibition against financial compensation, and against conceiving and treating sport as a vocation, obliging in the process both the structures of the capitalist marketplace (its financial reward for excellence), and the structures of sport in particular its dedication to established standards of athletic excellence. Professionalism is able thereby to give credence to Keating's claim that owing to the perfectionist imperatives of practices, "... the pursuit of excellence in athletics tends naturally and inevitably to some form of professionalism" (Keating, 1965: p. 267).

In his analysis relating to professionalism, Morgan (1993) certainly moves a long way towards substantiating his claim that 'professionalism' (which attempts to ignore or transform internal goods in favour of external goods) may seriously imperil the integrity of sport as a social practice. Where professionalism in sport may go seriously wrong as a moral image of sport is that it presumes an unalterable link between goods such as money and fame in sport. It is in this conception, that the only goods considered to be relevant and appropriate to sport are internal goods, which are supposed to go all the way to capturing everything that is essential to a sports practice, which may not necessarily be the case. As Morgan (1993: p. 478) writes, "The mere offering of financial compensation for athletic performance is not in itself morally troubling or suspect".

In fact financial rewards can, and often do, play a salutary role in human enterprises, when distributed justly. With regards to sport, and the concept of professionalism, what is morally, not to mention conceptually, problematic between the alleged linkage between goods like money and sport itself is that this linkage provides practitioners of sport no reason not to cheat, and every reason to cheat, in order to acquire the external goods they seek. What might the barriers to such decay look like in relation to the practitioners themselves?

Personal standards of integrity and pride on the part of the athlete, may make all thoughts of deceit or cheating irrelevant. Honestly attained fame or money can be as attractive and desirable in sport as they can be in any other profession undertaken for the obtainable external rewards.

The standards for excellence that sportspersons aspire to, and the skills, challenges, judgements and values sports excite, capture what it is about sporting practices that make them meaningful undertakings. However, perhaps most importantly of all, the goods attainable through sports, furnish the practitioners of sports with a compelling reason for engaging in sports which makes the pursuit of the goods they stand for, if not the whole, then certainly the chief reason for engagement in sport.

As a case-study exemplar of a set of sporting practices, rugby in general, and rugby in Wales in particular, provides an opportunity to illuminate some key distinctions very graphically. Over a century has now elapsed since the divergence of the then Amateur and Professional Codes of rugby. When the latter was formed in 1894, it was known as the "Northern Union", while the former retained the title "The Rugby Football Union". The schism between 'professional' and 'amateur' codes came about as a response to players who wished to be paid while taking time off from paid employment in order to play. Indeed it was a requirement of all Northern Union players that they be in employment so that they could play in what came to be known as the "League". Having contextualised some historical ambiguities surrounding the terms "professional" and "amateur", it is now important to be clear about how these terms are commonly understood.

What's in a name? Amateurs and professionals

The research upon which this chapter was based sought to challenge the assumption that professionals characteristically valued financial and other external rewards over those satisfactions and goods that were inherent within the sport. Historically, there has been a widespread assumption that there is something radically instrumental about the motivations of sportspersons who have sought wealth, status, recognition and the like from their engagement in certain British sports as we have noted above. It is not, however, immediately clear how we ought to think of these goods; what is to count as internal to an activity and external is not immediately obvious; what is definitive, what merely associated? That diffidence is increased by a less than clear account of the concepts of "amateur" and "professional". We shall turn to the latter of these tasks first.

Morgan (1993) sets out six clear but related senses of both terms. He notes that the term "amateur" may refer to one or more of the following: (i) the mythological sense; (ii) the British aristocratic sense; (iii) the liberal bourgeois sense; (iv) the moral sense; (v) the avocational sense; (vi) the non-specialist sense. It seems better to speak of these senses as dimensions or characteristics of amateurism rather than senses of the term. It seems that they represent criteria for a relatively open concept that may be conjoined to offer differing conceptions. We have greatly undermined senses (i) and (ii) in our historical remarks above, and recast them as being unworthy of serious scholarly attention except by way of unmasking a latent ideology. And the closely related third sense, that those who pay for play shall not count as amateurs, goes cap in hand with the Victorian dimension of (ii). Similarly, (v) allows that a player may be paid expenses for lost revenue but that they should not be paid directly for their sports "labour". Sense (vi) addresses by contrast the widely held, but misplaced, view that professionalism consists of merely technical expertise. Here the amateur is defined, by contrast, as a dabbler lacking in the relevant experience and ability. It will be clear that (v) is of most interest to us. The amateur, thus characterised, plays for the love of the game; sport is for him or her, an end in itself. It is precisely this motivation that Schneider and Butcher (1993) champion in their defence of the concept of amateurism. They premise the love of sport of the amateur on an appreciation for, and dedication to, the defining goods and standards of that sport. It should be clear immediately, however, that this raises a certain difficulty. Even where the meaning of "professional" is so etiolated as to mean merely that a player is paid to do something, there is no reason why he/ she might not be classified as "amateur" on the above account. Is this problematic? Some words on the notion of "professional" are required.

As with Morgan's senses of amateurism, the senses of "professional" are perhaps better thought of as dimensions or as criteria of conceptions that are the product of their various combinations. They are (i) the economic sense; (ii) the occupational sense; (iii) the legal sense; (iv) the moral sense; (v) the instrumental sense; (vi) the specialist sense. It will be clear that these senses partly mirror their would-be opposites. Senses (i)–(iii) build upon each other. To be professional one must be paid (i), such paid occupation may fit further criteria in which professional sports may be seen to be some kind of calling requiring the devotion of one's energies to the activity; which (iii) is encapsulated in a contractual framework. While sense (v) is a mere logical category — it covers those who play purely for ends extrinsic to sport — it is not particularly interesting. Moreover, one can question the psychological infelicity of thinking that one's motivations could ever be entirely external — or for that matter entirely internal — to the activity at hand. Thinking of pursuits that extend over years and require such emotional and identity constituting development in terms of simple ends and colourless means is extremely unhelpful (McNamee, 1994; McNamee, 1995). While (vi) speaks to the idea of professional expertise, the tendency in this sense is to cleave technical expertise away from the moral grounds that are thought properly to ground professions and the trust we place in them (Koehn, 1994; McNamee, 1998). We are left again, with the moral sense of the term that is of greatest interest to us. Here professionals engage in the activity not merely for external ends but for the particular configuration of mixed goods it offers them: internal and external.

It appears then that pursuing the goods of sport as an amateur and as a professional in the moral senses of the word have strong resemblances and that there is no logically necessary incompatibility between being an 'amateur'' and being paid to undertake the same activity under those particular rendering of the terms. On the one hand, amateurism, on the view of it that speaks of the goods internal to practices and the necessity of maintaining some positive ethical regard for them, is a moralised picture of sport properly understood. On the other hand, the ethical picture of professionalism we have sketched above, speaks too of sportspersons who are dedicated to the preservation and promotion of a certain moralised conception of sports as cultural practice worthy of inherent and instrumental value. Whether as amateur or professional, we will try to show how elite performers can and do perform in sport self-consciously conceived of as "practitioners" of sports conceived of as "practices" in the MacIntyrean sense, when they have a proper regard for the goods of the game and its best traditions, and for their place in relation to such.

Professionalisation and rugby

Just before the game of rugby union became officially professional on August 27th, 1995, Ian Ferrier, the Chairman of the New South Wales Rugby Union, asked the Australian Rugby Union to convey to the International Rugby Union Board his message that: "Amateurism as a concept is outmoded and should be dispensed with in the modern game" (in Pugh, 1995a: p. 33). Partly in response, Vernon Pugh, Q. C., then 'Chairman' of the Welsh Rugby Union and a delegate on the International Rugby Board (IRB) for nearly three years, denied that he brought about the dramatic change almost single-handedly in the game of rugby union becoming professional. He wrote a paper for Board delegates which dismissed the remaining significance of amateurism by taking issue with the central argument that, as he wrote: "… amateurism is responsible for the ethos — the game of rugby union does have a certain ethos but whether this is due to non-payment for playing/coaching is unclear" (Pugh, 1995b: p. 11).

Pugh's paper was realistic about the future of a professional game. It dismissed the argument that the game could not afford to go professional as "the least defensible, logical or relevant" argument of all. It pointed out that no one compelled unions or clubs to engage all of their employees full time; they were free to pay them what they could afford, be it thousands of pounds or five. Pugh also derided the idea that amateurism could somehow be sustained if players were paid indirectly through press funds, an option widely canvassed by member unions: "There is no justification for a pretend amateurism. Any halfway house will fail" (Pugh, 1995b: p. 11).

The changes announced by the IRB swept away all regulations governing amateurism. The reforms, which have paved the way for a transfer system, player contracts and win bonuses, are the culmination of almost twenty years of emerging professionalism within the game. The changes were a reflection of the way in which the sport has changed since the seventies when players were not only unpaid but barred from making money even indirectly from the game — for example writing their memoirs or writing for newspapers. But by the early eighties under-the-counter payments known as "boot money" from kit manufacturers and inflated expenses became increasingly commonplace.

However, in recent years these kinds of rules have been relaxed across the world. Top English players have been allowed to endorse products, providing they are not wearing rugby kit when doing so. In the Southern Hemisphere, the rules were even more relaxed with 'star' players receiving well-paid coaching and administrative sinecures. The difficulty of putting such rule changes into practice involves trying to work out how the new professional game is to operate, and how to sell the notion to the mass of rugby union's global membership, to whom amateurism is more a practical necessity than an article of faith.

Apart from a handful among the sixty-seven countries that form the membership of the IRB, most member countries have hardly any money to provide pitches, let alone pay the players. For example, although the Rugby Football Union has officially embraced the principles of a professional sport, rugby union's bruised mutilated amateur ethos it seems, has not gone away. For the most part, the game in the British Isles has been unaffected by the adoption of an "open game" (which is the official term). So the English Rugby Union team, who finished as Five Nations Champions in 1996 after being an indifferent fourth in the 1995 World Cup, have now entered the ranks of paid entertainers. Or have they? In this new world, where euphemism too often is still the name of the game, the England Rugby Union squad are not being paid only to play. The £40,000 or so they receive from the RFU is also for promoting the game — coaching clinics, personal appearances, and celebrity dinners.

It was clear that the governing institutions of rugby were particularly worried about the increasing dominance of financial considerations within the game. The extent to which these may or may not be founded are not commented upon here in a general sense. One might argue that there was a widespread lack of financial probity or public accountability of the funds generated by amateur rugby. Equally, one could argue that what they considered troubling was the corruption of the ethos or values of the game. It is the latter interpretation that we have focused upon here, having earlier highlighted the historical legacy of this view.

A methodological note

From the outset, the empirical thrust behind the research for this chapter was based on an ethnographic approach to 'exploratory research'. The epistemological and theoretical rationale for the use of the ethnography has been discussed at length elsewhere (see, for example, Atkinson, 1990; Hammersley and Atkinson, 1983), and need not be elaborated here. More significant for understanding the research process here, however, is the relation of the principal researcher [RA] to the research participants. With autobiographical detail being emphasized increasingly in the accounts of qualitative enquiries in sport and leisure, the background of the 'participant-as-researcher' is fundamental to framing the project itself, and to conceptualizing the validity of the findings.

The sociological imagination: history and biography

The pattern of movement of economic sporting migrants from rugby union in South Wales to rugby league in the North of England has been a well-established phenomenon (Williams, 1994). In the late 1980s in particular, a significant number of high profile Welsh rugby union internationals switched codes (some of whom later switched back). RA was amongst this group, and was therefore socialized into the cultural practices that are addressed in this paper. This is an important feature of the basis for this research. The success of the collection of empirical data relied on 'insider research' — research undertaken on a group or constituency by a member of that group (Pink Dandelion, 1997).

In methodological reflections soon after undertaking the data-collection, the following observations were noted:

> As assistant coach to the Welsh Rugby League team in the recent Halifax Rugby League Centenary World Cup, during October 1995, the opportunity arose to do some ethnographic research. Being in daily contact with a large number of players who had played International Rugby Union as amateurs, and then after switching to rugby league had played for Great Britain as professionals, gave me a unique opportunity

to participate in their daily lives for an extended period of time... I watched what happened, listened to what was said, and asked questions; in fact collected whatever data were available to throw light on the issues that concerned me. This role provided qualitative depth by allowing interviewees to talk in terms of their own 'frames of reference', and afforded me the opportunity to understand the meanings and interpretations that the individual players attributed to events, and their own values.

There is a key epistemological and ontological point here. We are not arguing that first hand experience is logically necessary for a proper understanding of social phenomena. What we are arguing, however, is that the insider role provided certain distinct advantages that could not have been gained easily in any other way. These can be summarised, as Pink Dandelion (1997) indicates, under the following headings:

(a) access to participants;
(b) familiarity with the context and practices; and
(c) trust of motives of research.

Access to participants

The uniqueness of this study, emphasised above, rests primarily on the kinds of participants who were involved. In this sense, it is the ethos of a group of elite level rugby players who had reached the ultimate heights of an international representative career (for some, in both of rugby's codes). The privileged access is alluded to in further methodological reflections:

I chose to interview seven players, five of whom had played rugby union for Wales as amateurs. Two of these five had also represented the British Isles Rugby Union Touring Team in Test Matches, which is the ultimate achievement for rugby union players in the British Isles. Two of the other three players who had played rugby union for Wales (though not for the British Isles), had gone on to represent Great Britain after turning professional and switching to rugby league. Of the remaining two players (who had not represented Wales at rugby union), one of them had been an amateur rugby league International, and had represented Great Britain. The other was approaching the end of a distinguished playing career in which he had achieved nearly everything that there was to achieve in the game of professional rugby league in England – he had represented Great Britain and had been victorious at Wembley in the Challenge Cup Final on seven occasions.

The credentials as a rugby player and coach (in both rugby union and rugby league) that RA brought to the research process were important in securing access to his contemporaries and peers. As he observed at the time:

> This 'rapport' between the interviewees and myself, had been developed over a period of months with some of them, and over a period of years with the others, going as far back as when I used to play International Rugby Union with one particular player some ten years [previously]. This helped me enormously.

Familiarity with the context and practices

The main advantages of familiarity with context and practices relate to the empathy that is brought into the recognition and interpretation of data that become pivotal to the empirical process. These are also important for the purposes of synthesis and the generation of an appropriately contextualised theoretical analysis. On one level, it is concerned with the ability of the participating actors to share a collective understanding of language (for example, through the use of esoteric jargon). On another level, however, it relates to common meanings and understandings within the discourse of the practice. This is evident through the ways in which players interact with each other, and as with particular specialist and/or committed sub-cultural groups, structure, activity and language are not necessarily coherent (Pink Dandelion, 1997). That is not to suggest that research cannot generate important insights and theoretical advancements without this kind of familiarity with the practice; rather that, when it does, there is often a necessarily prolonged period of familiarisation It is truistic, though significant, that familiarity obviates the fears of the unfamiliar. For social researchers entering an unfamiliar 'field', there can be considerable anxieties associated with the unknown. This unease is commonly felt by interviewees who may either be skeptical of the researcher and of their knowledge of the subject of the investigation. We are not, however, suggesting that the insider role is entirely free of its own difficulties and complexities. For instance, there are concerns about 'knowing too much' and 'taking too much for granted' (Pink Dandelion, 1997); about affective participation (for example, Pryce, 1986); and about 'premature saturation' — where the researcher's roles merge and create their own conflicts (Fleming, 1997). What we are arguing, however, is that, on balance, the advantages of being an insider significantly outweighed the shortcomings.

Trust of motives of research

The final thrust of the methodological argument for the efficacy of the insider role is linked to the first two. The access that RA was able to secure, and the trust that the other players had in him as a researcher, makes us more convinced in the validity of the findings. This position is in stark contrast to the position advanced by Norris (1993) in which he argues that some ethnographic fieldwork involves inevitable deception and brings into question the notion of 'trust'. His analysis (based on an ethnographic account of the police) is that the notion of trust implies mutuality of interest (Norris, 1993), and he argues that these were absent in his own field-worker role. What we argue here, however, is that RA's role was characterised by exactly these features, and that there was mutual trust, even to the point (perhaps) where the participants were actually empowered through the empirical data collection.

There are two further points to add. The first is analytical. These data were gathered in 1995 through a series of semi-structured interviews, and were analysed at that time (Ackerman, 1995). Subsequent retrospective re-evaluation provides for a more reflective and reflexive synthesis and analysis of the data. Throughout the process (which has now been on-going for five years), the participants have been willing and supportive verifiers of the analytical themes that are presented in the remainder of this paper. The second point relates to the ethics of research. The participants in this study have give fully informed consent for their identities to be revealed. This is somewhat unusual, for often the particular identities of participants is not directly relevant to the general points that emerge as key findings. In this instance, however, individual identities are important; and for readers who are familiar with them, this additional biographical detail may assist in contextualising the data and the overall findings further still.

Discussion

In this section we address the main substantive point to emerge from the research, and by drawing upon the empirical data we hope to illuminate the theoretical dimensions of the argument that we are advancing. As a consequence, we are concerned to collapse the false binary divide about conceptualisations about the nature of the 'amateur' and the 'professional', and particularly when such conceptualisations are couched (crudely) in terms of the economics (cf. Morgan, 1993). Rather, we argue that it is the individual's frame of reference, value hierarchy and relation to the practice of playing the game that is pivotal. To actually play the game or, be involved in it in some capacity, is often regarded by many as being more important than the final result of any match. People who feel the same way towards the practice of rugby (paid or unpaid) in this case, share in the same kind of values towards the game. As Gibson (1993: p. 108) writes:

> Out on that practice field in the cool pool of light that splits the darkness, the athletes weave the patterns of the game. In a ritual of action they unfold their relationship to the practice and each other. The seasons sweep (…). But always the relationship of the player to the craft and the practitioners are there, rain or shine, to make those magical touches on the ball and drive themselves further and deeper into themselves, the practice and the tradition.

As a brief synthesis of the overall view, it was critical that concern for excellence and recognition of standards of excellent performance were values logically connected to the practice of elite competitive sport. Indeed even when a competitor's main concern was winning rather than achieving excellence, there is still a sense of comparative (if not absolute) superiority. Inevitably, this presupposes a conception of better and worse play, and hence a conception of standards of evaluating performance in the sport. In this regard, a common theme amongst the participants in this study was the centrality of 'pride in their own performance' within each individual's value hierarchy — and this was not connected to an individual's amateur or professional status. Importantly too, this notion of 'pride' was not merely self-referenced. Understanding 'pride' for the players was about situating themselves in a social and historical context; as one of a (particular) team, with particular expectations and obligations to be satisfied, levels of excellence to be achieved. Iestyn Harris captured the essence of the point when he remarked:

> I think that pride is the biggest point in playing professional rugby, you always want to be the best, and I have always wanted to be the best.

Pride *of* the individual, and collective pride *through* the individual

All of these players set themselves particularly high performance standards (as international players they may have had to), but the continued maintenance of these standards required pride in their own performance. Without this personal motivation there was a real fear that their standards would drop, this pride would evaporate, and their self-esteem would be eroded. In this regard, the mere labelling of their motivational or value-hierarchy as 'instrumental' in virtue of their payment is hopelessly inadequate. It is true that they played for the external end of money; but this was not to be seen as distinct from the playing of rugby but as the reward appropriate to excellent performance. Each individual actively evaluated his own playing performance — and all were stern critics. They had their own standards to maintain and in order to maintain them required a dedication to a certain level of commitment and a certain picture of the enterprise of rugby which matched the practice conception. Moreover, it was not merely a matter of performance levels reflecting solely on the player concerned, there was a wider constituency of people affected. As Jonathan Davies explained:

> ... it is not for myself really, it is for my team mates and to feel that I haven't let any of them down by making a mistake that has cost us the game..... you want to play well because all your family and friends are watching.

Playing performance was not only a source of individual pride for the player, but a source of collective pride to his significant others.

The money-commitment (non)relation

In spite of the tabloidesque rhetoric that sometimes clouds uninformed analyses of the impact of money on sports performance, it was clear that for these elite-level rugby players financial reward was not causally linked to, or even significantly correlated with, the level of commitment demonstrated by them. As Kelvin Skerrett indicated, financial reward had did not impact on his cognitive processes whilst playing, and had no bearing on his own personal level of commitment on the rugby field:

> ... money can't drag you through an extra six tackles, it's personal pride which is the main thing.

Pride in the performance was not affected by a contractual obligation to perform as a professional. It was a view shared explicitly by Alan Bateman:

> ... that goes by the by, when I was in rugby union I always turned up for training and I always trained and played to the best of my ability.

He continued:

> ... before you go into a game you don't think "I'm on three hundred pounds this week, better win because of the money": you want to win because of self respect.

Indeed, Kelvin Skerrett took the theme a stage further when he argued that the consequences of not performing to the highest personal standards had implications for his own approach. For him, the pride in performance became intimately linked with the dread of defeat:

> ... fear of being beaten, and the fact that I would have been in the side that failed at Wembley ... it becomes mundane after so many times and you have to find something else to spur you on and we look towards fear of being beaten.

What these players have indicated is that they were reflective and critical practitioners, and that their practice was not cast in the contractual arrangements of the economics of elite sports performance. Importantly too, individual pride in their own performance was often expressed through the wider constituent parts of their identity as players and as persons.

Conclusion

There are, of course, variations between individuals in relation to their own values, one particular individual may value having pride in one's performance as important whilst, for another individual, this may not be the case. Cultural variations may also account for differences in values between individuals, for instance rugby players in Wales are likely to have different values to rugby players in England, South Africa or New Zealand and the significance they attach to the game for rugby is somewhat different. The empirical work that has informed this study does not lend itself easily to generalisation in any case. The data reflect a particular historical 'turning point' in the development of the game of rugby — that is to say, the data are rooted in a certain time and a specific place. The sample of the data that has been presented are, however, representative of the wider views of all of the players that were included in the study. Through the vignettes, we have tried to show how the data have corroborated our view that even elite sports, what are referred to sometimes euphemistically a 'professional' sports, can be viewed in the idealized manner that has been captured by the term 'practices'. We have tried to show further how elite performers can share in a particularly moralised picture of the sports where they understand themselves and their performances in their social and historical rootedness. Moreover, we have tried further to undermine the bourgeois view that payment for performance necessarily undermines the values and goods of sporting practices.

References

Ackerman, R. (1996) Amateurism, Professionalism and Rugby League, Unpublished dissertation. University of Wales Institute, Cardiff.

Atkinson, P. (1990) *The ethnographic imagination — textual constructions of reality*. London: Routledge.

Baker, W. J. (1988) *Sports in the western world*. Chicago: University of Illinois.

Brown, W. M. (1990) 'Practices and prudence', *Journal of the Philosophy of Sport*: pp. 71–84.

D'Agostino, F. (1981) *The ethos of games in the philosophic inquiry of sport.* Champaign, IL: Human Kinetics.

Fleming, S. (1997) 'Qualitative research of young people and sport: The ethics of role-conflict', in A. Tomlinson and S. Fleming (eds) *Ethics, sport and leisure: Crises and critiques.* Aachen: Meyer and Meyer, pp. 137–150.

Gibson, J. H. (1993) *Performance versus results: A critique of values in contemporary sport.* Albany, NY: Suny Press.

Hammersley, M. and Atkinson, P. (1983) *Ethnography — principles in practice.* London: Tavistock.

Hargreaves, J. A. (1994) *Sporting females.* London: Routledge.

Holt, R. (1989) *Sport and the British.* Oxford: Clarendon Press.

Keating, J. W. (1964) 'Sportsmanship as a moral category', *Ethics* Vol. LXXV, pp. 25–35.

Koehn, D. (1994) *The grounds of professional ethics.* London: Routledge.

MacIntyre, A. (1984) *After virtue.* Notre Dame: University of Notre Dame Press.

Mandell, R. (1984) *Sport: A cultural history.* New York: Columbia University Press.

McNamee, M. J. (1994) 'Valuing leisure practices: Towards a theoretical framework', *Leisure Studies* Vol. 13, No. 1: pp. 288–309.

———— (1995) 'Sporting practices, institutions and virtues: A critique and restatement', *Journal of the Philosophy of Sport* XXII: pp. 61–83.

———— (1996) 'Values in sport', in D. Levinson and K. Christenson (eds) *Encyclopaedia of world sport.* Massachusetts: ABC Clio Press, pp. 1123–1128.

———— (1998) 'Celebrating trust; Virtues and rules in the ethical conduct of sports coaches', in M. McNamee and S. J. Parry (eds) *Ethics and sport.* London: Spon-Routledge, pp. 470–493.

Morgan, W. J. (1993) 'Amateurism and professionalism as moral language. In search of a moral image of sport', *Quest* Vol. 45: pp. 470–493.

Norris, C. (1993) 'Some ethical considerations on field-work with the Police', in D. Hobbs and T. May (eds) *Interpreting the field — accounts of ethnography.* Oxford: Clarendon Press, pp. 122–144.

Pink Dandelion, B. (1997) 'Insider dealing: Researching your own private world', in A. Tomlinson and S. Fleming (eds) *Ethics, sport and leisure: Crises and critiques.* Aachen: Meyer and Meyer Verlag, pp. 181–201.

Pryce, K. (1986) *Endless pressure* 2nd edition. Bristol Classical Press, Bristol.

Pugh, V. (1995a) Untitled commentary, *Sunday Telegraph*, p. 27.

———— (1995b) Untitled commentary, *Sunday Times*, 3 September 1995.

Sansone, D. (1988) *The Greek athletics and genesis of sport*. Berkeley, California: University Press.

Schneider, A and Butcher, R. (1993) 'For the love of the game: A philosophical defense of amateurism', *Quest* Vol. 45: pp. 460–469.

Sugden, J. (1997) 'Field workers rush in (where theorists fear to tread): The perils of ethnography', in A. Tomlinson and S. Fleming (eds) *Ethics, sport and leisure: Crises and critiques*. Aachen: Meyer and Meyer Verlag, pp. 223–244.

Williams, G. (1994) 'The road to Wigan Pier revisited: The migration of Welsh rugby talent since 1918', in J. Bale and J. Maguire (eds) *The global sports arena*. London: Frank Cass, pp. 193–211.

Young, D. C. (1983) *The Olympic myth of Greek amateur athletics*. Chicago: Ares.

——— (1988) 'Professionalism in Classical and Archaic Greek athletics', in J. O. Seagrave and D. Chu (eds) *The Olympic Games in transition*. Champaign, IL.: Human Kinetics, pp. 27–36.

'GOING ALL THE WAY': FEMALE FOOTBALL FANS AND 'LADETTE' CULTURE IN THE UK

Joyce Sherlock and Nicola Elsden
De Montfort University

Introduction

Debates about postmodernism have significant implications for the female identity. Rejection of modernity's 'grand narratives', especially patriarchy and capitalism, means that female identity is no longer defined according to feminist theories associated with modernity which forefront attempts to find the cause of women's oppression (Scraton, 1994). This view highlights the way that masculinity and femininity are socially constructed in material cultural conditions (Scraton, 1994). If a rupture from modernity is accepted, a postmodern view of gender signifies decreased differentiation and discrimination. This implies that the universal categories and binary opposites-women/men, femininity/masculinity cease to be meaningful (Scraton, 1994). Gender divisions, in postmodern culture, it is argued, are more fluid (Crook, Pakulski and Waters, 1992 quoted in Scraton, 1994: p. 251), allowing females to adopt "different identities at different times" (Hall, 1992: p. 277). The contention is that this results in women being able to experience a less restricted and freer identity than previously, rendering the possibility of a diversity of female social experience.

The 'Ladette': the rise of the postmodern sporting experience for women?

One example of such diversity emerges in reports such as Moore's (1996, p, 5) when she wrote "The 'Ladess', 'Ladette', the babe with attitude is now upon us". She is said to be "taking Britain by storm" (Weaver, 1998: p. 5). Moore (1996) describes the 'Ladette' as lippy, raucous, brazen and confident, while Weaver (1998) adds that she chooses to drink vast quantities of beer and is sexually liberated. A parallel can be drawn with her male counterpart, the 'Lad'[1].

Redhead (1997) argues that British post youth is epitomised by immersion in football and music fandom out of which has emerged the 'Ladette'. Coddington (1997) further acknowledges the link between football and the 'Lad', 'Ladess'/ 'Ladette' culture in what has been a traditionally male environment (Whannel, 1992). Mass media reinforce the association between the 'Ladette' and football in singling out such celebrities as Helen Chamberlain, an avid football fan and host of Sky television "Soccer a.m." programme. Television presenter Zoe Ball is also recognised as a football fan, having reported on soccer for the *Sun* newspaper during the 1998 World Cup. She has been branded the "Ultimate Ladette" (Hoggart, 1998) or the "Ultimate Geezer Bird" (Brimson, 1998).

The 'Ladette' reflects a fragmented and fluid lifestyle within a culture challenging modernity's universal binary opposites. Such a celebration by females taking on behaviours, traditionally seen as masculine, indicates an open identity for women to experience sport as they choose. Status is no longer the defining social constraint, for one signifies identity through the codes with which one engages, such as choice of leisure pursuit, mode of dress and products one consumes (Crooke *et al.*, 1992, in Scraton, 1994: p. 251). The implication for the female football fan is that she can adopt a masculinised identity such as the 'Ladette' and experience the freedom to define her own identity through her chosen leisure experience, unrestricted by gender conventions.

Feminisation

The example of the 'Ladette' provides support for the possibility of a postmodern gender identity. In contrast a relatively new practice regarding female football fans, the 'feminisation' of football, is consistent with traditional feminine qualities such as being spiritual and nurturing (van Vucht Tijssen, 1995). The 'feminisation' idea was born directly out of Lord Justice Taylor's report on the Hillsborough disaster and claims that a greater presence of women at football matches will serve to pacify aggressive and macho behaviour of some male fans. It was, though, developed independently of the experiences and opinions of female fans themselves, which strongly suggest that actual women have very little influence on major issues within football. *The National Survey of Female Football Fans* (Woodhouse, 1991) reveals that a large percentage of such fans agreed that a greater presence of women at matches would have a subduing effect, but that it could lead to them becoming unpopular with male fans. The women primarily wanted to watch the game and, rather than seeing themselves as non-aggressive, said that much of their enjoyment came from participating in the masculine atmosphere. Almost half of the respondents in the 30 years and under age group said that they experienced sexist behaviour.

Coddington (1997) also showed that a modernist stereotype of the female football fan had not been adequately challenged. She pointed out that Tottenham continue to display signs indicating that because of the presence of women and children, care should be taken over what is said. Lindsey (1996), Moore (1996) and Redhead (1997) echo the notion that women are not free from modernist social constraints. According to Redhead (1997: p. 72), the 'Ladette' is "a figment of the advertising, marketing and popular culture industry's over imagination". Even the notion of the 'Ladette' could be said routinely to communicate messages of restriction over the freedom of identity choice proffered. Moore (1996) argues that it is only women with the image of beautiful good looks demanded by the industry who are allowed to act in a brazen and raucous manner on television. Even so, she notes that the limits to which women can go are very much bound by conventions of ladylike behaviour. They can act like the boys so long as they don't go too far. Lindsey (1996: p. 10) notes that a female fan does not belong in football, because without a "beer gut" she is labelled "lightweight" and with one, "a hard bitch". Brimson (1998: p. 13) is unequivocal in his use of "Geezer Bird" as a "derogatory term of the highest order, to be aimed primarily at ugly 'wimmin', overgrown tomboys and lesbians".

The journalistic and autobiographical accounts above, as well as the tiny amount of academic research, fail to expand into empirical research on the actual existence of the 'Ladette', or her relationship with football fandom. It is not surprising that research on football fans has focused almost exclusively on males, predominantly on hooliganism (for example, Moorhouse, 1984; Dunning, Murphy and Williams, 1988). In contrast, the research described here aimed to provide pioneering empirical material of the Saturday to Saturday 'lived experience' of female fans. It focused on whether being female influences experience within football culture and whether adopting the identity of a football fan enables enjoyment unrestricted by gender conventions. Analysing this in relation to claims about 'Ladette' freedom, it has the potential to give us an opportunity to comment on whether postmodern theorisations about new found diversities in female behaviour and identity apply in a specific leisure context.

Methodology

The chosen methodology aimed to 'give voice' to the perspectives of female football fans to gain an understanding of and insight into their experience of the cultural setting. Ethnographic methods were utilised in the form of participant observation and open-ended interviews. The long standing experience of football fandom of one of the researchers ensured her entry into the field. Once this was underway, the decision to attend away matches was crucial, since it meant breaking with her usual routine of attending with a male companion. She was left feeling vulnerable as an unaccompanied female, part of a fragmented tiny minority attending football matches. The necessity of planning coping strategies together and supporting progress made, highlighted for both of us how exposed is a lone female to the chauvinism of males on the football coach and during matches. Because of the personal nature of her research experience, Nicola's voice now takes over, accompanied by the voices of her female companions at the matches.

Recording the "lived experience" of a female Watford fan

The cultural setting of football is an environment with which I am very intimate, since, for the past six years, I have attended football matches on a regular basis as a Watford fan. My status as a female fan allowed me to immerse myself in the surroundings and become fully receptive to my thoughts, feelings and experiences. These I recorded in the form of a diary since I was convinced that they were a valuable source of data (Coolican, 1996). The diary was kept from the end of the 1998/1999 season, a period during which Watford were promoted from the second to the first division, the platform for a place in the Premiership, achieved shortly after the completion of the empirical research. Data was recorded within an hour of the events taking place. The personal account was extended in the away matches with participant observation of two female companions.

These overt observations were important to the research. I shared an equal relationship with the participants as a genuine football fan. A comfortable form of interaction between observer and participants was achieved. Practicalities prevented me from observing all five participants in the study. Female fans, I found, typically attend matches with a number of males, rather than with other female fans, and since their numbers are relatively small, they are very spread out, making it difficult to observe other than those close at hand. Thus, although a seasoned football fan, the requirements of the research went beyond simply donning a participant observer persona. To achieve the objective of my research, I had to engineer a collectivity of females not normally in the natural setting, abandoning my own usual practice of attending with a male colleague. Even given the overwhelming presence of male supporters in relation to female ones, and the usual practice of individual females of attending with a group of males, there were limits to the extent to which I could control my proximity to other females at the match.

I primarily adopted standardised open-ended interviews (Quinn Patton, 1990) which I conducted either in the fan's home or in a local café, on a non-match day, because of the difficulty of gaining in-depth information on reflections at the actual match. Interviews allowed me to gain an understanding of how the participants thought and felt about the topics of concern to the research. The technique allowed easy organisation and analysis of information. Such research techniques were valuable as those best suited to the type of research I wished to conduct. Tape-recording and almost immediate transcription aided the process and allowed me to be familiar with what had been said and sensitive to themes and patterns emerging for the analytical stage.

The participants

Female fans of Watford Football Club were approached to participate in the research since my personal association with the club made them accessible participants for study. Age was a factor in selection, with participants ranging between twenty-one to twenty-eight. Since the 'Ladette' was of interest in the related literature, it was felt appropriate to select participants whose age corresponded. The sample size of five was a number of female fans I felt comfortable about approaching and with whom I felt able to build up a good rapport in the time-scale available. Additionally, five participants was appropriate for such qualitative research, allowing each participant to be focused on in-depth. The participants, whose names have been changed for confidentiality, I shall call Hannah, Karen, Laura, all university students and aged 21, and Sally, a paramedic, and Emma, a customer service advisor, both aged 28. All were interviewed for one hour and Hannah and Karen were also observed in the football setting during two away matches. The 'Saturday Lads' is my collective term for us.

The 'Saturday Lads' most memorable day

> We're on the march with Taylor's army
> We're not going to Wemb-er-ly
> And we don't give a fuck
> 'Cause the 'Orns are going up
> 'Cause Watford are the greatest football team
> [Sung to the tune of 'Ally's Tartan Army']

May 2nd 1998: the atmosphere was electric in Watford town centre on that warm Saturday evening. It was approaching closing time and large numbers of people began to spill onto the high street. Watford Football Club had won the *Nationwide* Division Two Championship. The town was still buzzing some six hours after the Championship Trophy had been lifted. With my hands held high, clutching a can of beer, proudly displaying the yellow and red colours of my club, singing and chanting from the top of my voice, I stepped into the litter-ridden quagmire which is 'The Watford Pond' and embarked on my perilous journey through the broken beer bottles and empty fag packets to join my fellow compatriots revelling in the centre. As I stood submerged to my knees in the murky and fetid water, surrounded by the sonorous voices of men high on beer and high on the moment, I, a lone female, was at the very heart of the atmosphere. In complete harmony we sang and chanted the words "Championé, Championé, Olé Olé Olé", a phrase which had not been heard in Watford for two decades. The lights of the upper street reflected into The Pond. Those not brave enough to enter looked on and joined us in our singing and chanting. The whole town became united to create a raucous, jubilant, euphoric atmosphere. Fully participating in these predominantly male scenes of celebration, intoxicated by both the occasion and vast quantities of alcohol, were the 'Saturday Lads'.

This was the 'Saturday Lads' most memorable day as football fans. For each, after the short trip to Fulham on the train, the day started in *The White Horse*, a pub a short distance from Craven Cottage, the Fulham ground. The sun was shining on the mass of Watford fans overflowing onto the pavement outside, who were adorned in yellow shirts, scarves, hats, wigs, flags with faces painted in the club's colours creating a dazzling glow. As I entered the pub, I was hit by a cacophony of noise, the booming male voices vibrated round the small bar, groups of fans singing, laughing, shouting orders at the overworked barmen, glasses chinking in anticipation of victory, or clashing as people struggled to be served. There was a distinctive aroma of greasepaint evident amongst the overpowering smell of beer and tobacco hanging heavily in the confined space. As the match drew nearer, the pub began to throb in anticipation and excitement, more and more people crammed into the already heaving rooms, the barmen now becoming frantic in their efforts to keep pace with the empty pint glasses thrust in their faces. The boom of male voices intensified and grew to a deafening pitch pulsating through my whole body. The floor became a sea of beer and the tables rattled and creaked, struggling to take the strain of the excited fans dancing on top of them. I clambered on to the table, clutching my pint, to join these fans. As I swayed to and fro amidst the raucous and wild scene my face muscles ached from grinning broadly with complete happiness. I became totally absorbed by the atmosphere, truly relishing the moment of being 'as one' with the other fans. As 3 o'clock finally approached, the pub quickly emptied and we Watford fans surged towards the ground and found our places on the packed terrace behind the goal.

Yet, our involvement is certainly not unique to this occasion. Every match day, donning denim jeans, sports sweatshirts with a baggy yellow Watford shirt over the top, bulky jackets, clompy boots or trainers, and bright yellow and red scarves, wearing minimal or no make-up, turns the young women into the "Saturday Lads'. Tucking their season tickets into their back pockets, Emma and Laura, however, are much more concerned with finding a good seat within the ground, while Hannah, Sally, Karen and Nicola thoroughly enjoy the pre-match ritual 'down the pub', drinking pints with the lads where our attention is focused solely on football matters, discussed over a few beers.

Chants and songs reverberate around the North End of the stadium where the vociferous and animated supporters gather to watch the game in the bright, modern Vicarage Road stand.

I'm Watford till I die
I'm Watford til I die
I know I am,
I'm sure I am,
I'm Watford till I die
[sung to the tune of 'I'm H-A-P-P-Y']

Elton's Taylor made army
Elton's Taylor made army [Terrace chant]

It is the North End which charges the stadium with energy. Each matchday it is the place which is buzzing with activity. Pop music pumps out over the newly installed, high-tech, Tannoy system and competes with the resonant chanting, singing crowd. This chanting, singing, shouting mass is made up of a collection of groups, each with the same enthusiasm, combining together to create the excitement and passion of a Saturday afternoon.

It is precisely within these groups that the 'Saturday Lads' are to be found. "I love being a lad, being with the lads": this statement, made by Laura, epitomises their sentiments. "I've always stood with the lads", explained Sally. "I love getting involved with all the singing, its just part of the game really". Emma believes that being 'one of the lads' is a "very big part of football", while Hannah and Karen both relished their status as 'one of the lads'. During the long coach trips, to the bleak grounds of Bury and Stockport, both women sat at the back with their gang of lads, and joined in the quick, witty and continuous crude banter, uninhibited by topics often related to sex and often derogatory to women. Thus Hannah and Karen joined in abusing the opposing supporters, fighting for a position among the lads and shouting and displaying crude hand gestures. Banter with the lads could escalate into pushing and shoving, no allowances being made for Hannah and Karen.

When too enthusiastic, the male fans would haul them from their seats. At one match, a chant directed at the police led to the arrest of two males from the group. Hannah recalled that the police "could have arrested any of us really". Karen added "We've actually got video evidence and I'm apparently worse than most people … one of the mothers of the blokes that were arrested and has seen the video in court said that I'm going mad on it". The 'Saturday Lads' all engage in behaviour which has the potential to lead to trouble with the police. One example was climbing a perimeter fence and joining a mass fan invasion of the pitch.

Karen says: "All the people we go with, the lads, say they don't see me and Hannah as girls, they see us as lads, they just treat us exactly the same". Asked how she felt about being called a lad, Karen confided: "I don't mind, they know I've got my feminine side as well. I wear skirts, I do my nails and my make-up, but it's just the same level as them when it comes to football".

It is clear from all the accounts that it is not just the game that makes match-days so special — there are other vital rituals which give them meaning; the singing, the chanting, the pre-match pints, the after-match pints as 'one of the lads'. Thus far it appears that the 'Saturday Lads' are able to enjoy an equal standing with their male counterparts within the culture of football.

The 'Ladette' and identity fluidity

At this level, then, 'the Saturday lads' mirror the 'Ladette', as both are lippy, raucous, brazen, confident (Moore, 1996) and drink beer (Weaver, 1998) at least, by the pint, the epitome of British masculinity. The 'Ladette', a new female identity, does have some resemblances within football culture as Redhead (1997) and Coddington (1997) suggested. However, the women in this study adopted behaviours, which, at times, were more extreme than those suggested by Moore (1996) and Weaver (1998). They extended into being aggressive and abusive. The women do emphasise their closer relationship with the fan who does not set out to conflict with the police, but if fandom means invading the pitch and taunting the opposition then that is part of the full fan experience. Football is "a place where you can let yourself go, where you can be totally absorbed in the atmosphere" of 'escapism'. Sally "certainly behave (s) differently inside the ground: I wouldn't stand up and shout 'f--- off to anyone in the street, whereas I might to a ref'". As for the 'Ladette' being sexually liberated, as Weaver (1998) suggested, in this context passion is directed at the game.

The fan shared identity is also defined through her style of dress. Each 'Saturday Lad' strongly wishes to celebrate her casual football appearance above more female stereotypical images which she despises. This is where she parts company with the media 'Ladette' who can behave like a male so long as she achieves the media's standard of beauty at the same time (Moore, 1996). The masculinised attributes which the 'Saturday Lads' portray, conflict with the definition of a female as spiritual and nurturing (van Vucht Tijssen, 1991), just as much as the sexually provocative 'Ladette' does. Far from being like the 'Ladette' in the latter respect, the last thing that the fans in this study wish to signify, is sexual availability. The dress code of the 'Saturday Lads' mirrors that of the male fans, not only for practicality and warmth and to look like a fan, but to cover up signs of femininity. Wearing a football shirt and jeans with one's ticket in the back pocket is freedom from the constraints of figure revealing skimpy sweaters and handbags. In sometimes being more aggressive than the male counterpart there is a celebration of the freedom to be absorbed into masculinity, which, in media reports, is often presented as an extreme form of masculine behaviour. The very atmosphere of crowd behaviour is particular to football and its expression of passion for the game. It is this which is so liberating for the fans. Inside the game they feel free being 'one of the lads' in a way that they feel unable to be outside the game.

A blurring of universal categories and binary opposites appears present in the above actually observed females' behaviours (Scraton, 1994). There is not just one way for women to behave in late twentieth century consumer culture, but possibilities, liberating females from expectations of feminine gentleness, weakness, quietness, neatness, softness and demure modesty. Outside the football environment, the behaviours exhibited as a fan are replaced with, if not necessarily spiritual and nurturing qualities, those more readily consistent with norms of femininity. Such a distinction conforms with Hall's (1992) argument that the individual is able to adopt contradictory identities at different times and supports the contention that leisure now provides opportunities for the adoption of a variety of social identities. This does, however, fade as a full interpretation as further analysis tackles contrasting experiences. Each woman in the study has been subjected to this prejudice which, it will be shown, serves to restrict the carefree behaviour which she adopts during match day, and to diminish her sense of belonging among male fans.

"Get your tits out": uneasy belonging

As Nicola celebrated a Watford victory over Crewe Alexandra in the local pub, bellowing out songs and chants, enjoying her camaraderie with the lads, her sense of belonging was abruptly shattered when these same lads singled her out and directed the following chant at her.

Get your tits out
Get your tits out
Get your tits out for the lads
Get your tits out for the lads
[sung to the tune of 'Bread of Heaven']

Emma and Laura are very much aware of chants and comments referring to their gender. Laura has been subjected to wolf whistling and cries of "all right luv?", "looking for your boyfriend luv?", "been stood up?" from male football supporters. Emma finds this "offensive" as these same men, she believes would not treat women in the same manner outside football, and protests "what right have they got to shout at women at football?" Both women adopt strategies in order to avoid such unwanted attention from men. Laura chooses to sit near older men rather than a group of young lads who, she believes, would make her feel self-conscious. Laura also selects her clothing with great care, always avoiding "a short top or anything like that because it's not worth it with that many men there". She regrets that this is necessary because "I want to think it's the same, it's equal opportunities, but it's not". Whilst attempting to join in a conversation about football with a group of male fans, Hannah was subjected to the following comment from one of the men: "Oh shut up, you're a girl you don't know nothing". The others have also been made to feel that their passion and commitment to the game is not taken seriously by their male counterparts.

Disgusting and distasteful misdemeanours

Attitudes demonstrated by male fans, the police and the club have an effect on the behaviour of the 'Saturday Lads', such that Laura feels that the women are unable to experience the same freedom as their male counterparts. She states: "some of the things men do, women couldn't". The instigation of a football chant, which involves leading large numbers of fans in song, would make a woman a target for ridicule, she claims.

Hannah has been at matches where she has received looks of disgust and been told by male fans to "calm down, calm down, stop swearing, it's not ladylike".

Men, she protests "can … say what they like and don't get any looks of disgust or anything", whereas (she argues) a female behaving in the same way is frowned upon and regarded as behaving in an unacceptable manner. Nicola too has been singled out and received looks of disapproval and disgust whilst joining in the raucousness of the occasion. An example is of a male fan on the championship day at Fulham last May who, seeing her standing on a pub table, pint of beer in hand, joining in with the chants and songs, looked her up and down and, as he caught her eye, shook his head in distaste.

> Old Macdonald had a farm, ee ii ee ii oh
> On that farm he had some pigs, ee ii ee ii oh
> With an oink oink here, and an oink oink there
> Here an oink, there an oink, everywhere an oink oink

The above children's song, turned into an anti-police chant, a favourite of football fans, would according the Hannah, Karen and Laura, be more likely to go unpunished when sung by female football fans. In their experience, the police do not acknowledge male and female fans as equals, and feel that there have been occasions where their gender has influenced the police handling of particular situations. Karen believes that the police "see women as inferior at football" because "obviously … a weaker sex" and they "didn't think I could handle it". The women believed that often, because of their gender, they were not apprehended. The lenience shown to the female fans is not appreciated since, for them, being a full fan mans being treated the same as well as doing everything the men do.

Contradictory treatment of women has also been identified as coming from the organisers of Watford Football Club. The club has recently introduced cheerleaders, 'The Hornettes', a group of minimally dressed young women wearing tight fitting Watford shirts and hot pants. Laura and Emma are very critical of this form of entertainment which Laura describes as "terrible", finding demeaning the chant directed at these young women:

> Horney Hornettes
> Horney, Horney Hornettes
> [sung to the tune of the pop song 'Horney']

Emma agrees: "the 'Hornettes' are degrading … for the women there".

A further degradation to women is the organisation of penalty shoot-outs which often take place at half-time. Male teams are taken seriously by the club's compère and their efforts are met with encouraging cheers from the crowd but, on the rare occasions that female teams compete, the commentary from the compère is "so degrading and patronising". Mocking phrases such as "come on luv give it a good old kick" are met by jeers and laughter from the crowd.

Emma explained that during matches she first attended with her boyfriend, she was "quiet" and "didn't get up and shout too much in case he thought 'oh my god what the hell am I doing with her'. I didn't want him thinking that I was very masculine and a tomboy and I tried making more of my appearance". According to Hannah, when her dad is watching the game: "I don't think he'd like it if I got up and started swearing right, left and centre". There seems always an awareness of being female that prompts the women not to "let themselves go" fully.

Belonging or not?

Analysing these themes reveals that on one level the 'Saturday Lads' reflect a fluid, contradictory and multiple identity which shares strong consistencies with postmodern theory. The identity is less degendered than masculinised in many ways: an imitation of a football fan defined as male. "Letting oneself go" to these fans means acting like 'the lads'. That is the definition of freedom desired. Yet it has been found that male fans, the police and the club impose restrictions and limitations on the behaviour of female fans, indicating an identity which the females object to in a modernist manner. Interestingly, though, they also police their own behaviour in ways which are quite Victorian.

The club provides a context of varying femininities. The Watford cheerleaders clearly signify women as more gentle, passive and alluring than men, being used for male heterosexual pleasure. Add to this the compere's reinforcement of the distinction between male and female characteristics by mocking the physical capacity of female football teams participating in half-time competitions and that the presence of females at matches will have a pacifying effect on the crowd. In being alternately presented with images of females as provocatrices, promising skilled physical satisfaction of men's sexual needs and with females as inept in physical sporting skills, but with others having the aura of a naturally civilised and civilising influence, contradictions confound the idea of identity fluidity.

They indicate that gender categories and binary opposites are still influential within football culture. The 'Saturday Lads' do not want women to be presented as sexually provocative, when they themselves want to be taken seriously as knowledgeable fans of the game, and downplay their own sexuality in the football context. They want women to demonstrate competent football skills. They want to celebrate their own and others' not so civilised behaviour when it expresses an affiliation to a passionate fan identity.

Such discourses reveal a conflict between the way that women are thought of within the football club, and the way actual female fans think about themselves. Club portrayals strongly relate to capitalist and patriarchal "grand narratives" (Scraton, 1994: p. 251) through consumer marketing and essentialist gender discourses. The women fans challenge these, but the awareness affects the way they consciously negotiate an acceptable route through the social contradictions. Although they join unashamedly in the male banter of the terraces, which is often derogatory towards females, it is salutory for them to realise that one's moments of most free behaviour are seen by some males as disgusting or distasteful. This is especially ironic, when one's own views of how a woman should be portrayed are transgressed by public images which the 'Saturday Lads' see as disgusting and distasteful. Female fans sense that male fans still monopolise the social power to lead ritual chants, but they see it as their own responsibility to protect the traditional rituals of male/female interaction in which female sexual power is deemed tacit. They imply that they should not bring sexual harassment upon themselves but maintain enough credibility with a feminine sexual identity, to be able to return outside football culture to the norms expected of them domestically. Far from even touching on modernist, feminist discourses of gender, this smacks of a traditional myth of female heterosexuality as dangerous. There is little sense of power to challenge the idea that if males approach them sexually, they have invited the approach. There is little evidence of women's actual views being heard in football culture.

The subjective accounts from a small group of female fans provide some empirical support for the journalistic insights of Moore (1996) and Lindsey (1996). Moore (1996: p. 5) states "you can do what the boys do, but only up to a point.. don't go too far, or otherwise.. it's just not ladylike, is it?". Furthermore, there is no indication of 'Ladette' role reversal with 'Lad' behaviour in football, whereas television 'Ladettes' counter 'Get your tits out' with 'Gets your dicks out'. Hargreaves (1994) noted that Victorian norms allowed women to play sport only so long as they remained ladylike. In sporting practice it is well recognised that some remnants of this attitude persist. The findings of our study support Moore (1996) that in the broader context of contemporary society and the social life of the football fan, there is still a limit to the extent a female can take on those traits associated with the 'Ladette'. Hargreaves (1994) observed that Victorian women played sport like gentlemen while behaving like ladies. Female fans at the turn of another century are able to behave like the men at football matches, yet are never free from consciousness of a spectre not unlike expectations becoming a Victorian lady. Uninhibited freedom is compromised by their own restriction of their behaviour, prompted by a patriarchal look, word or dismissal. In the context of the club's positioning in consumer culture, criticism of sexism is going against the flow of power.

Change towards belonging

Although the 'Saturday Lads' have identified and experienced belittling of women within football, they all agree with Emma's view is that it has "become more socially acceptable for women to go ... especially over the last five years". Once she was looked at as if she were an "alien" and felt "a novelty sometimes". Karen acknowledges that the culture of derogatory remarks aimed at women is "not as bad as it used to be", in spite of the reply to a letter which she received from Dougie Brimson (1999). He agrees with the female fans that there has been an increase in females attending games. He gives three reasons: "the first is the feminist case; if men do then they should ... for many ... it's the only chance they get to spend time with their husband/boyfriend/dad/kids.. and it's the only chance they get to spend time in the company of huge quantities of men ... in a testosterone fuelled frenzy". Nicola has not found that the increase has coincided with a decrease in the sexist treatment of women. Brimson (1999) confirms the view that "many of us males resent the invasion of our *game* ... forced on us by the media and the clubs ... who see only pound signs and bums on seats ... whilst men lo*ve* football, women only *like* football".

These female fans love football and wish that male fans would fully accept them as fans, without reference to gender. They wish that the club would perpetuate an image of the woman as committed fan, competent in knowledge of the game, not pacifier or body to be ogled, and that the police cease their double standard with regard to male and female fans.

Conclusion

On the surface female football fans are free to take on a flexible identity theorised by postmodern debates. It has been found, however, that there is a limit to the extent to which young women feel able to don such an identity before it is reclaimed by the mechanisms of modernity. It is evident that the attitudes and beliefs challenged by modernist definitions of the female, defining her as gentle, caring, spiritual and controlled are deeply rooted within patriarchal football culture. The female fan is free only to enjoy her fandom while negotiating the subtleties of how far to go. For young women in the 1950s, going too far was a discourse of sexual behaviour, where neither heterosexual nor homosexual liberation was what the fathers of 'nice girls' had in mind for them. Approaching the year 2000, many would claim this as an outmoded idea for females with the achievement of social liberation. In the football grounds of Britain visited for this research, female fans are leery of going too far in the context of showing passion of another kind, as a football fan. Yet, their identities as 'one of the lads' encompass an engagement with a discourse of heterosexual purity, which extends much deeper, and locks back into very traditional discourses of female virtue. Their 'lived experience' sits uneasily with the claim of Crooke *et al.* (1992, in Scraton, 1994: p. 251) of a postmodern experience of sport, which assumes that women are able to choose sporting activity unrestricted by gender considerations. Identity does seem to depend on gender status. Access to codes of dress and behaviour, entry into the male domain of the football ground still do not mean that the female fans can go all the way. They are clearly seen as different from the lads and expected not to go too far. On the big screen of an away ground, the image filling the frame is of the taut buttocks of West Ham Football Club's "Hammerettes", bending over in their male-approved, provocative routine encouraging a perpetuation of sexist attitudes towards women. These lie at the very heart of the way the female fans do not themselves want to be seen, but they have no say in club marketing decisions. Their dilemma is summarised by Nicola with her own telling words.

May 2nd 1998, Championship Day: as the lone female amongst the mass of revellers in The Pond, I glanced beyond the abundance of exultant fans to the queue rapidly growing outside a nightclub, at the core of Watford's nightlife. I had been part of this queue the previous night, where I was indistinguishable from the rest of the 'girls' there, teetering along in my high heels, freshly showered and perfumed, with carefully applied make-up, wearing a skimpy dress and clutching a dainty purse. Just one day later I stood in The Pond, a complete contrast as I waded through the murky, foul smelling water, dressed in my Watford shirt and jeans that I had put on early that morning, now beer stained, sweaty and muddy. Clutching a bottle of beer in one hand with the other clenched, punching the air in triumph, singing and shouting loudly, I was at the high point of my fandom. At this high spot of emotion, however, I could not help thinking that I would be a lot more accepted in the queue for the nightclub along with the 'girlie girls' rather than in The Pond as 'one of the lads'.

Note

[1]   For an interesting discussion and contextualisation, see (for example) Carrington, 1998: pp. 106–110; Carrington, 1999: pp. 77–88.

References

Brimson, D. (1998) *The geezer's guide to football: A lifetime of lads and lager.* Edinburgh: Mainstream Publishing Company.

Carrington, B. (1998) '"Football's coming home", but whose home? And do we want it?: Nation, football and the politics of exclusion', in A. Brown (ed) *Fanatics! Power, identity and fandom in football.* London: Routledge, pp. 101–123.

———— (1999) 'Too many St George crosses to bear', in M. Perryman (ed) *The Ingerland factor: Home truths from football.* Edinburgh: Mainstream Publishing Company, pp. 71–88.

Coddington, A. (1997) *One of the lads*. London: Harper Collins Publishers.

Crook, S., Pakulski, J. and Waters, M. (1992) *Postmodernization: Change in advanced society*. London: Sage.

Coolican, H. (1996) *Research methods and statistics in psychology*. London: Hodder and Stoughton Educational.

Dunning, E., Murphy, P., and Williams, J. (1988) *The roots of football hooliganism: An historical and sociological study*. London: Routledge and Kegan Paul.

Hall, S. (1992) 'The question of cultural identity', in S. Hall, D. Held and T. McGrew (eds) *Modernity and its futures*. Cambridge: Polity Press and the Open University, pp. 274–323.

Hargreaves, J. (1994) *Sporting females*. London: Routledge.

Hoggart, S. (1998) 'Simon Hoggart's Diary', *The Guardian*, 25th April: p. 12.

Lindsey, E. (1996) 'Old habits die hard for the new woman', *The Observer*, 25th January: p. 12.

Moore, S. (1996) 'Babes still not out of the woods', *The Guardian*, 18th January: p. 5.

Moorhouse, H. F. (1984) 'Professional football and working class culture: English theories and Scottish evidence', *Sociological Review* Vol. 32: pp. 285–315.

Redhead, S. (1997) *Post fandom and the millennial blues*. London: Routledge.

Scraton, S. (1994) 'The changing world of women and leisure: Feminism, "postfeminism" and leisure', *Leisure Studies* Vol. 13, No. 4: pp. 249–261.

Quinn Patton, M. (1990) *Qualitative evaluative research methods*. California: Sage.

van Vucht Tijssen, L. (1995) 'Women between modernity and postmodernity', in B. Turner (ed) *Theories of modernity and postmodernity*. London: Sage.

Weaver, C. (1998) 'How they see us: Long live the English rose', *The Guardian*, 18th July: p. 4.

Whannel, G. (1992) *Football after Taylor. Factsheet 2*, Leicester: The Sir Norman Chester Centre for Football Research.

Woodhouse, J. (1991) *A national survey of female football fans*. Leicester: The Sir Norman Chester Centre for Football Research.

THE MEDIA SPECTACLE OF WOMEN AT THE OLYMPICS: DISSIMULATION, LEGITIMATION AND ISSUES OF PATRIARCHY

Gill Lines
Chelsea School, University of Brighton

Introduction

This chapter identifies the differentiated nature of female representation in the world's largest mediated sporting event with female performers. The focus on sporting women, in this instance during the 1996 Atlanta Olympics, identifies ways in which the sporting spectacle can act to perpetuate gender division and/ or function as a transforming agency for unity between the sexes. For as Thompson (1990) suggests, ideological strategies in media constructions act to reinforce power relations. It is argued here that through ideological modes of legitimation and dissimulation the selection of female media sporting imagery at the Atlanta Olympics acts to question women's legitimate place in the world of sport. The ideological mode of dissimulation works here to deflect attention away from women's sporting success by focusing on issues of vulnerability, triviality and sexuality. The under-representation of women in mediated sport works to question the legitimacy of their place and worth in contemporary professional sport and to affirm the myth that women have neither the interest nor the aptitude to compete at the same sporting level as men. This reinforces the hegemonic dominance of men across a variety of sporting terrain.

A code of difference operates around sport and gender constructions which attempts to legitimise "a gendered account of behaviour in which it is seen as unnatural for women to want to compete in the same way as men" (Blain, Boyle and O'Donnell, 1993: p. 10). For as van Zoonen (1991: p. 37) states:

> Since the mass media are in the hands of male producers they will
> operate to the benefit of a patriarchal society — the power of the media
> to affect women's behaviour and women's perceptions of themselves.

Patriarchy refers here to the unequal social relationship in which men are seen
to dominate, exploit and oppress women (Edgar and Sedgwick, 1999). The
concept of patriarchy has direct relevance within discussion focusing on ways in
which sports women are represented by the male dominated world of media
sports professionals as the naturalisation of media representations masks
ideological strategies which reflect certain ways in which sportswomen are
constructed. It is argued here that dominant discourse and media imagery
operates to offer a mythical sports world where serious sports women are
outnumbered in their representation by pretty, heterosexual females or vulnerable
women perceived as unable to offer a serious challenge to male sporting
dominance.

Where women are perceived to be contesting patriarchal sporting space,
relations of domination are affirmed through signifiers of distinct differences
from male sporting performance. Feminine appropriate sports and sexual
imagery predominate as distinct from strong, powerful male sporting imagery.
Images of vulnerability such as tears and injury, dependence on male 'others',
such as coaches, partners and fathers, in addition to issues propagated about the
masculinisation and sexuality of female athletes all connote the dangers to
women who seek to challenge the status quo. This serves as a warning to those
females who might wish to emulate them, and confirms ways in which
patriarchal control of the media and the sporting world seeks to rationalise the
role of women across their terrain.

The methodology draws upon a wider investigation into text and audience
responses to the 1996 'Summer of Sport' (Lines, 1998; 1999; 2000)[1] . This
chapter reports most specifically on the content and textual analysis of a selection
of English tabloid and broadsheet newspapers and the 'end-of-coverage'
television highlights[2]. Focus concentrated on the nature of the images and events
selected as representative of women's participation during the competition
together with the discourse surrounding the key performers and events.

The media spectacle — global unity or gendered division?

The Olympics, irrefutably, are the global sporting event, relayed to more countries and people than any other event around the world in a shared mediated experience and spectacle. The Atlanta Olympics provided 3,000 hours of television and radio coverage to an estimated audience of 35 billion people in 200 countries and was covered by a total of 12,000 media representatives, actually exceeding the number of athletes performing at the event. The marketing programme of the Games was estimated to have raised £500 million in partnership with ten major sponsors. Coca-Cola, based in Atlanta, spent nearly a quarter of its £2.5 billion annual budget on the Olympics (*The Times*, 15th July 1996).

The BBC screened more than 300 hours of live and recorded coverage, sometimes with coverage simultaneously on both BBC1 and BBC2. On the first Tuesday, for example, there was almost blanket coverage on BBC1; 7–9am; 9.05–12.35pm; 1.40–5.35pm; 7–8.30pm and 10.10pm–4.25am with BBC2 occupying the 8.30–10.10pm slot. Due to time differences much of the 'live' broadcasting was scheduled in the early hours of the morning. The bill for costs and rights of domestic coverage was £30 million with the total global television rights at £600 million. Britain was estimated to have approximately 600 media professionals at the Games (*The Times*, 15th July 1996). The *Independent on Sunday* (4th August 1996: p. 1) confirmed the popularity of Olympic viewing:

> Despite the dearth of medal hopefuls and the tricky time zone differences between the UK and Georgia, the BBC has posted massive audiences, with as many as two million tuning in, even in the small hours of the morning.

The Olympics are mythically billed as an event of sporting unity and friendship, promoting peace and co-operation amongst the youth of the world. Mystical images of the Olympic flame, torch bearers, doves of peace, the symbolic five rings and amateur sporting heroes provide a link with traditions of the past and act to authenticate the traditional ideals of the modern Games. During the Atlanta Olympics traditional imagery was superseded by the resemblance of the flame to a McDonald's fries packet, the endless billboard advertisements of Coca-Cola,

Swatch and other sponsors outside the stadia, the bomb blast in Centennial Park and doping controversies surrounding gold medal winners. In essence, the mediated spectacle provided a platform for political conflicts and rights, a global market for commerce and economic profit, a means for the home nation to promote their social status and identity, and for the hierarchical representation of different groups within society (Tomlinson and Whannel, 1984). This suggests a reinforcement of social distinctions and divisions rather than global unity and solidarity.

The mediated experience of the Olympics is inevitably a disparate one for audiences. Real (1996) refers to the contemporary nature of the 'designer Olympics' brought about by media professionals defining their own agendas and selecting, fragmenting and framing specific events to suit their particular local consumer groups. This is a point worth consideration as, according to Andrews (1998)[3], the Atlanta event was a designing of the Olympics as a feminine-appropriate product and confirmed that sports media consumption is perceived to be gender differentiated. The media professionals' means of determining the ways in which coverage should be altered to accommodate women might, in reality, be contrary to the perceptions of the female viewers.

An increase in the coverage of female sportswomen, and consideration given to female viewers, will not necessarily transform inherent traditional patriarchal attitudes and ideologies. For if the nature of the coverage continues to reflect stereotypical and mythical gender differences in the world of sport, hegemonic values and myths are reinforced rather than transformed. Whilst female consumers, through negotiated or oppositional readings, might resist such patriarchal and hegemonic codes, little empirical evidence has been gathered to substantiate such claims.

The spectacle of women and the Olympics — performers, media portrayal and the female audience experience

The role of women as performers at the Olympics has always been one of omission, oppression and contestation. Patriarchal control and inequalities have been consistently reinforced since the inception of the Modern Games. One might point to the sexist remarks of Baron Pierre De Coubertin who remarked that the Olympics, "were to be dedicated to the solemn and periodic exultation of male athleticism... with female applause as reward" (Cashmore, 1996: p. 122). In more recent times a simple examination of statistical data demonstrates continuing inequalities: male performers (63.53%) outnumbered females (36.47%) during the Barcelona Olympics of 1992 and there were sixty-four more men's events at the 1996 event. At the 1992 Barcelona Olympics there were 34 countries with no female representation and Iran's Islamic government has excluded Iranian women from Olympic competitions since the Revolution in 1979 (Feminist Majority Foundation, 2000). These examples reflect the continued discrimination women face, but conversely reveal ways in which women are seeking to empower themselves through sport:

> With the goal of reaching the Summer Olympics in Atlanta, members of Iran's women's kayaking team practise on an artificial lake near Tehran. They train in chadors, hooded robes, adhering to Iran's strict dress code. (*The Detroit News*, 10th December 1995)

In reality, the expanding percentage of women currently taking part, together with the number of events they participate in, reflects a growing acceptance of female sports women. Yet there is a relative mismatch between reality and representation as reflected by Conniff's (1996: p. 11) comments about the Barbie doll :

> Even Barbie is becoming an athlete. Olympic Barbie comes in a gymnastic uniform, complete with her gym bag and hairbrush. At thirty-five, Barbie is about twenty years too old and rather unbelievably proportioned to be a believable member of the US gymnastics team ... It's no surprise that Barbie chose to go out for gymnastics, the most lady-like of women's sports, where you can be a great athlete and still be compared to a doll.

Whilst there is a positive element that a doll for girls is seen to be sporty, 'Olympic Barbie' reinforces femininity through accessories such as the hairbrush and her womanly curves, and the selection of gymnastics reflects the feminine-appropriate nature of acceptable sport for women. Barbie and gymnastics embody the 'doll-like' qualities promoted by the media concerning young adolescent female gymnasts at elite level. The under-representation and lack of female acceptance in some sporting events continues to question issues of equality that the Olympics purport to support. Whilst the emergence of 'Soccer Barbie' in the USA reflects the growing popularity and acceptance of soccer for women in the USA, only when 'Olympic Barbie' sweats, bruises and wears boxing gloves, and Action Man takes up synchronized swimming can we truly acknowledge a sporting cultural transformation in gender ideals.

Inequalities in the sporting world are further exacerbated by the media representation of women at the Olympics. For as Kane and Greendorfer (1994: p. 29) suggest:

> Gender difference is translated into gender hierarchy because in existing social arrangements females are defined not only as 'other', but as 'less than' their male counterparts.

This is especially the case in sporting representations. A number of content analyses such as Duncan (1990) and Daddario (1994), exploring female representation in the print media, photographic images and television commentaries, confirm the ways in which Olympic sportswomen are under-represented, trivialised and marginalised. Examples below suggest that equity reform has offered women athletes greater opportunities for Olympic success and better media coverage than ever before. Conniff (1996: p. 11) argues that the 1996 Games advanced women's athletics in a thrilling fashion, providing more attention to images of powerful, female athleticism than ever before. Similarly, Weidman's (1997) quantitative content analysis of selected segments of the NBC broadcasts of the 1996 Olympics suggested that there was no longer significant evidence to support gender differentiated use of commentary:

> This is the second study of 1996 US television broadcasts of men's and women's sports in which I have found no statistically significant differences in the ways that sport announcers talk about male and female athletes and men's and women's sports. ... Recent advances in the popularity of women's and girl's sports — among participants, live audiences and media audiences — are further indications of the increasing acceptability of female athleticism and improved status for women's sports. (Weidman, 1997: p. 24)

However it is the underpinning ideologies and power stakes, rather than the statistical data, which offers more interesting and revealing gender issues that are still apparent in media sport coverage. Mikosza and Phillips (1999: p. 12) focus on the positioning of the female athletic body 'as a site of heterosexual pleasure' through analysis of an Australian magazine entitled *The Atlanta Dream*. Their work reveals that the majority of naked female bodies are presented in similar poses and photo spreads to those of naked sports men. Yet the visibility of female pubic hair and concealment of male genitalia, together with the privileging of a particular body type over a larger more muscular female imagery, suggests that gender differentiated and feminine appropriate selections were made.

Although I would argue that changes identified by Weidman (1997) and Conniff (1996) do not provide convincing evidence for absolute gender unity in sports media coverage, the Olympics do provide one of the most prominent stages to highlight images of female athletes across a range of physical disciplines and from a range of different cultural backgrounds. The sights of successful female, Muslim athletes crossing the finishing line wearing western athletics clothing, transmitted around the world, are focal points for reflection on the nature of social change and consciousness-raising about the role of women in other cultures. Athletes such as Hassiba Boulmerka from Algeria who won the 1500m and Derartu Tulu from Ethiopia, the first black African woman to win a gold medal in the Barcelona Olympics, exemplify the contradictory nature of female sporting achievements. For Boulmerka, on her return home, received abuse from Islamic Fundamentalists against her running in western athletics clothing and Tulu's father only finally gave his official permission for her to run after her Olympic success (*Electronic Mail & Guardian*, South Africa, 21st May 1998).

Media imagery reflecting the acceptability and desirability of physical strength, power and stamina shown by women participating in marathons, pole vault, soccer and other such contested sporting terrain, clearly shows the sporting capabilities of women, refuting physiological and medical myths, whilst providing positive female role models for girls and women. However, much depends on the ways in which such images are selected and portrayed, for if feminine-appropriate sports and sexualised images and commentary are prioritised over more powerful, sporting representations then the persisting stereotypes of sporting women will not change. For these reinforce rather than challenge the patriarchal dominance of sport.

Attempts to target women by the English Football Association, and the deliberate focus of NBC to 'feminise' the Atlanta Olympics, raise a number of discussion points about the stereotypical ways in which such targeting and marketing has been deployed. Conniff (1996: p. 11) suggests that the Olympic coverage in the United States was strategically aimed at women, who made up more than half of the television audience. According to her, NBC accommodated women by redesigning the event in a "sappy, soap opera style" (Conniff (1996: p.11). Andrews (1998: p. 10) also acknowledges that '1996 witnessed the discovery of women as an important and hitherto largely neglected market segment'. This was a deliberate attempt by NBC to ensure the widest possible ratings. In order to do so, they had to target and appeal to women, who whilst more likely to be drawn into the Olympics than many other sporting events, are less likely than men to watch whatever the event or situation. To ensure adherence by female viewers NBC interviewed 10,000 people prior to the event to ascertain their viewing preferences (Impoco, 1996: p. 36). This resulted in NBC, through their economic influence within the International Olympic Committee (IOC), obtaining an increased gymnastic, diving and swimming programme of events coinciding with prime viewing time. It would be interesting to note the gender composition of the production team here, whether female producers were involved in determining the final practices, and how males, as outsiders, can accurately predict what female viewers might want to watch.

Several comments from Pollack (1996: p. 8) suggest ways in which production practices were considered inappropriate:

> Apparently pandering to female viewers in hopes of raising ratings, but actually insulting mature and intelligent women who are not excited by immature, skinny, pale, drawn Barbie Dolls ... the *New York Times* noted that appealing to female viewers does not require shooting every background feature with amber lighting and swelling music that suggests the finale of *Lassie Come Home*.

An article in *The Times* (24th July 1996: p. 45) also criticized the nature of the agenda, seemingly unaware of the feminine-appropriateness of the activities and the aesthetic (and sexual) appeal of women's bodies:

More gymnastics, and more swimming? Wasn't that what we had last night and the night before? It is and it's what we get tonight and tomorrow night as well ... gym, swimming and a bit of boxing for those of us doing the Atlanta Olympics the live way ... they are hardly proving the spice of sporting life. Quite why gym and swimming are providing such good television is a mystery ...

The methods through which NBC strove to produce feminine-appropriate discourse and imagery, suggest that it saw its female consumers as a traditional, stereotypical and uniform group, with priority given to feminised, vulnerable, aesthetically body-focused imagery. Andrews (1998) confirms that despite their relative success, the USA women's football, basketball and softball teams received less prime-time coverage than gymnastics, swimming and diving, whilst traditionally masculine events, such as weightlifting, boxing and wrestling were subjected to day time coverage. Pollack (1996: p. 8) indicates the fragmented coverage of some events, and suggests more viewers "would have liked to see an entire half of a women's soccer game."

Whilst media producers' consideration of female consumers is a positive advance, and soap operas are clearly one of the most enduring of popular cultural forms, it is disappointing that their philosophy perpetuates ideologically entrenched ideals of feminine appropriate sports. This acts to trivialise women's interest in sport for its own sake, by redesigning sport as 'soap'. A more radical approach to the re-design would have advocated the opportunity to transform women's and girl's consciousness, by presenting new, powerful images of female athleticism, across a range of diverse and growing sports. This, accompanied by positive and forward thinking commentary accepting the variety of female shapes and looks, could have provided a powerful innovative platform for cultural reinforcement and acceptance of new female sporting imagery.

Legitimation and dissimulation — female sports stars for the 'male gaze', or as transforming role models for women?

This section looks at the ways in which the British press coverage and television highlights of the Atlanta Olympics presented photographic imagery of female Olympians. It also questions the ways in which female consumers are positioned in the sporting agendas during such a global event. Such an analysis illustrates methods through which gender inequalities are interwoven in the representational imagery of sporting women. It confirms the ideological process in which, despite women's increasing and improving acceptance within the sporting culture, such acceptance still functions within a wider framework of hegemony and patriarchy. Whilst some images do act to empower both the athletes themselves and the ways in which the female audience might come to perceive their own opportunities within the sporting world, a wider range of images trivialises, stereotypes and reinforces notions of female vulnerability. The variety of ways in which women readers position themselves in relation to these preferred meanings are under researched as women are not perceived to be the target readership of the sporting texts:

> Sports writing as a popular form must engage with a large, predominantly working class and male readership. (Rowe, 1992: p. 109)

If the dominant positioning of the media sports viewer is regarded as male, then the female sports star within sporting texts could be perceived to be framed predominately for the 'male gaze':

> A core element of western patriarchal culture is the display of woman as spectacle to be looked at, subjected to the gaze of the (male) audience. (van Zoonen, 1994: p. 87)

If this is so, sportswomen represented by sexualised and passive 'to be gazed at' imagery could be perceived to function as sport for the male voyeur, rather than for the benefit and promotion of female sport. From within the total range of female events taking place during the Atlanta Olympics, viewers and readers received a fragmented and selected part. The argument proposed here is that the agenda set for the nature and type of images selected and constructed by media professionals continues to reinforce the notion that 'women in sport' are a contested issue. Kuhn (1985) believes that sports photography offering powerful athletic representations of sports women is contentious, as there are indeterminate codes of difference from men.

Photographic images during the Atlanta Olympics firstly acted to show inherent dangers if women do choose to take part (for example with references to the injured, vulnerable gymnastic dolls). Secondly they more frequently provided aesthetically femininised and often sexualised images (a good example is the bikini clad 'beach volleyball babes') appropriate for the 'male gaze' (men are, after all, perceived to be the dominant sports media consumers). Whilst there were some powerful images of strong, athletic women represented in the same ways we have come to expect sports men to be represented these were more frequently in the minority or offered as images questioning the femininity or heterosexuality of the competitor. Duncan (1990: p. 24) suggests sport offers "a market setting of photographic imagery for the relative disempowering of women."

The range of female sports represented across the four daily UK papers analyzed provided for the categorization of three types of sporting images: (a) aesthetic body-focused images, (b) team games-focused images and (c) combat/target-focused images. Seventeen different female sports were selected from the 97 different events that women participated in at Atlanta. The broadsheet papers offered a wider range of photographic images whilst in comparison, only six different sports were visually represented in *The Sun*. As an example, consider the differentiated representation of male and female photographs, and the nature of the female photographs selected by one broadsheet paper, *The Independent*. Here, in the relevant period, only 34% of the sports photographic images and coverage was devoted to females, with 66% given over to images, etc., of males. Moreover, the coverage of the women participants at Atlanta Olympic Games was dominated by athletics (65%), with swimming (10%), hockey and gymnastics (each 5%) also represented, as were rhythmic gymnastics, beach volleyball, syncronised swimming, fencing and canoeing (with yet smaller percentages). These figures are representative of a number of commonalties in the photographic coverage within the sampled newspapers. Beach volleyball, gymnastics, athletics, hockey and swimming were evident across all newspapers. Neither of the first two events was expected to bring British medal success and home performers had little prior 'star' status. The now disgraced Michelle Smith's quadruple medal haul partially explains her dominant image within the swimming news. The high profile of athletics is attributed to the relatively few, but well-known British athletes: Sally Gunnell, Denise Lewis, Kelly Holmes and Liz McColgan. Such women provide the powerful reality of successful female athletic images. The Great Britain women's hockey team was also worthy of news coverage during its successful run in their respective competition. However, if success is deemed as newsworthy, then this still was not proportionally equal coverage to that of the less successful men's team (Brennan, 1997).

Whilst male imagery in swimming, hockey and athletics was also evident, in contrast, despite male competitors in both beach volleyball and gymnastics, female images completely dominated. If beach volleyball imagery was high on the agenda due to its status as a 'new' Olympic sport, then we might similarly have expected to see male images. In contrast, there were no images to accompany the new Olympic event of women's soccer. News value, it seems, has more to do with gender appropriateness and 'sexuality' than sport. The International Beach Volleyball Association's recent remit, that bikini bottoms should be no more than two inches wide from upper thigh to waist, confirms sexual female images rather than sportswomen in their own right are a more highly valued commodity (*Daily Mail*, 12th January 1999: p. 16).

Gymnastics too, continually draws in large television audiences at the Olympics, one of the reasons for NBC's promotion of the event. I argue that the youth of the female performers makes it more acceptable — girls clearly will grow out of it when they become 'real' women. Additionally, the decrease in age of the gymnasts, accompanied by increasingly complex tumbling and vaulting routines has led to media amplification, contrasting the thrills and spills of the performances, with its associated emotional and physical health of the (vulnerable) female competitors. Both beach volleyball and gymnastics are focal points for this case study, in an attempt to understand why 'sporting babes and dolls' receive amplified attention. Clearly both sports have the opportunity to provide powerful, athletic images and this could be viewed as a positive feature in representation. However, it is the nature of the representation that is under question in the following section.

In relation to the events that media professionals selected for coverage, the number of female performers raises issues about the depth and nature of sporting role models for women and girls. A total of thirty-five females, across a range of ages, ethnic and national backgrounds, were chosen. Only three received photographic status across all of the newspapers. The remaining performers, apart from Liz McColgan, Denise Lewis, Kelly Holmes and Jamaican sprinter, Merlene Ottey were unlikely to be widely recognisable to the general British public, which confirms the lack of female sport stars who receive consistently high profiles across a range of media texts. This notion of invisibility is particularly marked at the Olympics where there is no justifiable argument for the lack of coverage of elite female performers. An analysis of the events and performers represented on the BBC highlights programme, scheduled at the end of the Olympics, revealed that whilst a relatively wide range of events were shown, men's events outnumbered women's events by 20%. The female sports stars covered were those who featured predominately in the newspapers and a higher proportion of individual, as opposed to team, performances were shown.

Sally Gunnell, as a British athlete and 1992 Olympic gold medallist, might have anticipated receiving considerable media attention. Her fight back from injury and subsequent collapse in the second round of her event, ensured newsworthiness during Atlanta. References to her homeliness and cheerfulness below detract from the seriousness and significance of her sporting success:

> Britain's most cherished athlete for her successes, homeliness and cheerful demeanor, admitted yesterday that she might be at the end of her glorious career. (*The Times*, 31st July 1996: p. 44)

Significantly, when "Gunnell, defending 400 metres hurdles champion, swept aside her injury fears with a comfortable debut yesterday" (*Independent*, 29th July 1996: p. S9), there were no accompanying action photographs. However her subsequent race featured a number of images across the newspapers either of her distraught and collapsed on the track, or being carried from the track and on crutches. Such captions accompanied the photographic images:

> Final anguish: Gunnell carried off. (*Daily Mail*, 29th July 1996: p. 48)

> Injured Gunnell considers retirement. (*The Times*, 31st July 1996: p. 44)

Readings of the text indicate considerable focus on her recent injuries, her imminent retirement and her opportunity to concentrate on starting a family, thus re-affirming her femininity and role for motherhood.

The second athlete featured across the newspapers was Kerrie Strugg. Prior to the Olympics it is unlikely that the American gymnast would have been widely known to the general British public. The priority given to television coverage of the gymnastics competition, and her involvement in one of the 'mythical' moments of the Games, catapulted her to the attention of the audience.

Newspapers also provided amplified attention, and photographic images resembled similarities with the Gunnell themes — injury focus, tears and being carried by her coach to the medal podium. *The Times* dual references to the heroine and the 'wounded bird' underlined the fragility of female sporting heroism:

> Kerrie Strugg became an all-American heroine and the wounded bird of gymnastics with her last vault heroics as the US team won the gold medal. (*The Times*, 29th July 1996: p. 29)

The Sun trivialised the moment with its points of references to a cartoon character and an acrobat deflecting attention away from her gymnastic ability:

> She cried, audiences cried and everybody gasped in disbelief when the teenage acrobat, with a voice like Minnie Mouse, was carried to the medal ceremony. She had enough strapping around her leg to supply St. John's Ambulance for a year …. (*The Sun*, 3rd August 1996: p. 36)

More positive action images of other successful individual female gymnasts, such as the individual all round Olympic champion Lilia Podkopayeva from the Ukraine, were not deemed to be so newsworthy. These forms of ideological constructions ensure that more vulnerable and trivial female images are brought to the forefront of readers' attention, and thus legitimised, whilst those of sporting success and power are more regularly omitted.

Michelle Smith, Irish swimmer and Ireland's first ever female flag bearer (at the 1992 Barcelona Olympics), as might be expected, received high profile for her spectacular four medals in the swimming events. The photographic images of her, represented by both, action and posed shots reflect her success as an athlete. However, the positive features are overridden by constant references to the American-led drive to discredit her achievements by doping allegations[4]. An article focusing on Michelle Smith and issues around women in sport, helps to draw readers' attention to the oppression women in sport have had to face. An alternative reading might suggest that Smith's controversial improvement in performance and the doping insinuations, reaffirm concerns about women's participation in sport, as indicated by the Archbishop below:

In Ireland, Smith's success is being celebrated widely as a long overdue resurgence in women's sport ... mass euphoria has yet to touch the Irish World Cup campaign levels ... her golds were also the first Irish success at Atlanta by either male of female. The breakthrough by Smith and O'Sullivan is part of a wider Irish women's emancipation. In sport this has been nothing short of revolutionary. Irish women's athletics was in effect wiped out for over a decade by the Archbishop of Dublin. In 1949 with women's sport on the increase he wrote a Lenten pastoral letter damming it as unbecoming. (*The Independent* 24th July 1996: p. 30)

A positive feature of the doping controversy was the media focus on Smith's training methods, and its impact on her performance. Such information is rarely reported in coverage of female sports stars unless it gives medical cause for concern. One image of Smith, arms aloft after victory, shows a powerful and well-defined upper body. *The Times* (22nd July 1996: p. 28) in the accompanying article stated that:

Smith puts her new found musculature and strength (made all the more noticeable by her 5ft. 3" height) down to hard work in the gym as well as the pool.

The Sun (24th July 1996: p. 29) could not resist gender stereotypical references to her hair (photographed with her long hair loose and flowing), whilst positioning her within the doping issue:

Michelle — Our Belle ... flame haired Michelle, 26 ... Golden girl said my success is sheer hard work not hard drugs.

Appraisal of the three dominant female sport stars across the British press raises concern about how and why their images appeared across all of the daily papers analysed. In this case it seems that active images of athletic success are less likely to be amplified than media images of female vulnerability that are selected, reinforcing the dangers that being a physically active and successful female can bring.

With regard to other female sportswomen who received photographic representation, a number of themes emerged. Firstly, images of sexuality for the 'male gaze' posed or focused on scantily clad body images. These images were evident in beach volleyball, for example, with several camera angles focusing on close ups of the players from the hips upwards, and linguistic messages about 'Baywatch babes', bikinis and breast implants. Such images were also to be found in coverage of archery. The photograph and article on British archer Alison Williamson entitled "Pin-Up aiming for a perfect profile", was presumably covered because of her potential for the 'male gaze':

> Remembered by many as 'that bird' with the bow and arrow who appeared starkers in some glossy magazine, *Esquire* ... Archery being such a minority sport, even an Olympic medal will provide Alison with less lasting fame than the notoriety she achieved when taking her kit off for the lens. (*Daily Mail*, 27th July 1996: p. 77)

Secondly, such comments confirm media agenda-setting that gives higher profile to sexual, body poses than female athletic success and supports Lenskyj's (1998: p. 20) identification that:

> Women tend to be shown in submissive, sexualised poses, with camera angles that focus on the breasts or crotch.

The Sun, when reporting on two successful athletic performances, chose to represent them with rear view photographs: the female hockey players bending over ('Rear we go...' 23rd July 1996) and the women's 100 metres winning trio whose shorts had ridden up ('Top of the Bots', 3rd August 1996). Clearly sexualised and revealing body imagery, selected here in preference to action shots, provided more visible opportunities for male gaze than female empowerment.

There were also images of vulnerability, signified by photographs focusing on injuries, tears, disappointment and distress, and comments such as

> Sonia O'Sullivan failed to qualify as she has not recovered from the severe stomach problems that caused her such distress in the 5,000 metres. (*The Sun*, 1st August 1996)

> Synchronised snivelling ... Kerrie Strugg ... shed enough tears to fill an Olympic pool. (*The Sun*, 3rd August 1996)

Thirdly, evidence of trivial and frivolous imagery connotated a lack of seriousness about women's participation in sport. For example, discourse around beach volleyball, focused more on Baywatch and breast implants, trivialising the performances:

> Silicone Volley! Baywatch it ain't but nobody could spot a Pamela Anderson look-alike in the daftest game of all. If competitors had dabbled with silicone implants then the ops had failed or the contents melted in the heat. (*The Sun*, 25th July 1996: p. 65)

If beach volleyball is billed as the 'daftest game of all' this explains why only female imagery is selected to represent it. The audience is encouraged to forget that men take part too! Consider also, a sailing photograph showing two female competitors sunbathing whilst waiting for the race to start:

> Olympic team skipper, helming with her crew, sunbathes ... she covered up with a towel when photographers' boats converged on theirs. (*The Times*, 30th July 1996: p. 22)

A photograph of a gold medal winning female windsurfer, smiling and waving on the board, connotated a light-hearted and non-serious approach by these sportswomen. Action shots of these women were deemed less newsworthy than the trivial imagery, which deflects attention away from their sporting success.

Duncan and Messner (1998: p. 178) use Foucault's concept of the 'formulae of exclusion' to suggest that practices in media sport discourse operate a selective agenda where:

> Some attributes of the players are socially visible by bringing those qualities to the audience's attention; simultaneously commentators make other characteristics of the athletes socially invisible.

In the selection of photographic images taken at the Atlanta Olympics, the inclusion by the newspapers of examples identified in this chapter has been clearly prioritised whilst more active, powerful less 'feminine-appropriate' images are excluded from the reader's vision. This verifies ways in which ideological strategies of legitimation and dissimulation operate through the sporting texts to oppress sportswomen.

There was evidence of athletic, powerful, strong and successful imagery portrayed by action photographs particularly in the hockey, swimming, diving, basketball and athletics. Shots, such as those of the Chinese diver Fu Mingxia, were accompanied by positive comments such as "Grace and power were evident as she captured the springboard gold" (*The Times*, 2nd August 1996: p. 38). Judo commentary was similarly positive and empowering:

> Watching these women ... power, energy, purpose: it was splendid to be close to such things ... these judo fighters offer something a little more substantial than chocolate box femininity (*The Times*, 20th July 1996: p. 46)

The US basketballer Sheryl Swoopes was positively promoted as a role model for girls and recognition was also given to the favourability of Swoopes over other male role models:

> Young girls fanatical about basketball now have hoop heroes of the same gender. They want to be like Swoopes and her team mates, not Grant Hill and his. (*The Times* supplement for Young People, 20th July 1996: p. 7)

Although the effects of such media portrayals are uncertain, a wider range of similar articles focusing on female performers as role models could assist in both the acceptances of, and desirability in becoming a successful sportswoman. Such articles could be included on the sports pages of newspapers and women's magazines, rather than simply felt as appropriate for young girls, for adults too might like to read them.

The coverage of handball, synchronized swimming, rhythmic gymnastics and beach volleyball, whilst positively represented with female imagery in various articles across the papers, was accompanied by texts criticising the inclusion of such sports in the Olympics:

> Sport or spectacle? The Russian swimming team makes patterns in the water whilst the rhythmic gymnasts of the American team jump through hoops in order to impress the judges. (*The Independent*, 1st August 1996: p. 26)

The article above ran the headline "Rhythms out of sync with Olympic spirit" and criticised two Olympic sports that have female-only participation. The photographs whilst visually appealing, showing athleticism, aestheticism and co-ordination, are trivialised by the accompanying text. Indeed, if women had designed the Olympic motto it might have been 'balance, ultra endurance and flexibility' instead of 'faster, higher and stronger' (Hargreaves, 1994). As such, activities requiring differing sporting qualities to the patriarchal determined mottoes are undermined. Both handball and beach volleyball had male competitions taking place, yet where headlines questioned the validity of the sport, the accompanying photographs were of female participants.

> Sublime or ridiculous? Welcome the Olympics of the Absurd. (*The Independent*, 24th July 1996: p. 1)

By criticism being given to feminine appropriate sports, and those considered inappropriate signified with female images, hegemonic values continue to be perpetuated about the place and value of women in the Olympics. The 'formulae of exclusion' acts to disempower women in sport.

'The Beach Volleyball Babes and Gymnastic Dollies'

Beach volleyball and gymnastics, as two of the most highly media profiled female sports during the Atlanta Olympics, provide some of the more interesting areas of contestation for women's sporting representation. The 'Beach Volleyball Babes', in the Olympics for the first time, drew sell-out crowds at Atlanta. This confirmed the high profile of the sport in the USA, as its status as one of the most lucrative for females. It is suggested that the biggest selling point for the game is its sex appeal, rather than the sporting prowess on display:

> Rear we go — Mexican Velia has bot what it takes. (*The Sun*, 25th July 1996: p. 46)

Tanned, well-toned, scantily clad women are on display. And although Gabrielle Reece is the only one who has been named "one of the 5 most beautiful women in the world" by *Elle*, there are plenty of prominent players who look terrific in bikinis (Silver, 1997).

Holly McPeak, the volleyball player who received media coverage focusing on her perfectly sculptured build as a result of breast implants, raised the difficulty with female coverage of the sport:

> Men's volleyball sells sex and it does so effortlessly, without being judged ... men aren't uncomfortable being perceived as sexy, because no-one questions their legitimacy as athletes. With women's athletes there's always the question of whether we're sex objects who aren't being taken seriously. (Silver, 1997)

In the case of British press coverage, the women's beach volleyball players received high photographic coverage, yet there were no photographic images of scantily clad muscular male volleyball players for its women's readers to gaze at. The sports pages remain predominantly for heterosexual, sports loving men anyway who would prefer to gaze at female bodies,

> ... any man who tells you that he's watching beach volleyball for any other reason than those muscular costumes is telling porkies.[5] (*The Sun*, 28th July 1996: p. 31)

References to the female players, such as Gabrielle Reece, (even though she didn't make selection for the US Olympic teams) as the 6'3" Amazonian, a model who has lucrative sponsorship deals, is on TV chat shows and who has written a book on her career entitled "Big girl in the middle", suggests that it is possible to be athletic, strong and sexy. This can project new interpretations on notions of acceptable feminine body shape and image, and the ways that sport can provide successful and lucrative careers for women as well as men. In this vein female sporting images portrayed by the media of the 'Beach babes', whilst offering sexualised images for the 'male gaze', could also be read as redefining 'athletic' and 'sporty' as compatible, rather than conflicting, with sexual appeal.

By contrast, the imagery of gymnastic performance connotes dangers and concerns about female participation in sport:

> It is the place where little girls fly, where little girls pout and preen, where little girls fall to the ground and weep. (*The Times*, 27th July 1996: p. 46)

The nature of the amplified attention given to the 'Gymnastic dolls' reflects the patriarchal media jealousy of societal ideals, which prevent male gymnasts from attracting the same kind of historical adoration and attention given to female gymnasts. Since the performance of Olga Korbut in the 1972 Olympics, the increasing complexity of tumbling routines and the grace and aesthetic nature of more mature female bodies becoming seemingly less appealing to the subjective marking of the judges, gymnastics has been for girls rather than women. Whilst it can provide images of amazing athleticism, balance, co-ordination and suppleness, newspaper portrayal at Atlanta focused instead on images of vulnerability, weakness, reliance on male coaches, tears and the prevention of developing into 'real' women by delayed puberty and long term implications of infertility and injury.

A US team nutritionist, (*The Times* 27th July 1996: p. 13), suggested that such discourse relies on old myths that can no longer be substantiated as the health and welfare of the girls are closely monitored. Concerns about the involvement of boys in gymnastics does not seem to receive any media focus, yet presumably males have similar injury, if not medical, risks. Yet, when male performers take part in sport the inherent injury risks and overcoming of such obstacles are part of the challenge, and a means of proving manhood.

Gymnastics has traditionally been seen to be a more feminine-appropriate sport, although historical ideals promoted it as both remedial and therapeutic for women, rather than serious sport. Perhaps it is this dichotomy that now creates a contested sporting site, for the amplification of injuries, little girls made up as 'Barbie', and the tearful releases at the end of competitions in many ways contravene healthy ideals. Conniff (1996: p.11) makes two significant observations. First, although gymnastics does draw in a huge audience, the viewing experience itself may not be a pleasurable one: "A lot of viewers were disturbed by network coverage of those weeping dolls, little girls under enormous pressure". Second, that girls' gymnastics could be perceived to be degrading rather than empowering by "subjecting the contestants to a kind of merciless, critical gaze while they dance and preen in front of the judges" (Conniff, 1996: p. 11).

There can be no argument that women's gymnastics is now highly competitive and 'big business'. The USA women's gymnastics team attained a high profile following their success in Atlanta. Dominique Moceanu, when 14 years old, had already appeared on the front cover of *Vanity Fair* and had her story in the *New York Times*. Kerrie Strugg, at 19 years old, had earned $1.3 million since the Olympics. She also endorsed Danskin and Ace bandages and had written her autobiography. The whole team toured 34 cities after the Olympics, and each received $6,000 per performance (Leavy, 1997).

The active, sporting image of female gymnasts was subsumed by connotations of vulnerability through one mythical moment, amplified by close-up of injuries, tears and the ultimate dependence on a male coach to carry Kerrie Strugg to the medal podium. For the media, it was seen as one of the defining moments of the 1996 Olympics. In essence, references such as those attributed to 'The Pixie Queens', of the US gymnastics team, provided a number of elements confirming patriarchal control, for example: Kerrie Strugg: "... a girl just four feet and six inches tall and weighing just a bag of sugar over five stone ... cradled like a baby in the arms of her coach"; Dominique Moceanu: "huge brown eyes, giant dimples and a tiny body make her the most marketable gymnast around" (*Daily Mail*, 25th July 1996: p. 77). This discourse and its accompanying imagery gave readings of girls made up like dolls, in continual need of male protection, and exemplified warnings of the dangers to females taking sport too seriously.

Conclusions

Considering the claim in the opening sections for the re-designing of Atlanta as a feminised product, the stereotypical ways in which this appeared to have happened, and whether such an event did provide positive imagery for women can begin to be questioned. The values and status attached to male dominance and power within the sporting spectacle were sustained through a predominance of male over female imagery around sporting success and achievement. There clearly were some positive features — to see women performing at all on prime time television is one step forward in the equity battle. Equally, some of the empowering images from athletics, hockey and swimming did show athletic, female bodies in action. However with highly profiled moments illustrating the tears and injury of both the gymnast Kerrie Strugg (seen as a defining moment of the Games) and the British athlete Sally Gunnell, focus on the more successful female athletes in events was dissimulated. The way in which women were framed as weaker than men reflects the ideological modes of dissimulation and legitimation operating through imagery and discourse that not only distracted attention away from the sporting action and success of female Olympians but also legitimised the dangers to women who do take part. In addition, imagery surrounding female beach volleyballers confirmed the importance attached to the sexual commodification of the female athlete for the 'male gaze', with a predominance of rear view shots and close ups of bikini bottoms and discourse around beautiful girls and breast implants. This coverage further served to legitimise the significance of the male viewer and reader in the sporting genre and deflected attention away from the attributes of female athletes.

Such readings are only some in a range of polysemic images across a variety of texts. The way in which female audiences were interpellated and read the texts requires another level of analysis. Even if the Atlanta Olympics did draw in more female viewers, audience figures do not inform us if women felt part of global sporting unity, or whether they too sensed that the mediated sporting versions of events were selected within a patriarchal, stereotypical framework. For if such messages are internalised we can question the extent to which women are disempowered in their perceptions about their place within and across sporting terrain, through the ways in which men can reinforce assumptions that women are not serious sporting contenders.

Notes

[1]   A reflexive account of the research framework can be found in Lines (2000) and provides a summarised discussion of both the methodological approach and the wider results. A further application of this textual analysis and its relationship to sport stars as role models for young people entitled 'Villains, fools or heroes? Sport stars as role models for young people' is forthcoming in *Leisure Studies*. This article identifies the contradictory nature of females as sporting heroines and their relative omission as role models.

[2]   The newspapers referenced within the text are selected representations from a broader content and textual analysis across the daily and Sunday equivalents of *The Independent*, *The Telegraph*, *The Times*, the *Daily Mail*, and *The Sun* throughout the months of July and August 1996.

3   Andrews (1998) offers a perspective on the redesigning by NBC of the USA television coverage of the Atlanta Olympics to accommodate a larger female audience.

4   Michelle Smith's image as a sport star clearly is contested in itself — her success and incredible four medals, tarnished by the drug scandal which consequently was proven. Smith (now Michelle De Bruin) was banned for four years by FINA, the international swimming federation in 1998 after being found guilty of tampering with a urine sample. Her appeal to the Court of Arbitration in Sport (CAS) in June 1999 was unsuccessful, although she continues to maintain her innocence.

5   'Porkies' is a British colloquialism for 'lies'.

References

Andrews, D. (1998) 'Feminizing Olympic reality: Preliminary dispatches from Baudrillard's Atlanta', *International Review for the Sociology of Sport*, Vol. 33, No. 1: pp. 5–18.

British Broadcasting Corporation (1996) Recorded highlights of the Atlanta Olympics. July–August.

Blain, N., Boyle, R. and O' Donnell, H. (1993) *Sport and identity in the European media*. Leicester: Leicester University Press.

Brennan, S. (1997) Media portrayals Of male and female athletes: An analysis of newspaper accounts of the 1996 Olympic Games as reported in the quality and tabloid press. Unpublished BSc dissertation, University of Brighton.

Cashmore, E. (1996) *Making sense of sports*. London: Routledge.

Conniff, R. (1996) 'A new day for women's sports-favourable tv images of the Atlanta Olympics', *The Progressive* (September) Vol. 60, No. 9: p. 11.

Creedon, P. (ed) (1994) *Women, media and sport. Challenging gender values*. California: Sage.

Daddario, G. (1994) 'Chilly scenes of the 1992 Winter Games. The mass media and the marginalisation of female athletes', *Sociology of Sport Journal* Vol. 11, No. 3: pp. 275–288.

Detroit News (1995) 'Iran gives women athletes a sporting chance.' (10 December) retrieved 15 September 2000 from World Wide Web   HYPERLINK http://

detnews.com/menu/stories/2789.html http://detnews.com/menu/stories/ 2789.html

Duncan, M. (1990) 'Sports photographs and sexual difference: Images of men and women in the 1984 and 1988 Olympic Games', *Sociology of Sport Journal* Vol. 7, No. 1: pp. 22–43.

Duncan, M., and Messner, M. (1998) 'The media image of sport and gender'. in Wenner, L. (ed) (1998) *Mediasport*. London: Routledge, pp. 170–185.

Edgar, A. and Sedgwick, P. (1999) *Key concepts in cultural theory*. London, Routledge.

Electronic Mail & Guardian (1998) 'Women runners who blazed the revolutionary trail'. 21st May retrieved 15th September 2000 from World Wide Web http   HYPERLINK   http://www .mg.co.za/mg/news/98may2/22may- women.html ://www   .mg.co.za/mg/news/98may2/22may-women.html.

Feminist Majority Foundation ëWomen in the Olympicsí retrieved 15th September 2000 from the World Wide Web   HYPERLINK http://www   http:// www.feminist.org/research/sports5.html

Hargreaves, J. (1994) *Sporting females. Critical issues in the history and sociology of women's sports*. London: Routledge.

Impoco, J. (1996) 'Live from Atlanta. (TV broadcast of the 1996 Olympics)'. *US News and World Report* (July 15) Vol. 121, No. 3: p. 36.

Kane, M. and Greendorfer, S. (1994)'The media's role in accommodating and resisting stereotyped images of women in sport', in P. Creedon (ed) *Women, media and sport. Challenging gender values*. California: Sage, pp. 28–44.

Kuhn, A. (1985) *The power of the image: Essays on representation and sexuality*. London: Routledge.

Leavy, J. (1997) 'Happy landing', *Sport Illustrated* (August 11) Vol. 87, No. 6: pp. 54–59.

Lenskyj, H. (1998) '"Inside sport"or "On the margins"? : Australian women and the sport media', *International Review for the Sociology of Sport* Vol. 33, No. 1: pp. 19–32.

Lines, G. (1998) 'A case study of adolescent media consumption during the summer of sport 1996'. in U. Merkel, G. Lines and I. McDonald (eds) *The production and consumption of sport cultures: Leisure, culture and commerce*. (LSA publication No. 62) Eastbourne: Leisure Studies Association, p. 111–132.

——— (1999) 'Young people and mass mediated sports events: Consumption, impact and interpretation'. Unpublished PhD thesis, University of Brighton.

——— (2000) 'Media sport audiences — young people and the "summer of sport '96": Revisiting frameworks for analysis', *Media, Culture and Society* Vol. 22: pp. 669–679.

Mikosza, J. and Phillips, M.(1999) 'Gender, sport and the body politic', *International Review for the Sociology of Sport* Vol. 34, No. 1: pp. 5–16.

Pollack, J. (1996) 'NBC cheated Olympic viewers', *St Louis Journalism Review* (September) Vol. 26, No. 189: p. 8.

Real, M., (1996) *Exploring media culture: A guide*. London: Sage.

Rowe, D. (1992) 'Modes of sports writing', in P. Dalgren and C. Sparks (eds) *Journalism and popular culture*. London: Sage.

Silver, M. (1997) 'Beauty and the beach'. *Sports Illustrated* (Winter) Vol. 86, No. 7: p. 216.

Thompson, J. (1990) *Ideology and modern culture.Critical social theory in the era of mass communication*. Cambridge: Polity Press.

Tomlinson, A. and Whannel, G.(eds.) (1984) *Five ring circus. Money, power and politics at the Olympic Games*. London: Pluto Press.

Van Zoonen, L. (1994) *Feminist media studies*. London: Sage.

Weidman, L. (1997) In the Olympic tradition: Sportscasters' language and female athleticism. Unpublished paper presented to the annual meeting of NASS, Toronto, November 7.

Wenner, L. (ed) (1998) *Mediasport*. London: Routledge.

TEACHING MORAL VALUES THROUGH PHYSICAL EDUCATION AND SPORT

Andrew Theodoulides
Chelsea School, University of Brighton

Introduction

It is a commonly held view that Physical Education (PE) and sport are an effective means of promoting children's moral development. The philosophical claim that moral values, such as fair play, sportsmanship and respect for others (to name but three), which children can learn through participation in sporting activities is well made. However, in practice, the task facing teachers and coaches in attempting to promote these and other socially desirable values is more problematic. Within the literature on moral education, the argument that outlines why PE ought to promote children's moral development is strong. Yet, research that examines how teachers can effectively implement strategies for promoting children's moral learning has not been forthcoming. Lee (1996) believes that in order for teachers and coaches to be more effective in promoting children's development in this area, a greater awareness is needed of how theories of moral development impact upon the way in which it is taught. If Lee's claim is borne out, then one aspect of moral education that might help teachers and coaches in planning appropriate teaching and learning strategies is athlete's perceptions of moral dilemmas in PE and sport (Drewe, 1999).

This chapter seeks to raise some important questions about how athletes, and in particular child athletes, see moral issues within PE and sport. First, a case will be made for the need to explore this issue from the perspective of the child athlete. Like many areas of research within education and sport, it is argued that much of the current research in this area has been carried out "from the perspectives of 'legitimate adults', i.e. parents, teachers and other educationalists" (Groves and Laws, 2000: p. 19). Second, research in which children have expressed value judgements about matters of fair play and sportsmanship will be examined. This will focus mainly upon issues of unsportsmanlike behaviour. At the same time, the value of understanding how children think about ethical issues will be examined with regard to how this knowledge might assist in developing effective teaching and learning strategies. Third, the implications of this are considered and some tentative suggestions made for the future of PE. It is argued that a number of research questions about the way in which children view moral issues within PE and sport need to be addressed. For example: 'Do children see PE and sport as a vehicle for promoting their moral development?'. If so, 'Where do children believe moral issues arise?'.

Children's perspectives

If children are to learn morally desirable values through sporting activities then teachers must be able to teach such values effectively. Rees (1998) argues that one reason why teaching children ethical values through physical activity has been so difficult is that, for some time now, physical educationalists and coaches have believed that the development of these values occurs naturally within sporting activities. Children's moral development must be planned for, that is, teachers and coaches need to implement strategies which are specifically aimed at promoting children's ethical behaviour (Rees, 1998). However, effective teaching strategies have not been easily identified. One reason may be the lack of understanding about the way in which moral theories impact upon the way in which moral development is taught (Lee, 1996), and in particular the different ways in which children and adults perceive moral issues. By exploring children's ethical values, and the way in which they perceive moral issues within PE and sport, teachers, coaches and researchers might be able to devise a range of teaching strategies which they can incorporate into their work with children (Drewe, 1999).

Children's values play a prominent role in determining behaviour (Lee, 1993; Shields and Bredemeier, 1995). Lee (1993: p. 38) states that, "values refer to priorities about personal goals and standards of behaviour", and it is these priorities which are organised into an enduring hierarchical structure from which people make their choices. It is believed that within sport children and adults can hold different moral values (Lee and Cockman, 1995). Consequently, what adults see as appropriate or inappropriate behaviour, may not be seen in the same way by children. If children and adults do indeed view the same situation from different moral perspectives then this has important consequences for teachers and coaches who are charged with developing children's ethical behaviour. In order for PE teachers and coaches to plan to promote children's moral development more effectively (planning implies some pre-determined action, and this can only be done effectively if those who are doing the planning have some understanding of the likely obstacles they will face), a clearer understanding of how children perceive moral issues in sport may help (Drewe, 1999).

Dyson (1995) believes that researchers often fail to seek the views of children with regard to their experiences in physical activity and consequently fail to explore a valuable source of evidence that may be used to inform good practice. Groves and Laws (2000) highlight the value of research in which it is not the questions of the researcher(s) that form the central focus of the study, but rather children's own understanding of reality and their experiences. Within the ethical domain of physical activity, Vallerand *et al.* (1996: p. 91) state that:

> The most meaningful and ecological understanding of the nature of sportsmanship should be obtained from the very individuals who participate in sport settings.

If the views of children are important in understanding their experiences then it appears that asking children about how they see moral issues within sport becomes a salient factor in moral education research. Drewe (1999) has argued that researchers have been slow to examine athletes' perceptions of moral dilemmas in sporting situations, and that in order to be more successful, teachers and coaches need to develop a greater understanding of the reasons athletes give for their moral behaviour. However, before discussing this further and its implications for teachers and coaches, a brief review of the relationship between levels of moral reasoning and participation in physical activity will be conducted.

Athletes' moral values in sporting activities

Research studies have found a direct link between children's level of moral reasoning and participation in sporting activities. Bredemeier and her colleagues (Bredemeier, 1985; 1994; 1995; Bredemeier *et.al*, 1986) have studied children's levels of moral reasoning by asking children about how they think they would act in hypothetical sporting dilemmas[1]. Bredemeier (1994) found that lower levels of moral reasoning are congruent with more aggressive behaviour, and result in children more readily accepting deliberate acts which may injure other competitors (Bredemeier, 1985). A further study found that the type of sporting activity in which children engaged was a significant factor in the way in which they reasoned about moral issues. Boys who participated in high contact sports, and girls who took part in medium contact sports, exhibited less developed levels of moral reasoning than those children who took part in sporting activities where there was less bodily contact (Bredemeier *et al.,* 1986). As a result of their research, Bredemeier and her associates conclude that, children's moral reasoning is more egocentric within sport than in other life contexts (Bredemeier, 1995). Bredemeier (1995: p. 455) points out that:

> Competitive sport may allow the temporary suspension of an equalised morality and encourage a more egocentric style of moral engagement as an enjoyable and non-serious moral deviation.

The work carried out by Bredemeier and her colleagues points to a negative relationship between moral reasoning and sport. The methodology employed by Bredemeier *et al.* (1986) has essentially centred upon children indicating the way in which they think they would respond to a moral dilemma within a sporting situation. The use of hypothetical situations to measure moral reasoning has been criticised on the grounds that respondents may not always act in the way they indicate when faced with real life situations (Haan *et al.*, 1985). Consequently, moral reasoning does not always result in moral action (Shields and Bredemeier, 1995).

If children's responses to hypothetical dilemmas fail to fully explain why children do not always act in a morally acceptable manner, then perhaps another approach to the study of children's moral action might prove useful. Lee

(1993) argues for understanding moral behaviour by exploring children's moral values, as the strength with which individuals hold particular values is a salient factor in determining action. For example, if a child values honesty above success, then that child is less likely to cheat in an exam. In providing 'ready made' dilemmas for the interviewees, Bredemeier and her colleagues fail to give "voice" to the children they studied (Groves and Laws, 2000). By giving young athletes the opportunity to express their understanding of moral issues within physical activity, researchers open up a new field of investigation with a potentially rich source of valuable data, one which may shed further light on how children interpret moral issues within PE and sport. A fundamentally important question needs addressing, 'How do children see moral issues within sporting activities?'

Although Drewe (1999) explored the reasons university athletes (and not children) gave for their moral behaviour, the comments of one athlete appear to support the argument put forward by Bredemeier (1995), that participation in sport may result in a short term suspension of equalised morality. The interviewee drew a distinction between his own moral perspective as an athlete, and that of the researcher and fan:

> for a person like yourself (the researcher) or a fan, you may think, "well, he's sending him out to beat someone up! That can't be ethical." But from the player's perspective, I mean, you see that as part of the game. (Drewe, 1999: p. 121)

The comments of the athlete quoted above highlights the discrepancy that is sometimes apparent in the way in which people in different 'locations' perceive ethical issues within sport. From the athlete's point of view, fighting is seen as acceptable. He has been socialised into the game (Pilz, 1995) and consequently sees this type of behaviour as normal and therefore acceptable. But, all is not lost. The athlete is also able to realise that from the perspective of the researcher, or the fan, this type of behaviour is regarded as unacceptable. By exploring further how the athlete is able to step outside of his position as someone who condones this type of behaviour, whilst at the same time showing appreciation that others do not, a clearer picture of how athletes think about moral issues within sport may emerge. From this, more effective teaching strategies might be developed.

Drewe (1999) draws some interesting analysis from her research, concluding that the athletes interviewed in her study reasoned about moral issues in terms of one of three moral theories ('doing unto others' [Kantian theory], out of loyalty to the team or the game [virtue theory] or out of fear of getting caught [consequentialist theory]). The value of this, continues Drewe (1999), is that it attempts to relate theories of moral development and real life sporting experiences, in part addressing Lee's (1996) claim of the need for a clearer understanding of the relationship between the theory and practice of moral education. Drewe's (1999) work with university athletes provides an initial insight into how athletes perceive moral issues within the context of their experiences of physical activity. Although there have been no studies which directly examine children's perceptions of ethical issues within PE, a number of studies within the wider context of youth sport have been carried out. If as Drewe (1999) claims, her analysis of athletes' moral reasoning is to prove fruitful in helping teachers and coaches promote moral education in children, then it might be valuable to examine this in the light of studies that have explored moral values within youth sport. Whilst doing this, where possible, some suggestions for the way in which teachers and coaches structure opportunities for promoting children's moral values within PE and sport will be made.

One study that has considered children's sporting values is that carried out by Gonçalves *et al.* (1998) who compared the values of sporting and non-sporting adolescents. They found that those children who did not take part in sport showed a greater tendency towards issues of fair play than children who regularly took part in sporting activities. In eliciting children's responses through semi-structured interviews, Gonçalves *et al.* (1998) were able to examine more closely children's understanding of moral issues within sporting activities. Of particular interest was children's understanding of how they saw issues of cheating and unsportsmanlike behaviour. Almost half of the children in the study (48%) saw it as the job of the referee to control the game and to decide upon matters of fair play. Thus many children felt little responsibility towards controlling their own moral behaviour. A similar number (46%) felt that it was okay to cheat if they didn't get caught. Gonçalves *et al.* (1998: p. 297) concluded that fair play was "not a question of principles or mental attitude, but rather a question of opportunity". This finding appears to support Drewe's (1999) claim that many athletes reason about moral issues in terms of personal consequences. The value of this for teachers and coaches lies in how they might use this information in their approach to teaching ethical issues through PE and sport.

If in fact some children reason about moral issues in this way, and teachers and coaches are aware of this, they can set up learning experiences which require them to use others ways of reasoning, such as virtue theory. For example, rather than allowing children rely on the referee to determine what is or is not fair, in practice situations why not let children play without a referee? In such cases dealing with transgressions in the rules may become more evident, that is, those players who are nearest the incident have a responsibility to bring the matter to light. Consequently, if some children reason about moral issues in consequentialist terms as Drewe suggests, they are more likely to be caught and receive the condemnation of their peers. In addition, when rule infringements occur, children will be forced to deal with these incidents and enter into moral dialogue, rather than relying upon the referee to make the decision and then carrying on with play. Disputes could be settled through group discussions, in the initial stages with guidance from the teacher or coach. Once children become competent in resolving disputes for themselves, the teacher or coach need play no further part in this process. Over time children will come to appreciate the importance of virtues such as fair play and respect for others, which they can hopefully then use to reason about other moral issues in sport. It can be seen then, that children's 'voices' can be a salient factor in deciding upon teaching strategies for promoting ethical behaviour.

Listening to children's 'voices'

What may appear straightforward and unproblematic to adults, may not be perceived in the same manner by children. Groves and Laws (2000) report the case of a 15-year-old pupil who chose to participate in weight training because he saw it as a good chance to compete against the other pupils in the class, an interpretation which the researchers had never considered. Children's perceptions of fair play can bring to light some interesting insights as to how they perceive moral issues. For example, Pilz (1995: p. 393) reports the comments of a youth football player who said, "Fair play means only to play unfair when it is necessary". Views such as these in young children are worrying, because if left unchallenged they set the pattern for future participation in sport.

In a study into the moral values of university athletes, one athlete (an ice-hockey player) did not see fighting as unacceptable, commenting, "I mean, that's just the way the game's played by nature" (cited in Drewe, 1999: p. 119). If some athletes see fighting, cheating and unsportsmanlike behaviour as legitimate forms of behaviour the difficulty for teachers and coaches then, is to make these children realise that these are moral issues. For those children who see unethical behaviour as an acceptable 'part of the game' are unlikely to appreciate the moral implications of their action. Shields and Bredemeier (1995) argue that for moral action to occur, an individual must realise that the decision upon which action was based was a moral issue in the first place. Therefore, whilst adults are more likely to perceive fighting and breaking the rules as moral issues, this may not necessarily be true for all children. If teachers and coaches are to be effective in promoting moral behaviour, they need to understand which types of behaviour children see as moral issues and which they do not. The athlete interviewed by Drewe (1999), who was able to appreciate the moral implications of fighting from the researcher's and the fan's perspective, might need a different learning task in order to promote his moral education, than one who does not see the moral implications of this type of behaviour at all.

From a philosophical perspective, it would be difficult to justify, as the youth football player interviewed by Pilz (1995) attempted to do, when it would be 'necessary' to break the rules. However from the practical standpoint of this young player, it was seen as unproblematic. Although Pilz (1995) does not probe the player's perceptions further, the comments of another player may shed some light on the way in which children think it 'necessary' to play unfairly:

> Fair play means not to foul a player without reason. In an important and very hard fight you have to foul in the interest of the team, but you are not allowed to make unfair fouls. (Pilz, 1995: p. 393)

The interest of the team, and team-mates, appears to be a central factor that underlies why some athletes are prepared to engage in unsportsmanlike behaviour. Drewe (1999) found that some athletes were prepared to 'play dirty', 'trash talk' opponents and break the rules in order to support a team mate or in the interest of the team. Pilz concluded that the interest of the team is winning, that players, coaches and managers believe that the desire for success justifies playing unfairly. Gonçalves *et al.* (1998) made a similar conclusion, attributing success orientations to the message portrayed by professional sport. Loyalty to the team is one example of athletes using virtue theory in order to reason about moral issues (Drewe, 1999). Consequently, if this type of reasoning is used by some children to justify unethical behaviour, then teachers and coaches could discuss the relevance and relationship between competing values such as loyalty, fair play and respect for others.

Although both Pilz (1995) and Gonçalves *et al.* (1998) claim that winning is highly valued by athletes they do not examine why children perceive it to be so important. The reflections of one athlete may provide part of the answer. For young children and adolescents who value recognition and the opinions of their contemporaries: "Winning means peers, so you wanna win" (a university athlete recounting his/her perceptions of high school values in Drewe, 1999: p. 122).

However, Lee (1993) questions whether winning is the most significant value of participation. Lee acknowledges that winning is important, it was the most frequent reason given by children for participating in sport. But when forced to prioritise their values children placed winning fourth or fifth on their list. If winning is not the most highly valued reason for playing sport, then in order to promote moral values through physical activity, it may be that teachers and coaches need to implement teaching strategies which challenge children's perceived values, forcing them to reappraise why they take part. Once children themselves have a clearer understanding of what sport is about, they may be more willing to recognise the moral value of this activity.

It appears that for many children unsportsmanlike behaviour is common place (Pilz, 1995; Gonçalves *et al.,* 1998). Pilz concluded that many of the players he interviewed believed that it was okay to foul an opponent. Pilz (1995: p. 399) goes on to argue that players came to see the 'fair foul' as acceptable, even the norm.

> Rule violations aren't regarded any longer as pathological, but as an absolutely rational form of conflict resolution. The declaration of an intentional foul as an emergency break for the prevention of a goal, proves this is an impressive manner. This even leads to the paradoxical fact that the renunciation of rule violations are denounced as pathological, naïve, just plain stupid. (Pilz, 1995: p. 399)

As a result of his research Pilz (1995) states that through socialisation into sport, children learn to behave in ways that are regarded as unsportsmanlike. The work of Gonçalves *et al.* (1998) certainly appears to support such claims. For example, Gonçalves *et al.* (1998: p. 297) report the views of one young child who commented "I would probably play fair if it was expected of me". For this child, and many of those interviewed by Pilz (1995), the expectation is that it is thought to be acceptable to behave in an unsportsmanlike manner. Pilz concludes that this expectation frequently emanates from the team's coach. However, the expectations of others, such as opponents, may also be an important factor. Frequently, children attempt to justify their behaviour by claiming, 'everyone else is doing it'. Consequently, certain types of behaviour, such as breaking the rules, may come to be regarded as acceptable on "negotiated terms" (Groves and Laws, 2000, p. 23) and it is argued here that breaking the rules may be one example of this. Wigmore and Tuxill (1995: p. 70) assert that, "To will that everyone in a game should cheat would be to render cheating impossible". Consequently, if those children who are prepared to break the rules believe that other players are doing the same, then in the eyes of the child cheating becomes "impossible"; it is an acceptable part of the game.

One may loosely draw upon Drewe's (1999) analysis of the way in which athletes use one of three moral theories to reason about ethical issues. Perhaps, from the child's point of view, behaving in an unethical manner may simply be a case of 'doing unto others as you think they do unto you'. In order to encourage fair play then, teachers and coaches need to challenge perceptions that breaking the rules is a common occurrence. This might involve discussing and reinforcing instances of fair play and rewarding appropriate behaviour (at least in the short term) until this becomes the norm. In addition, showing video clips of sportsmanlike behaviour could be a powerful tool in alerting children to the fact that it may be much more common in professional sport than they believe. In recent years the practice of throwing the ball back to the opposition in association football when they have kicked it out of play for a player to receive medical attention has become common at a junior level. If the message is put across in the correct manner, then success will be more likely.

Promoting children's moral values within sport may not be an easy task. In fact, as highlighted above, sport has the potential to be mis-educative. To promote children's moral learning through sport, Rees (1998: p. 283) states that:

In order to be effective such (moral education) programmes need to be endorsed by all elements in the sports world — education, media, the sports industry, and pro sports.

Add to that the general public and governments (Houlihan, 1998), and the task facing teachers and coaches would appear to become significantly easier. However, Houlihan (1998: p. 292) believes that:

In the increasingly competitive pursuit of international success, one must feel a degree of scepticism about the willingness of governments to sacrifice gold medals for the maintenance of ethical standards ... The likelihood of the media, and particularly television, using its resources to lead a campaign for ethical standards is remote.

To make matters worse:

To date the public has shown little sign of disillusion or revulsion at the standards of behaviour of their elite sportsman or women. (Houlihan: 1998: p. 293)

Houlihan's pessimism is understandable, considering the constant attention that is given to unsporting behaviour in the media although the situation may not be as desperate as he suggests.

With the increased emphasis on the 'win at all costs' culture that has become more prevalent as a result of the globalisation of sport, and the subsequent effect this has had on youth sport (Rees, 1998), changing prevailing attitudes might well prove difficult. Miller, Bredemeier and Shields (1997) point out that PE ought to be a more effective vehicle than sport for promoting children's moral values for four reasons: first, because of the compulsory nature of PE participation rates are higher; second, PE is less commercially, and therefore, success orientated; third, moral development is a whole school issue and taught across the curriculum; and fourth, PE teachers have a responsibility to promote moral values within children's experiences of physical activity, sports coaches do not. However Pilz (1995) provides a cautionary note, pointing out that the youth football players he studied saw those groups and individuals who attempted to promote the notion of fair play as idealists who lack the drive to be successful in sporting activities.

If this argument holds together, then perhaps some children are likely to resist attempts to promote their moral learning, in which case the teacher or coach will need to proceed with more care than if the children were enthusiastic and receptive. From the perspective of the teacher or coach, knowing how children will receive attempts to promote sportsmanlike behaviour has important implications for the way in which strategies are implemented. In recognising the difficulty of the task facing teachers and coaches, it is worth asking what, if anything, can be done to change the prevailing attitudes? If, as Houlihan (1998) indicates, these 'other' groups are unlikely to take the initiative in setting a moral example, that does not absolve the PE profession from its responsibility to do what it can to promote children's education in this area. Burt (1998) believes that PE has the capacity to alleviate some of society's more pressing problems, but has yet to realise this potential. If so, by developing a more critical approach to the way in which PE promotes moral values within physical activity part of this potential value may be realised. In addition to developing a greater understanding of how children think about moral issues within PE and sport, moral learning needs to take a more central role in curriculum design.

The way forward — promoting moral learning within PE and sport

To promote children's moral values within PE and sport the teaching of these values needs to be a more central focus of teaching and coaching within physical activity. Moral learning outcomes must be planned for. The planning of moral learning outcomes is unlikely to occur within youth sport outside of school. There are two reasons for this. The first has already been made, that is, youth sport is generally performance orientated (Pilz, 1995; Miller *et al.*, 1997), and promoting moral values is frequently ignored by coaches. Whilst some coaches may take the opportunity to reinforce moral values as they arise within games and practice situations, it appears from the work carried out by Pilz (1995) and Gonçalves *et al.* (1998) that others do not. Where it does occur, it seems likely that those coaches who are promoting moral values within sport are being reactive rather than proactive. The second reason is that even if coaches were keen to promote the ethical values of the children they work with, it is doubtful they have the coaching skills or strategies to do this effectively.

Yet within PE, where a strong moral education knowledge claim has traditionally been made, one might expect the situation to be better. However, there is little empirical evidence to suggest that it is, despite educational claims that "the game is not the thing — the child is" (Department for Education and Science, 1991: p. 15). If, as Miller *et al.* (1997) suggest, PE is more likely to be an effective vehicle than sport for developing ethical values in children, then the physical education profession needs to develop some innovative ways in which this can occur. Learning programmes that have been specifically aimed at promoting ethical values through physical activity have been reported as having some success.

In the USA the work of Don Hellison in 'Teaching Personal and Social Responsibility' is one such programme. For Hellison (1996: p. 271), responsibility:

encompasses *both learning to become more responsible and learning to take responsibility.* [original italics]

Hellison identifies five progressive steps in this process. At the lowest level, pupils are irresponsible, blaming others for their behaviour. At the second level, whist pupils might not be involved in learning themselves, they do not interfere with others' right to learn. The next level sees pupils actively participate in the learning process, whilst at level 4 they are able to work independently of the teacher and plan their own learning activities. Finally, at the highest level, children are able to show concern for others and are willing to help fellow pupils during learning activities. Miller *et al.* (1997) attempted to develop four aspects of children's moral education; empathy through co-operative learning, moral reasoning by promoting the moral atmosphere within the group, personal success through task mastery, and self-responsibility through increased decision making. Both Hellison (1996) and Miller *et al.* (1997) claim some success for their programmes, although their evidence is largely anecdotal. Although important, moral learning programmes of this type may only provide part of the answer for teachers of PE.

Unsurprisingly, the learning programmes of Hellison (1996) and Miller *et al.* (1997) have, as a central feature, aspects of moral learning. It is doubtful if such a great emphasis would be placed upon this facet of children's education within main stream PE lessons. In addition to children's moral learning, any PE curriculum is likely to encompass a range of other learning outcomes, such as skill development, tactical understanding, information and communications technology learning, language development, and health and fitness. However, the important point to bear in mind is that if any teaching strategies are likely to be successful, it will be those which directly focus on children's moral education. It is worth considering the implications this may have for curriculum design.

In Britain the National Curriculum for Physical Education (NCPE) sets out the "knowledge, skills and understanding" children should learn within PE (Department for Education and Employment, 1999: p. 6)[2]. Whilst not a central component of the NCPE, the statutory requirements make it incumbent upon teachers of PE to promote children's moral education. In using this as an example of a curriculum structure for everyone (although its use should not be seen as implying that this is a 'model' of curriculum design — for the record I do not believe it is — but this is another matter beyond what is being suggested here), and more specifically for England and Wales, two interesting questions arise. 'What would the NCPE look like if pupils' moral education was made an integral part of the programmes of study (PoS)?' and 'How would it be taught?' (Theodoulides and Armour, 2000). The NCPE that was implemented in September 2000 has four key aspects as the focus within the programmes of study (PoS). Perhaps future changes may see a fifth strand added, to promote pupils' moral education (Theodoulides and Armour, 2000). After all, the development of pupils' planning and evaluating skills only became a central feature of PE in England and Wales since they were incorporated into the PoS. Perhaps the same will be true of pupils' moral education. If, as both Hellison and Miller *et al.* seem to suggest, PE is the context in which moral learning takes place, the changing nature of the PE curriculum may be moving towards a situation where the inclusion of a fifth key strand might be possible. The philosophy that now underpins the NCPE, attempts to de-emphasise the content of the different activity areas, in favour of the key aspects.

Any future changes to the NCPE are likely to be some way off. In the meantime other more urgent questions need addressing. It has been argued here that in order to promote children's ethical behaviour through PE and sport a greater understanding is needed of how children perceive moral issues within physical activity. Graham (1995) argues that researchers, teachers and coaches can learn a lot about the way in which children perceive the value of PE and sport simply by asking them and listening to their answers. If, as Graham (1995) suggests, listening to children's 'voices' is valuable, then this can prove an effective means of understanding how they see moral issues within physical activity. Once a clearer picture emerges, more effective teaching strategies can be adopted. Many important questions remain unanswered. Graham (1995) points out that frequently children do not have a clear understanding of what PE is about. What appears to be required therefore is research that explores what children think about moral learning within PE. Opening questions might be, 'Do children see physical activity as a means of promoting their moral education?' If so, 'What do they believe the moral issues to be?' Other useful questions could include, 'What do children see as central values to PE?' and 'How different are these from sport?'

Conclusion

Studies into youth sports such as those discussed above, suggest that sport can be mis-educative, that is, through sport children learn to behave in ways that are unethical. In order to realise any potential sport has for promoting children's ethical values the role of the coach in setting up moral learning experiences is of *especial* importance. In the same way that a coach would teach a skill or tactic, teaching moral values through sport must be planned for. Yet, it is unlikely that coaches will have the skills and strategies, if indeed they have the inclination, to promote children's moral learning through physical activity. If Houlihan's (1998) scepticism is founded, then the part youth sport might be able to play in developing children's moral learning appears limited, in which case another avenue is needed.

This other avenue might be PE. The conceptual nature of PE, the aims and the way in which these aims are realised through the school curriculum make PE, at least in a theoretical sense, a potentially more effective means of promoting children's moral development than youth sport. The structure of the PE curriculum and its requirements may be more conducive to teaching moral values through physical activity, particularly if moral learning is made a central feature of curriculum policy. The PE profession has often tried to distance itself from the performance orientations of sport, by claiming it is more concerned with the development of the 'whole child'. But it is not clear how much importance teachers of PE place upon pupils' moral learning. Although there is a strong ideological argument for the role PE can play in promoting children's moral education, there has been little empirical research which substantiates this claim.

Whilst coaches working in the area of youth sport might find it difficult to realise moral learning outcomes because of a lack of effective teaching and learning strategies which meet the aims of moral education in this context, the same point might also be directed towards teachers of PE. It has been argued here that a greater understanding of the way in which children perceive moral issues within PE and sport can help teachers and coaches when considering how to promote ethical values more effectively. Further research that examines children's understanding of ethical issues within PE is required in order to see how, if at all, these are different from those of children who participate in youth sport. Some opening research questions have been suggested. In the meantime, the extent to which teachers and coaches implement moral learning tasks will depend upon a number of factors, not least of which will be the usefulness of these strategies for achieving intended outcomes. If the tasks used prove to be ineffective and/or difficult to implement then more appropriate tasks will need to be developed, and so begins the process of critical debate with regard to effective teaching strategies which is so desperately needed. It is only by planning for children's moral education, by making moral learning more explicit within the context of PE and sport, and by implementing relevant and successful learning tasks that ethical values will effectively be developed.

Notes

1 The work of Bredemeier and colleagues has been criticised by Gough (1998), who rejects the claim by Shields and Bredemeier (1995) that their research is essentially objective and value-free. Gough's (1998) comments are based on a critique of Haanian Interactionist Moral Theory upon which Bredemeier and her collaborators rely heavily. Gough (1998) points out that Haan's final stage of moral development (Stage 5 – Equilibrium) signifies an 'end-state' of moral maturity, which relies upon value judgements ('thick values') which set out what it means to be a morally developed person. It is these 'thick values' which Gough (p. 144) believes undermine scientific objectivity as they "essentially define both how and what is to be judged as morally right or wrong, mature or immature, and so forth". Consequently, Gough (p. 146) concludes the research of Bredemeier and her colleagues should not be regarded as "the conclusions of objective science but as moral opinions of a particular liberalist ideology clothed in the language of scientific detachment".

2 The National Curriculum (NC) is a centralised curriculum that sets out statutory requirements with regard to what children in all state schools in England and Wales should be taught. The curriculum is organised into four Key Stages (KS), KS 1 for children from 5–7 years of age, KS 2 (7–11), KS 3 (11—14) and KS 4 (14–16) (for a review of the structure of the NC and the background surrounding its implementation see Maclure, 1989). As a foundation subject within the NC, PE is taught in all four key stages. The NCPE programmes of study (PoS) require teachers to promote children's knowledge, skills and understanding across 4 key aspects, "(1) acquiring and developing skills, (2) selecting and applying skills, tactics and compositional ideas, (3) evaluating and improving, and, (4) knowledge and understanding of fitness and health" (DfEE, 1999: p. 6). It is through the different activity areas, athletics, dance, games, gymnastics, outdoor and adventurous activities and swimming, that learning in the key aspects takes place. For a more detailed account of the NCPE in each of the four KS before the implementation of the new orders, see Jones, 1996; Williams, 1996; Martin, 1996; McConachie-Smith, 1996.

References

Bredemeier, B. J. (1985) 'Moral reasoning and perceived legitimacy of intentionally injurious sports acts', *Journal of Sport Psychology* Vol. 7: pp. 110–124.

———— (1994) 'Children's moral reasoning and their assertive, aggressive and submissive tendencies in sport and daily life', *Journal of Sport and Exercise Psychology* Vol. 16: pp. 1–14.

———— (1995) 'Divergence in children's moral reasoning about issues in daily life and sport specific contexts', *International Journal of Sport Psychology* Vol. 26: pp. 453–463.

Bredemeier, B. J., Weiss, R., Shields, D. L. and Cooper, B. A. B. (1986) 'The relationship of sport involvement with children's moral reasoning and aggressive tendencies', *Journal of Sport Psychology* Vol. 8: pp. 304–318.

Burt, J. J. (1998) 'The role of kinesiology in elevating modern society', *Quest* Vol. 50, No. 1: pp. 80-95.

Drewe, S. B. (1999) 'Moral reasoning in sport: Implications for physical education', *Sport, Education and Society* Vol. 2: pp. 117–130.

Department for Education and Science, (1991) *Physical education for ages 5–16; Proposals of the secretary of state for education and science and secretary of state for Wales*. London: NCC.

Department for Education and Employment, (1999) *Physical education: The national curriculum for England*. London: QCA.

Dyson, B. P. (1995) 'Students' voices in two alternative elementary physical education programmes', *Journal of Teaching in Physical Education* Vol. 14: pp. 394–407.

Gonçalves, G., da Costa, F. C. and Piéron, M. (1998) 'Values in youth sport: Comparative study between participants and non-participants', *Proceedings of the AIESEP-Adelphi World Congress*, Adelphi University, New York: 12-17 July.

Gough, R. (1998) 'Moral development research in sports and its quest for objectivity', in M. J. McNamee and S. J. Parry (eds) *Ethics and sport*. London: E & FN Spon, pp. 134–147.

Graham, G. (1995) 'Physical education through students' eyes and in students' voices: Implications for teachers and researchers', *Journal of Teaching in Physical Education* Vol. 14: pp. 478–482.

Groves, S. and Laws, C. (2000) 'Children's experiences of physical education', *European Journal of Physical Education* Vol. 5, No. 1: pp. 19–27.

Haan, N., Aerts, E. and Cooper, B. A. B. (1985) *On moral grounds: The search for practical morality*. New York: New York University Press.

Hellison, D. (1996) 'Teaching personal and social responsibility in physical education, in S. J. Silverman and C. D. Ennis (eds) *Student learning in physical education: Applying research to enhance instruction*. Champaign IL: Human Kinetics.

Houlihan, B. (1998) 'Fairness as a global issue in sport', Proceedings of the AIESEP-Adelphi World Congress, Adelphi University, New York: 12–17 July, pp. 287–294

Jones, C. (1996) 'Physical education at key stage 1', in N. Armstrong (ed) *New directions in physical education*. London: Cassell, pp. 48–61.

Lee, M. J. (1993) 'Moral development and children's sporting values', in J. Whitehead (ed) *Developmental issues in children's sport and physical education*. Leeds: Human Kinetics, pp. 30–42.

———— (1996) 'Psycho-social development from 5 to 16 years', in N. Armstrong (ed) *New directions in physical education*. London: Cassell, pp. 33–47.

Lee, M. J. and Cockman, M. (1995) 'Values in children's sport: Spontaneously expressed Values among young athletes', *International Review for the Sociology of Sport* Vol. 30: pp. 337–350.

Maclure, S. (1989) 'The national curriculum and assessment', in M. Preedy (ed) *Approaches to curriculum management*. Milton Keynes: Open University Press, pp. 3–20.

Martin, B. (1996) 'Physical education at key stage 3', in N. Armstrong (ed) *New directions in physical education*. London: Cassell, pp. 73–81.

McConachie-Smith, J. (1996) 'Physical education at key stage 1', in N. Armstrong (ed) *New directions in physical education*. London: Cassell, pp. 82–93.

Miller, S. C., Bredemeier, B. J. and Shields, D. L. L. (1997) 'Socio-moral education through physical education with at-risk children', *Quest* Vol. 49: pp. 114–129.

Pilz, G. A. (1995) 'Performance sport: Education in fair play (some empirical and theoretical remarks)', *International Review for the Sociology of Sport* Vol. 30: pp. 391–418.

Rees, C. R. (1998) 'Building character and the globalisation of sport', Proceedings of the AIESEP-Adelphi World Congress, Adelphi University, New York: 12-17 July, pp. 281–286.

Shields, D. L. L. and Bredemeier B. J. (1995) *Character development and physical activity*. Champaign IL: Human Kinetics.

Theodoulides, A. and Armour, K. M. (2000) 'Personal, social and moral development through team games: Some critical questions', paper presented at "Between a rock and a hard place: Philosophy, ethics and competitive sport" conference. St. Martin's College, Lancaster, 10–12 April.

Vallerand, R. J., Deshaies, P., Cuerrier, J-P., Brière, N. M. and Pelletier, I. C. (1996) 'Towards a multidimensional definition of sportsmanship', *Journal of Applied Sport Psychology* Vol. 8: pp. 89–101.

Wigmore, S. and Tuxill, C. (1995) 'A consideration of the concept of fair play', *European Physical Education Review* Vol. 1, No. 1: pp. 67–73.

Williams, A. (1996) 'Physical education at key stage 2', in N. Armstrong (ed) *New directions in physical education*. London: Cassell, pp. 62–72.

SPORT AND VALUES:
THE POLITICAL VALUE OF SPORT
IN GERMANY

Udo Merkel
Chelsea School, University of Brighton

Introduction

There is hardly a book on the political aspects of sport nowadays which does not at least refer to, or even dedicate some detailed attention to, the 1936 Olympic Games in Berlin. The key issue usually is the politicisation of sport in Nazi Germany and, in particular, the blatant use of sport as a propagandist tool by Hitler and his supporters. For them the Berlin Olympics provided a symbolically important resource to publicly demonstrate the physical supremacy of the Aryan race. Although the four gold medals of the black American athlete Jesse Owens made the doctrine of racial superiority look oddly out of place, most contemporary commentators view the 1936 Olympics as "one of the great public relations coups of all time" (Coe *et al.,* 1992: p. 127). According to Cashmore, the 1936 Olympic Games in Berlin was "a satisfactory and rewarding Nazi spectacle ....
In terms of propaganda, the entire Olympic essay was of value to the Nazis: as the world exulted, Germany stepped up its rearmament program and stamped down on Jews. No single games since has approached it in terms of ideological pitch" (Cashmore, 1996: p. 240). Coakley (1994: p. 366) describes these games as "one classic example of a government's use of sport to promote its own political ideology ... of Nordic supremacy", whilst Houlihan (1994: p. 11) stresses that "Hitler and the Nazi Olympics showed just how pliable sport was during the Berlin Games where almost every aspect of the Games was

manipulated to enhance the prestige of the Third Reich and national socialism". Johann and Junker (1970: p. 166) add that it "was impossible for other countries to perceive Hitler's actual intentions behind the skilfully-staged curtain of the Olympic Games in 1936".

There is no doubt that the 1936 Berlin Olympics are a prime example for the political use of sport. However, for many, these Games also mark the beginning of the general politicisation of sport. This chapter will show that this is only partly true as the political interest in sport by the German state and its ruling powers has a much longer tradition which goes back to the early 19th century. Since then, the states' involvement in sport has continuously been modified due to the changing socio-historical context and political values, has become larger, more refined and complex, and has played an important role in both political and civil society in Germany, which in the 20th century became increasingly intertwined. It will also be argued that this development, which has consistently been accompanied by various forms of social and political conflicts, requires an analytical and theoretical framework which is able to capture the subtleties of this process, the changing political nature and value of sport.

This chapter is not only motivated by my academic interest in the study of sport and politics but also by my growing sense of uneasiness about the state of theory and research in the sociology of sport in Germany which is very rarely concerned with critical inquiries into the political meaning of sport in German society. Furthermore, the dominance of the followers of Niklas Luhmann's Systems Theory in the sociology of sport in Germany has not helped improving an understanding of the political values and associated conflicts surrounding sport.

After these introductory comments, three significant events in the history of German physical culture will be outlined. Subsequently, they will be analysed employing a vertical and horizontal comparative perspective looking for both continuities and changes, commonalities and differences, respectively. Whilst the vertical comparisons will provide some valuable insights into the historical development, the horizontal juxtaposition with other European countries will stress the distinctiveness of some political characteristics of sport in Germany. Finally, some theoretical implications for the sociological study of the relationship between sport and power will be discussed.

2 January 1820: Prussian Government declares ban on *Turnen*

On behalf of the Prussian King Friedrich Wilhelm III, the Home Office Minister declares a ban on all forms of *Turnen* (gymnastics). Subsequently, many of the Prussian civil servants, who are responsible for the implementation of this ban, inquire what the term *Turnen* actually stands for. Neither the label nor the concept of physical exercises are that well known although they have been in existence for almost a decade. *Turnen* began in 1810 when the teacher and political agitator Friedrich Ludwig Jahn took his pupils to a hilly area near Berlin for physical exercises. Due to the increasing interest in these activities he opened the first *Turnplatz*, an outdoor space dedicated to physical exercises, in 1811. Jahn's short-term intention was to prepare the German youth for the forthcoming military struggle with the French occupiers. His long-term aim, however, was to contribute to the creation of a united Germany, free from feudal class distinctions and with a liberal constitution. It was his political values that motivated the ban on *Turnen*, which was to last for more than two decades during which Jahn spent six years either under house arrest or in prison.

14 February 1914: German parliament agrees on funding of 1916 Olympics in Berlin

After a lengthy and heated debate the German parliament, in which the Social Democrats are the largest fraction due to the electoral support of about one third of the German population, decides to fully support the 1916 Olympic Games which were to be held in Berlin. This decision means that the German state committed itself to provide the funding and many other forms of support. Furthermore, the exclusive responsibility for top-level sport in Germany was allocated to the Home Office. Prior to this decision the discussions focused upon the merits and advantages of the modern concept of international, competitive sport compared to the traditional German gymnastics and upon concerns of the working class representatives who argued that only bourgeois sport organisations would benefit from the Olympic Games and the state's support. Never before has a central government so openly demonstrated its will to fund the international representation of the state through top-level sport. The Olympics, however, had to be cancelled because of the First World War.

6 July 2000: Victory for Germany's bid to host 2006 Soccer World Cup

The German bid to host the 2006 Football World Cup is successful. The expensive and high profile campaign was led by Franz Beckenbauer who won the World Cup in 1974 as a player and in 1990 as the manager of the national side. For the final presentation to the FIFA executive the German Chancellor, Gerhard Schröder, provided a guard of honour standing silently next to the tennis player Boris Becker and the model Claudia Schiffer. Schröder's role was to publicly demonstrate the state's backing of this major sport event. Another man of the moment was the Home Office Minister, Otto Schilly, who was praised for cleaning up football hooliganism. Experts predict that hosting the World Cup could generate a profit of about 4.5 million Deutschmark (£1.5 million) for the German economy.

Vertical comparisons: continuities and change

In hindsight and apprehension of the social, historical and political context these three events are fairly symptomatic for the sportisation of German society over the last two centuries and reflect almost a linear development. Each of these three episodes represent a distinctive phase in the history of physical culture in Germany.

The first event succinctly sums up two related developments in the first half of the 19th century: the emergence of a new and distinctive concept of physical culture, *Turnen*, which combined gymnastic exercises with revolutionary ideas, in particular advocating political unification of the German people and democratic reforms; and the strict response of a fearful and weak state in apprehensive anticipation of the political influence of a civic movement. These two related issues occurred in the first half of the 19th century when Germany as a unified nation state did not exist and German society, which was spread over many smaller and a few larger states, still possessed essentially feudal structures. The aristocracy was the dominant class while the slowly growing middle class had hardly any influence on social life. The vast majority of people lived in rural communities (Fürstenberg, 1972: p. 25). Despite attempts to establish a nation state in 1848 and 1849, it was not until 1871 that the first German state was founded. However, the above episode happened in an era of dramatic social

change which culminated in the publication of Marx and Engels's Communist
Manifesto (1848) and in revolutionary outbreaks all over the European continent.

Despite the ban on *Turnen*, which in some parts of Germany lasted until 1842
whilst in other parts it was lifted soon after it had been declared, the *Turnbewegung*, the gymnastics movements, made a number of important contributions to
the creation of a national identity and the process of state formation:

1. The quickly growing and large network of independent gymnastics clubs
   were a significant element of German civic society in the 19th century. They
   provided a public forum for the articulation of their political cause at local,
   regional and national level and helped to disseminate their desire for national
   unity and political reforms. Members of the *Turnbewegung* were involved
   in a variety of political activities ranging from small-scale, local actions to
   the more spectacular involvement in the 1848/49 revolutionary uprising. Due
   to the public attention the *Turnbewegung* drew it was able to exercise
   political pressure which led to some modest reforms.

2. The regular participation in physical exercise, involvement in social events
   organised by the *Turnvereine* (gymnastic clubs) and interaction with other
   Turner provided the members of this movement with a sense of belonging
   in a rapidly changing society. It commenced as a simple group identity and
   developed into a national awareness. The annual national gymnastic festivals
   became an important expression of this new identity and helped to confirm,
   strengthen and diffuse the desire for national unity through rituals,
   ceremonies, speeches, flags and other symbolic displays.

3. The development of *Turnen* was accompanied by many efforts to define
   gymnastic exercises as a unique and distinctive element of German tradition
   and culture. Next to the German language it became a key element in the
   construction of Germanness.

In the aftermath of the ban various German states gradually appropriated and
simultaneously reconstructed *Turnen* and subsequently contributed to its
expansion via the education system which failed to undermine the popularity of
independent gymnastic clubs.

In the second episode, the initial hostility and rejection of *Turnen* has
successfully been replaced by a general political appreciation of the value of
physical culture which found it most explicit manifestation in the generous

practical and financial support provided by the state. Equally dramatic is the change of the socio-historical and political context. The political unification of Germany in 1871 marked the beginning of an accelerated economic development which led, particularly from the early 1890s onwards, to an enormous increase of the productive capacity of key industries, such as coal mining, iron and steel production. None of the other European economies grew faster during this period and Germany soon caught up with its main rivals. At the same time the urbanisation process continued and led to a fast growth of towns and cities. By 1914 about 60 percent of the population lived in urban environments. Although the aristocracy continued to enjoy many privileges the class system underwent some important changes. Whilst previously the middle class had attempted to demarcate itself from both the upper and the working classes, it gradually stopped to perceive the aristocracy as an opponent, moved closer to it and even adopted some of their norms, values and cultural practices whilst at the same time increasing their efforts to distance themselves from the working class. The latter, particularly the urban industrial working class, developed a distinctive class consciousness, which found its most explicit expression in the foundation of the Social Democratic Party (SPD) in 1875. However, the new state was also characterised by one important continuity: the existing governments remained in power and the German people were hardly able to influence the politics of the new state. Democratic reforms had yet to be achieved. Although many of the 25 states, which composed the German Empire, introduced restricted franchises for parliamentary elections, many governments and ministers remained in power.

When the above mentioned parliamentary debate happened in 1914, the concept of physical culture comprised two distinctively different pillars: competitive team games and individual events which had derived from England and German gymnastics. The generic term for both, 'sport', clearly shows the dominance of the former. The pronounced tensions and conflicts between German *Turnen* and the English concept of athleticism and sport, which preceded this development, were an integral part and reflection of the wider power struggle between the modernising and conservative forces of German society which the latter lost. Despite some strong resistance, English sports became eventually more popular than traditional forms of *Turnen*.

The initial rejection of competitive English sports extended to France and led to a dismissal of Baron Pierre De Coubertin's attempt to revive the ancient

Olympic idea at the end of the 19th century. The reluctance of the German *Turnbewegung* to be involved in the modern Olympic movement was not only caused by the attitudes of this French nobleman, who had made it very clear that he saw physical education as a means for restoring the vigour of French youth (against the arch-enemy Germany), but also by their dislike of the concept, the political tensions between Germany and France and by Coubertin's admiration of the English sport system. The *Turner* perceived the emerging Olympic movement as an anti-German conspiracy and felt threatened by their French neighbours expecting them every minute to seek revenge for the lost war in 1871. They also fundamentally disagreed on the international nature of sport and the Olympic Games as their concept of physical culture was clearly associated with national characteristics. The aristocratic upper class of the Wilhelmine Empire, however, strongly supported the concept of competitive international sport and the Olympic movement. By 1904, they had set up a national committee whose primary aim was to hold one of the next Olympic Games in the German Empire. Only five years later they successfully applied to stage the 1916 Olympics in Berlin.

The last episode then clearly shows that the cultural practice of sport has become so successful that at the beginning of the new millennium even the most important political figure of the democratic system, the chancellor (comparable to the Prime Minister in the UK or the President in the USA) is publicly playing second fiddle to a very successful and well known football player and manager. Again, this happened in an era of some dramatic political changes which had a fundamental impact on the sporting world in Germany, in particular the rushed 're-unification' process between the Federal Republic of Germany and the German Democratic Republic after the Wall came down in 1989. It took less than a year to formally legitimise the take over of East Germany. Subsequently, what in the past was usually referred to as the East-German 'sporting miracle' was systematically destroyed. This development found widespread public support, particularly in the West, due to orchestrated public discourses which focused on the drug abuse by East German athletes, their roles as spies, their privileged status in East German society, unethical selection and training methods, the exploitation of children, and disregard for the concept of amateurism.

Despite the very different socio-historical and political backgrounds and the very distinctive nature of these three events there are three fundamental commonalities: First, the political authorities in Germany have over the last two centuries consistently shown a keen interest in physical culture and never hesitated to intervene by either suppressing or supporting its development. Whilst initially and only for a relatively short period of time they feared and suppressed the activities of the *Turnbewegung*, the gymnastic movement, state encouragement for military, economic, political, social and ideological reasons became a key feature in the development of sport in Germany.

Second, in all three events the Home Office plays an important role. Although the number of governmental and voluntary organisations with an interest in sport has dramatically grown the Home Office has continuously held a central position in the world of German sport. However, the increased complexity of sport has also led to a clear division of labour between different political agencies: whilst nowadays the Home Office is in charge of top-level sport, the responsibility for Sport for All and Physical Education in schools lies with the regional governments of the *Länder*.

Third, all three events are part of or the outcome of social conflicts, are closely related to power struggles and reflect divisions in German society. In the first episode the main protagonists of the power struggle are easily identifiable. They are the ruling powers of the Prussian state and the members of a national movement which was to grow significantly in the following decades. In contrast, the different fractions and their values in the second episode have become more complex. On one hand, there were the conservative supporters of traditional forms of German gymnastics still arguing with the followers of the new concept of athleticism, competitive sport and team games about the right approach to physical culture; on the other hand there were the representatives of working class sport accusing the government of neglecting and excluding them from public support, whilst the bourgeois sport organisations were keen to ensure funds for the hosting of the next Olympic Games.

The third episode, whose televised pictures conveyed an image of harmony and unity, is even more complex. It is multi-layered and embedded in the politics of sport at local, national and global level. Immediately after the decision of FIFA's Executive Committee the quarrelling about where the 1964 World Cup matches would in fact be played began. The official bid contained the names and locations of 16 stadiums although eventually only a dozen will be needed. Whilst it has already been agreed that the opening ceremony and first match will take place in Munich and the final in the Olympic Stadium in Berlin, local government and football representatives joint forces and put forward some fierce arguments why their facility should be selected in favour of others. Local authorities in Germany have a particularly keen interest in this question as they usually own the football grounds which the top-level clubs simply rent for their matches. Whilst local authorities usually subsidise professional football in Germany, on this occasion they are keen to ensure their piece of the World Cup cake which comes in various forms. The central government has already approved 100 million Deutschmark for the renovation of the Olympic Stadium in Berlin, which staged the infamous 1936 Hitler Games, and the same sum for the construction of a new ground in Leipzig, in the old East Germany. Therefore local politicians are keen to ensure their share of the additional and generous governmental spending spray. Furthermore, they obviously want to cash in on the predicted 1.1 million visitors' spending of 1.75 billion Deutschmark and the global media coverage which might reach half of the world's population.

Whilst the global sporting audience hardly knows about these internal quarrels it is common knowledge that the selection process of FIFA was overshadowed by petty personal rivalries and power politics which led to angry scenes in Zurich after the announcement of the final decision. The main and most promising contestants to stage the 2006 World Cup were South Africa and Germany, whilst the English Football Association's bid failed miserably after Brazil had withdrawn their application only weeks before the final meeting of FIFA's executive committee. For many, the German success came as a surprise as South Africa was the clear favourite.

Despite the decreasing importance of the nation state as a consequence of the ongoing globalisation process the conflicts and negotiations at the national level are more important. Neither the German bid to host the 2004 Olympics in Berlin nor the tendering for the 2006 Soccer World Cup managed to succeed the unequivocal support of the German population who is still paying the price for the hasty and rushed 're-unification' of the two people after the Berlin Wall came down in 1989. Nevertheless, the populist German chancellor, Gerhard Schröder, fully supported the German bid, whose main private sponsor the BAYER AG was, one of the a largest multi-national pharmaceutical companies based in Leverkusen in the Rhineland. The town also hosts one of the top Bundesliga teams, Bayer 04 Leverkusen. Although the club was founded in 1904 there appears to be a lack of tradition as well as clear association with any specific social group or class. However, the name clearly reveals that the team is owned by the BAYER AG, who also employs the vast majority of the fans. Unsurprisingly, the football ground in Leverkusen (called the BAYARENA) is one of the few in Germany privately owned — by the BAYER AG. For the BAYER AG there seems to be no doubt that their stadium will be selected for some of the World Cup matches — although it only has a capacity of 22,000 seats and would require a major extension unless FIFA allows dispensation for the inadequate size. Similar expectations can be held by the manufacturer of the famous Mercedes cars, the Daimler-Benz AG, who is also the main sponsor of tennis in Germany. Its employee, Davis-Cup team captain Boris Becker, already a sporting hero in Germany and a member of the bidding team, is a well-known supporter of Bayern Munich, whilst the Daimler-Benz AG, based in Stuttgart, are more closely associated with the local football ground. The Gottlieb-Daimler-Stadium, previously known as (River) Neckar Stadium, changed its name only a few years ago when the car manufacturer moved in as sponsors. Gottlieb Daimler constructed the first motor cycle and car in Germany in 1885 and is one of the founders of the Daimler Benz AG.

Gerhard Schröder's agenda is very different. His short-term goal was certainly to associate himself with popular and successful sport figures as well as the world of glamour and fashion in order to increase his fading popularity. More importantly, however, the World Cup 2006 will fall into the last months of his second term of office as German Chancellor and — pending on the performance of the German national side — could have an impact on the outcome of his election campaign.

Both these issues (that is, the German state's involvement in sport and the continuos divisions and power struggles) will now be explored in a comparative European perspective which will confirm that both the development of sport in Germany as well as its sociological analysis contains some very distinctive elements, particularly concerning the role of the state.

Horizontal comparisons: commonalities and differences

Comparing the development of sport in Germany with other European countries a number of common features as well as some significant differences become quickly visible. As in several other societies, for example Britain, the Prussian rulers already showed an interest in physically active forms of recreation in the early 19th century and tried to suppress them. The key difference, however, between these two societies is that the British state already had a long tradition whilst the German nation state had yet to be founded. Whilst in most countries sport's contribution to the celebration of a national identity is a 20th century phenomenon, in Germany the *Turnbewegung* helped in various ways to create such an identity already in the 19th century.

Despite this fundamental dissimilarity and many other differences between Victorian England and the Prussian state, the largest and politically most influential configuration on the territory, which was later to become the first German nation state, their education systems shared some important characteristics: First, both German and English educationalists believed in the doctrine of muscular christianity, the apparently positive moral influence of physical exercise. However, while in Victorian England athleticism was regarded as a way to provide for the healthy mind in the healthy body as well as for character formation the latter aspect was clearly denied in Germany. The body was supposed to be only the "servant and carrier of the mind" (Denk and Hecker 1981: p. 147). Second, physical exercise became very early an essential part of school life in both societies. But while in England team games were preferred, in Prussia more mechanical gymnastic exercises were the dominant physical activity. Third, uncivilised, rough and wild behaviour among pupils and students was not limited to English public schools. In German universities duelling was common and in schools younger members of the middle class frequently organised themselves in pupils' associations who copied and imitated the practices of the student organisations, in particular their heavy drinking and fighting. When the repressive measures of the state failed to eliminate this public nuisance teachers were looking for an alternative which would satisfy the needs of pupils to socialise and was at the same time attractive due to its unseemly, wild and unruly nature. Consequently, from the early 1870s onwards, they introduced extra curricular activities, in which physical exercise played an important role.

Only a few decades after the formation of the German nation state in 1871, the government started to generously support and politically use international sport in a number of different ways — as early as almost any other country in Europe. In Britain, in contrast, at the beginning of the 20th century the central tenet of the dominant amateur ethos was that the state had no role to play in sport. Although there were extensive contacts and connections between sport and the state, they were predominantly informal, with members of the government, ministers and civil servants often also members of influential sport organisations. Although the Central Council for Recreation and Training was set up in 1935, which brought together various organisations concerned with sport, physical education and health, the British state only started to systematically support the development of sport at the beginning of the 1970s when the Sports Council was established by Royal Charter. However, the short history of state involvement in sport in Britain is full of discontinuities, lack of co-ordination, chronic financial under-provision and ad hoc improvisations. Until the 1990s none of the political parties in power had a clear policy or vision for sport. Consequently, the firmly established fragmentation of the organisational structures in British sport has not yet been cured and still exists. In contrast to this:

> ... with a considerable degree of continuity in personnel from Imperial Germany, through the Republic into the Nazi period and afterwards into the German Federal Republic, the knowledge and skill of international competitions and the propaganda that went with it was thoroughly maintained. (A. Krüger, 1998: p. 92)

The most prominent example for this high degree of continuity is clearly reflected in the biography of Carl Diem, a first-class scholar and the outstanding sports administrator in the 20th century. He founded his first sports club in Berlin in the age of 17 in 1899. Later he accompanied the German teams to the Olympics both in Amsterdam in 1906 and in Stockholm in 1912. One year later he became the secretary of the German government's Commission for Physical Exercise (*Deutscher Reichsausschuß für Leibesübungen*). In this role, he promoted sport, organised athletic festivals and travelled the world whilst at the same time producing a stream of scholarly writings focusing particularly upon the history and pedagogy of sport. As an uncritical admirer of De Coubertin and a devoted supporter of the Olympic movement Diem was in charge of the planning and preparation of the 1916 Olympics in Berlin.

After the First World War, in the 1920s, it was largely due to Diem's continuous lobbying efforts that Germany was re-admitted to the Olympic family in 1928 and that the 1936 Games were awarded to Berlin. Immediately after the announcement in May 1932, Diem travelled to Los Angeles where the next Olympic Games were held in order to learn from the Californian approach. When he returned to Germany, he was convinced that he would be able to surpass the Hollywoodian Olympics and started to plan the biggest and most lavish Olympic festival ever. As Diem had the full support of Hitler and Goebbels, and almost unlimited access to all kinds of resources, he was able to successfully design a spectacle of previously unknown magnitude which still remains unmatched in its blatant political use.

Although there is some anecdotal evidence which suggests that Diem was a committed supporter of the Nazi regime and its ideology, he was able to continue his career as a scholar and sports administrator in the newly founded Federal Republic of Germany. Diem was one of the founding fathers and became the first director of the German Sports University in Cologne in 1947. He died in 1962. Although in recent years more evidence of his genuine support for the Nazis has been discovered, his name is still used for many streets, parks, recreational facilities, sport and research centres throughout Germany. Diem's lasting role as a top sports administrator despite very different socio-political and ideological environments is somehow representative as many other survived the political collapse of the Third Reich and moved straight into powerful positions of the new sports system of the Federal Republic of Germany.

It was not only the British state which, at the beginning of the last century, hardly showed an interest in sport but also the British working class movement, "which was virtually uninvolved in the sports organizations and activities of the Second International" (Hargreaves, 1986: p. 212). In comparison, in France and Germany Socialist and Communist sport organisations had been formed already before the First World War. In 1912, the *Zentralkommission für Arbeitersport und Körperpflege* (ZK — Central Committee for Workers Sport and Physical Hygiene) became the umbrella organisation for a large number of worker sport organisations. It was heavily influenced and supported by the Social Democratic Party (SPD) as the parliamentary debate of the second episode clearly shows. Social Democratic members of parliament used the debate about the funding of the Olympic Games to highlight the tense relationship between bourgeois and working class sport after the latter had been suppressed for many years and had subsequently been excluded from financial support by the state. They argued that as long as the various benefits of working class involvement in active forms of physical recreation were completely ignored, the government should not support international competitions which celebrated notions of record and individual achievement and would eventually only benefit bourgeois sport organisations.

This development of worker sport has been extensively researched in Germany, in particular by sport historians. Their results are usually full of rich and detailed information but often suffer from two weaknesses. Many have looked at worker sport in isolation, without relating its development to wider changes in the social structures of German society, in particular to other classes. The focus has often been more on distributive rather than relational issues. Secondly, the research often lacks a theoretical framework and so remains rather descriptive.

In contrast to the history of worker sport, neither the development of the state's involvement in sport nor the more general analysis of power issues have hardly ever featured prominently on the research agenda of sports historians or sociologists. The most notable exception here is Arnd Krüger's detailed study of the relationship between 'Sport and Politics' (1975) since ancient times. However, it appears as if such fundamental sociological concerns do not play an important role in the sociology of sport in Germany. Instead, it is preoccupied with practical and applied investigations and only very rarely concerned with critical inquiries into the meaning of sport in society.

The very few critical and radical sociological studies focusing on sport in Germany go back to the late 1960s and early 1970s and must be seen in the context of the emergence of a New Left subsequent to the students riots. Bero Rigauer's seminal text on the structural analogies between sport and work (1969) was followed by G. Vinnais's analysis of soccer (1970) as an example a popular cultural formation which helps to socialise individuals into capitalist forms of production and consumption as well as authoritarian patterns of behaviour. Ulrike Prokop's critical sociological analysis of the Olympic Games (1971) concludes that sport helps significantly to sustain the power structures of capitalist societies. All these authors have in common that they used a (neo-)Marxist theoretical framework for their 'critical theory of sport' (Rigauer, 2000) which was largely influenced by the Frankfurt School and aimed to contribute to wider debates about sport and capitalism. Paradoxically, all of them dealt with sport without saying very much about the body. This changed in 1976 when Karin Rittner published her book on sport and the division of labour. Gramsci's ideas, however, (although widely used by scholars from other countries: see below) have so far hardly been recognised in the sociology of sport in Germany and thus not been employed as a theoretical framework for the study of sport.

Despite these fertile academic roots the 'critical theory of sport' in Germany never really took off and only very few scholars continued to develop it (Rigauer, 1995) or used it as a theoretical framework for their investigations (Rütten, 1988). In contrast, Gramsci's concept of hegemony became a key theoretical element in the critical and radical study of sport in the Anglo-American environment. Whilst it has been very fruitfully employed for the analysis of sport and power in British society (Hargreaves, 1986), in America (Sage, 1990) and Northern Ireland (Sugden and Bairner, 1995), no such attempt has been made in Germany.

Gramsci's hegemony concept and the increasing complexity of modern German society

The third episode clearly shows that the area of state action is continuing to expand into civil society (and popular culture) which means that civil and political society are increasingly intertwined. This development must be seen against the context of existing mass organisations, such as political parties and pressure groups, and the state's attempts to maintain the consent of the governed. Increased educational standards, universal suffrage, the increasing competition of ideas and practices have changed the meaning and process of gaining political leadership dramatically. In order to stay in power the ruling elites must win over and nurture the allegiance of the majority of the population which in modern democratic societies is achieved through reforms and compromises in which the interests of different groups are taken into account (or at least perceived to be recognised). In addition, leadership is not only obtained in political society but increasingly won within the private institutions of civil society, which mediate the individual and the state.

The concept of hegemony, although established already before the First World War, captures precisely this development and attempts to describe and explain how the domination of one social class or group of people over others is achieved by a combination of political and ideological means. Gramsci argued that modern states should be understood as an apparatus which combines power and consent.

Although the state has the monopoly over the use of physical force and is therefore able to coerce individuals and groups into the existing order, the role of the ideological apparatus in winning the consent of the subordinate groups has become increasingly important. For Marx, the primary task of the state was to defend the economic and political interests of the capitalist class: insteadf, Gramsci suggested that in the 20th century the state is the chief instrument of coercive force, with the winning of consent with the help of ideological domination happening in the institutions of civil society. He also stressed the state's instrumental role in creating and maintaining those institutions comprising civil society, such as the family, political parties, trade unions and other voluntary associations.

For Gramsci, hegemony is achieved when subordinate groups generally accept the fundamental and central structures, patterns, practices and relationships of a particular social arrangement as natural, normal and inevitable. However, as hegemony is hardly ever complete, the dominant group(s) always face potential demands and challenges from below. In order to sustain hegemony they employ a variety of political and social institutions and strategies to reproduce consent. Although this process of negotiating consent often leads to economic, political or cultural economic concessions, which appear to genuinely accommodate the demands of the subordinate groups, the outcome does only very rarely change the fundamental structures of an existing social order. Hegemony is essentially a synthesis of moral, political and intellectual leadership by one class which has successfully influenced and gained the consent of all other social groups. One environment, which has over the last decades increasingly gained in importance as an arena for negotiations of definitions of social reality, is the area of popular culture which obviously includes sport.

Using Gramsci's hegemony concept for an analysis of key moments in sports history and development offers a more subtle and flexible approach, which allows us to avoid monolithic and mechanical explanations of the workings of modern class societies. The three episodes from the beginning of this text show this convincingly. On a more general level, they clearly display a fundamental characteristic and continuity of sport in Germany: it is part of, and an arena for, hegemonic struggles as the development of sport, its parameters and the shape of sport is contested by different social groups. Although the three episodes are only typical examples for the development of sport in Germany, at least three aspects of the concept of hegemony can already be confirmed. First, achieving consent over social, political and moral leadership is a continual process and requires persistent efforts. Second, the precise composition of those groups trying to achieve hegemony changes constantly and new coalitions emerge all the time. Third, the borders between civil and political society become increasingly blurred.

Conclusion

The IOC awarded the 1936 Olympic Games to Berlin before Hitler came to power. The politicians of the Weimar Republic had hoped to celebrate the emergence of a democratic German state its re-admittance to the European and community of nations after its isolation in the aftermath of the First World War. Instead the Nazis used the Games to celebrate the ongoing destruction of that system, to improve their international reputation and to demonstrate their claims of racial superiority. This blatant political use of sport was followed by a more subtle approach. The Cold War and the separation of the German nation (state) meant that sport became part of a variety of political initiatives, for example the creation of distinctive national identities in the East and West. This approach had its roots in the 19th century when the *Turnbewegung* made some significant contributions to the emergence of the first German nation state in 1871. Its development also represents the gradual formation and extension of a differentiated civil society which has become increasingly important for the achievement of hegemony.

Whilst Hitler's totalitarian regime used sport in a very blunt, direct and overt way, the inclusion of sport in the struggle for hegemony is more subtle, indirect and diffuse. It has been suggested that the analysis of sport in Germany as an outstanding element of both civic society and poplar culture requires a critical and flexible theoretical framework which is able to capture the dynamics of power struggles and the nature, trajectories and outcome of social conflicts. Gramsci's hegemony concept offers such a framework which the sociology of sport in Germany has not yet employed.

References

Abrams, L. (1992) *Workers' culture in Imperial Germany — Leisure and recreation in the Rhineland and Westphalia*. London and New York: Routledge.

Anderson, B. (1991) *Imagined communities*. London/New York: Verso.

Bade, K. J. (1994) *Homo Migrans — Wanderungen aus und nach Deutschland.* Essen: Klartext.

Beck, U. (1986) *Die Risikogesellschaft*. Frankfurt/M.: Suhrkamp Verlag.

Cashmore, E. (1996) *Making sense of sport*. London, Routledge.

Coakley, J. J. (1994) *Sport in society: Issues and controversies*. St. Louis, Mosby.

Coe, S., Teasdale, D. and Wickham, D. (1992) *More than a game — sport in our time*. London: BBC Books.

Denk, H. and Hecker, G. (eds) (1981) *Texte zur Sportpädagogik*. Schorndorf:Verlag Karl Hofmann

Dann, O. (1996) *Nation und Nationalismus in Deutschland 1770–1990*. München, Beck.

Dixon, J. G. (1986) 'Prussia, politics and physical education' in P. C. McIntosh, J. G. Dixon, A. D. Munrow and R. F. Willetts (eds) *Landmarks in the history of physical education*. London: RKP, pp. 112–155.

Duke, V. and Crolley, L. (1996) *Football, nationality and the state*. New York: Longman.

Elias, N. (1996) *The Germans — Power struggles and the development of habitus in the nineteenth and twentieth centuries*. Cambridge: Polity Press.

Fischer, G. and Lindner, U. (1999) *Stürmer für Hitler — Vom Zusammenspiel zwischen Fußball und Nationalsozialismus*. Göttingen: Verlag Die Werkstatt.

Fürstenberg, F. (1972) *Die Sozialstruktur der Bundesrepublik Deutschland — Ein soziologischer Überblick*. Opladen: Westdeutscher Verlag.

Gehrmann, S. (1996) 'Symbol of German resurrection: Max Schmeling, German Sports Idol', in R. Holt, J. A. Mangan and P. Lafranchi (eds) *European heroes — Myth, identity, sport*. London: Frank Cass, pp. 101–113.

Gramsci, A. (1971) *Selections from the prison notebooks*. London: Lawrence and Wishart.

Gruneau, R. (1999) *Class, sports and social development*. Champaign (IL): Human Kinetics.

Hargreaves, J. (1986) *Sport, power and culture*. Cambridge: Polity Press.

Hobsbawm, E. and Ranger, T. (eds) (1999) *The invention of tradition*. Cambridge: Cambridge University Press.

Houlihan, B. (1994) *Sport and international politics*. New York, Harvester Wheatsheaf.

Johann, E. and Junker, J. (1970) *German cultural history of the last hundred years*. Munich: Nymphenburger Verlagshandlung.

Koch, H. W. (1975) *The Hitler Youth — origins and development 1922–1945*. London: Macdonald and Jane's.

Krüger, A. (1975) *Sport und Politik — Von Turnvater Jahn zum Staatsamateur*. Hannover, Fackelträger.

Krüger, A. (1996) 'The German way of worker sport', in A. Krüger and J. Riordan (eds) *The story of worker sport*. Champaign (IL): Human Kinetics, pp. 1–26.

Krüger, A. (ed) (1984) *Forum für Sportgeschichte*. Berlin: Die Entwicklung der Turn- und Sportvereine.

Krüger, M. (1993a) *Einführung in die Geschichte der Leibeserziehung und des Sports — Leibeserziehung im 19. Jahrhundert. Turnen fürs Vaterland. Vol. 9*. Schorndorf: Verlag Karl Hofmann.

——— (1993b) *Einführung in die Geschichte der Leibeserziehung und des Sports — Leibesübungen im 20. Jahrhundert. Sport für alle. Vol. 10*. Schorndorf: Verlag Karl Hofmann.

——— (1996) *Körperkultur und Nationsbildung. Die Geschichte des Turnens in der Reichsgründungsära — eine Detailstudie über die Deutschen*. Schorndorf: Verlag Karl Hofmann.

Lindner, R. and Breuer, H. T. (1982) *"Sind doch nicht alles Beckenbauers"*. Frankfurt: Syndicat.

Lindner, R. (ed) (1983) *Der Satz "Der Ball ist rund" hat eine gewisse philosophische Tiefe*. Berlin: Transit.

Mandell, R. D. (1971) *The Nazi Olympics*. New York: The Macmillan Company.

Mann, G. (1996) *The history of Germany since 1789*. London: Pimlico.

Merkel, U. (1995) 'The German government and the politics of sport and leisure in the 1990s: An interim report', in A. Tomlinson, M. Talbot, and S. Fleming (eds) *Policy and politics in sport, physical education and leisure*. Eastbourne: Leisure Studies Association Publications, pp. 95–108.

——— (1998) 'Sport in divided nations — The case of the old, new and 're-united' Germany', in A. Bairner and J. Sugden (eds) *Sport in divided societies*. Aachen: Meyer and Meyer, pp. 139–166.

———— (2000) 'The hidden social and political history of the German Football Association (DFB), 1900–1950', *Soccer and society* Vol. 1, No. 2: pp. 167–186.

Münch, R. (1993) 'The contribution of German social theory to European Sociology', in B. Nedelmann and P. Sztompka (eds) *Sociology in Europe. In search of identity*. Berlin/New York: Walter de Gruyter, pp. 45–66.

Prokop, U. (1971) *Soziologie der Olympischen Spiele*. Munich: Carl Hansa Verlag.

Pulzer, P. (1997) *Germany, 1870–1945. Politics, state formation and war*. Oxford: Oxford University Press.

Rigauer, B. (1969) *Sport und Arbeit*. Frankfurt/M.: Suhrkamp Verlag.

Rittner, K. (1976) *Sport und Arbeitsteilung — Zur sozialen Funktion und Bedeutung des Sports*. Bad Homburg: Limpert Verlag.

Rütten, A. (1988) *Sport, Ideologie, Kritische Theorie*. Frankfurt/M.: Lang.

Sage, G. H. (1998) *Power and ideology in American sport. A critical perspective*. Champaign (IL): Human Kinetics.

Senn, A. E. (1999) *Power, politics and the Olympic games*. Champaign (IL): Human Kinetics.

Teske, H. J. (1977) *FC-Gelsenkirchen Schalke 04. Zur Sozialgeschichte eines Fußballvereins in einer Industrieregion*. Essen (unpublished manuscript)

Ueberhorst, H. (1986) 'Sport, physical culture and political action in Germany during the Weimar Republic', in G. Redmond (ed) *Sport and politics*. Champaign (IL): Human Kinetics, pp. 109–116.

Verlag Die Werkstatt (ed) (1993) *Fußball und Rassismus*. Göttingen: Verlag Die Werkstatt.

Vinnaii, G. (1972) *Sport in der Klassengesellschaft*. Frankfurt/M: Suhrkamp Verlag.

FROM THE FIELD: SYDNEY 2000 AND AN OLYMPICS RESEARCH AGENDA

Alan Tomlinson
Chelsea School, University of Brighton

The best Olympic Games ever?

Within weeks of the closing of the Sydney Olympic Games — predictably hailed by IOC supremo Juan Antonio Samaranch as "the best Olympic Games ever. They could not have been better ... a perfect organisation" — this assessment was accepted as the evaluative orthodoxy on the 2000 Summer Games. Social commentators such as Pat Kane could ask, in the 'Life' section of the UK Sunday broadsheet *The Observer*, "Why was it such a good Olympics again?", and confidently announce that it was because "sport has become the drama that articulates the play ethic in its most accessible form" (22 October 2000, 'Play for today': pp. 20–30). Here, the "goodness" or high quality of the Olympics is taken-for-granted without comment. The premise is that Sydney was indeed some sort of pinnacle of human achievement. Simultaneously, the tawdry history of a tainted movement is also glossed in one innocent-sounding but revisionist-in-impact word — "again". In such commentaries the complexity of the Games, the motives of the organizers, hosts and participants are collapsed into an encomium of the everyday, in which the athletes are said to be really just like us. The Games and the play ethic that it is said to embody are diluted into a mirror for the narcissistic contemporary self: "What we love about great sportspersons is the fact that they are not robots, or mutants, or androids — but humans, recognisably, like us". So, Kane postulates rather than argues, we feel ourselves with them in the pool, on the track, on the baseball diamond or on court: "In an age where the

207

immateriality of capital, culture and technology rule supreme, we have a hunger for these heroes of the material and the physical".

During the lead-up to the Olympic Games in Sydney I was giving talks, seminars and public lectures on the Olympics and modern sport, and at one event in New South Wales, with Olympic fever heightening as the torch relay went through town and descended upon the Sydney area itself, I felt like a party-pooper, a sceptical spoilsport[1]. As the party was about to begin, questions concerning the dubious politics and economics of the Olympic movement, and of the involvement of the host state New South Wales itself, began to be sidelined in the bright spring sunshine of an excited Australian public. The imperative of every Games, Let the Games Begin, had an accompanying echo, Let the Criticisms Stop.

And Sydney was, as so many of us predicted and as Clive James has so irresistibly documented, in *The Independent*, some party[2]. But within a couple of days of the Game's closing extravaganza, the Nobel Peace prize was awarded not to the little Catalan unreformed Francoist fascist Samaranch, but to a politician from South Korea. Within hours of Sydney's spectacular firework finale — 3 million Australian dollars' worth of multicoloured explosives — Israel and Palestine were not smilingly represented by flagbearers in Homebush's Olympic Stadium, or frolicking athletes partying in the heart of the stadium, but were close to war as the body count of civilians mounted on the Gaza Strip. And the Aboriginal population of Redfern, just a couple of stops and a few minutes west of Sydney's Central Station, was no longer sought out by world media or asked for its views on Cathy Freeman, Australia's flame-lighter extraordinaire in the Opening Ceremony, and symbol-on-the-400-metre track of the country's aspirations to reconciliation around the Aboriginal question.

Sydney welcomed 15,000 IOC-accredited media, and the city, at its Media Centre, accredited another 5,000 or so. That figure of close to 21,000 media is almost double the number of participating athletes. Rose-coloured spectacles (or maybe good Hunter Valley reds) must have been widely available in Sydney, given the positive write-up of almost every aspect of the Games, fanatically and exhaustively so in the Australian press, and jingoistically so in the UK media. The presentation and the reception of the Games have suggested that the Olympics and the IOC have erased all problems and controversies. Spoilsport or not, a more sober, reflective and retrospective view than this, of key aspects of

Olympism, is surely called for. Offering an overview of the Games as spectacle, through the lenses of Sydney's opening and closing ceremonies, this piece provides a reminder of some of the recurring issues in Olympic research that must not be neglected in the triumphalist glow of the IOC's own myth-making, and the extraordinary interpretive myopia of a cosseted world media. The piece is based upon my media tours of the Olympic Park and the International Broadcast Centre at Homebush, prior to the Games, observation whilst in New South Wales of the build-up to the event, and time spent at a number of Olympic venues and attending a dozen different events during the Games (including the Opening Ceremony). A professional base in the Olympic Park's Main Press Centre and the city's Media Centre also afforded the opportunity to gather contextual material and watch at close hand the unfolding of the Sydney success as it seduced the working professionals within the media[3]. The piece is therefore pitched as analytical observations from the field, covering the claims and the impact of the Olympic Games, and alert to the research agenda that must be sustained if the social, cultural and economic impact of the Olympic Games is to be adequately contextualised, understood and, wherever appropriate, critiqued[4].

The Games as spectacle: bigger and bigger

US giant NBC forked out over seven hundred million dollars to get the rights to relay the Sydney Olympics to what it anticipated as vast consumer and sports-mad markets. NBC's Olympic maestro, Dick Ebersol, had a dream camera shot of Sydney 2000. It frames the leafy suburbs of North Sydney and the skyscrapers of the city centre alongside the Sydney Harbour Bridge, fronted by the roof of the Olympic stadium and the blazing Olympic cauldron. New South Wales' Olympic Minister Michael Knight shared the NBC aesthetic, ordering the demolition of power lines that blocked Ebersol's vision. The image producers at Sydney were looking to woo the global audience with the swishest technology yet, and visual effects that might make even Montjuic on the edge of the Mediterranean, at Barcelona 1992, look dull[5].

The Olympic Games has become one of the biggest television events in the world. At its most pompous the body that runs the Olympics, the IOC — International Olympic Committee — claims to put on the biggest show on earth, watched on television by 4 billion viewers, more people than for any other event in history, it reminds us, reported on by an army of media folk.

Grandiosity of scale has become a byword for those looking to stage a successful and media-friendly Olympics. In Sydney the 2000 Summer Olympics continued in this mode, notching up firsts and bests and showing off with reels of statistics. Sydney and the IOC had one goal in common, especially in the wake of waves of scandal and corruption engulfing both the IOC itself and the organizing committee (SOCOG) of the Sydney event. This was to make the Games work, to keep sponsors and television partners happy. In the midst of the IOC's biggest ever crisis, following revelations concerning bribery and corruption around Salt Lake City's successful bid to stage the 2004 winter Olympics, the Olympic juggernaut was beginning to wobble, with sponsors muttering about pulling out, television companies beginning to regret their investment. In January 1999 IOC executive board member and vice-president — and star smoothie — Dick Pound apologized to athletes who embodied the Olympic ideals, to volunteers who made the whole thing work, and to people and communities to whom the Olympics meant heartfelt ideals and values. We'll pull through was his message, echoing the mantra of the Olympic Charter "The Olympic Movement is founded on ideals such as Hope, Unity, Friendship and Fair Play ... the Sydney Games will be one of the greatest ever".

Touring Olympic Park in Homebush Bay, out in the western suburbs 19 kilometres from central Sydney, a barrage of statistics was presented in support of this claim. The hosts for the media tour were from SOCOG and its partner organization from the New South Wales government, the OCA (Olympic Coordinating Authority). Things hadn't gone too well that morning. The new Olympic Park train wasn't running that day, and some camera crews were late. Sydney knows what the press corps did to Atlanta when there were delays and transport problems. You don't get long in a 17-day event to overturn initial media impressions which within hours become worldwide opinion. So the organizers were nervous at the start of the tour. But it didn't put them off their stats. This will be the biggest sports event ever, with 34 sports and disciplines and an Olympic village catering "for the first time in Olympic history" for all athletes, and housing a total of 15,300 athletes and team officials. The Olympic Park is 160 hectares in size — "the largest land regeneration project in Australia", surrounded by the 440 hectare Millennium Parklands. Australia's made a 3.3

billion dollar commitment (two thirds from state taxpayers in New South Wales). More than 50,000 a day will come in to the park by train and bus, 100,000 flocking around Darling Harbour in central Sydney. The new station cost 95 million dollars. 5,500 will use the main press centre as their working base. The International Broadcast Centre, on the edge of Olympic Park, covers more than 70,000 square metres of facilities, including one monitoring studio housing 402 screens, servicing more than 180 broadcast organizations and 12,000 or so accredited Rights Holding Broadcasters. 47,000 volunteers have been trained to ensure that the event goes smoothly.

The stats were reeled off relentlessly. It went on. The Olympic Boulevard — a soulless driveway that when empty looks like nothing so much as a hastily constructed retail park — is 1.5 kilometres long. "The world's largest dining facility" will feed 4,900 people at once, and 50,000 meals a day will be served to Olympic athletes, officials and helpers. It's the "longest torch relay in history, 133 days, a major logistic exercise". The park's got "the largest Olympic stadium ever", a snip at 690 million dollars, holding 110,000. IOC president Samaranch was moved to mutter, in April 1998 well over a year before its completion, that it was "the best stadium I have seen in my life". And a mere 197 million dollars got "the largest Superdome with no columns, in the southern hemisphere". Oh, and not forgetting the tents to cover the equivalent of 5,000 three-bedroomed houses, and the 2,000 portable toilets, across the different Olympic sites. Homebush Bay was essentially a toxic dumping-ground for the Sydney area, and it took 137 million dollars to clean up the site to make this "Disneyworld of sport", as SOCOG's Steve Cooke put it, for athletes and participants from all levels from the Olympic elite to community teams and family groups — and it's still not clean throughout. The official Olympic telephone wait-in-line voiceover had said that "this will be the biggest event ever held in Australia". The stakes were raised on the trip around the park. Albeit a little sheepishly, our hosts announced that "this will be the biggest peacetime event in the world".

Origins and beginnings

Things were not always thus. The last time that the Olympics stopped off in Australia, at Melbourne in 1956 there weren't 10,400, but just 3,258 athletes, representing 72 nations. By 1996, Atlanta welcomed 10,310 athletes from 197 nations[7]. Post-colonial independence across imperial empires, and the collapse of the Soviet Union, had combined with television advances and global marketing power to make the Olympics a genuinely international and worldwide phenomenon. The event agenda had been expanded too, with the easy-on-the-eye sport of beach volleyball featuring for the second time at Sydney, down on Bondi Beach. Admittedly others have gone. The tug-of-war featured only from 1900 to 1908. And the British imperial sport of cricket only had one appearance, in 1900, when Great Britain won gold, thanks to Devon and Wanderers Cricket Club's stroll to victory over France, which was represented by a bunch of players from down the road at the British Embassy in Paris. In fact, the Olympic Games were in truly dire straits just half a dozen Olympiads ago. No-one wanted them. They spelt trouble.

Mexico City '68 is remembered for the brutal sweeping off the streets of political activists, and for the brave black power salutes by US Afro-Caribbean athletes Tommie Smith and John Carlos, on the victory rostrum for their gold and bronze medals respectively in the 200 metres. The massacre of Israeli athletes at the Munich Olympics of 1972 was one of those I-know-where-I-was death of Kennedy moments that stay with you forever[8]. Montreal in 1976 suffered not just a boycott by 22 black African nations over the issue of apartheid, but botched planning and soaraway budgets that still remain to be paid off a quarter of a century on. The US led the next boycott of the Olympics, Jimmy Carter marching his men away from Moscow in protest at the Soviet Union's invasion of Afghanistan, and leaving the field invitingly clear for Thatcher-defying British winners Sebastian Coe, Steve Ovett and Daley Thompson — the latter performing acrobatics of delight as he left the rostrum draped in gold, rows of empty seats in the stadium behind him testifying to the selective interest of the home audience. By now, for years nobody had wanted the Games. But Los Angeles rode to the rescue.

Los Angeles rewrote the rules for the hosting of the Olympics. The IOC had no choice. Only LA was left in the race when its main competitor — Teheran — decided not to go the whole way. The terrorism and the financial disasters of the 70s had made the Olympic Games an albatross. LA, supported all the way by Ronald Reagan, revived them. In the context of the Cold War, it showcased the Olympics and proved that you could make money with the event. Bringing in sponsors, working with an IOC now led by former Franco supporter Samaranch and aping the football body FIFA to bring in funds from global business, LA '84 made 225 million US dollars clear profit, helped by creative accounting that deleted the considerable contribution of the public sector. The money men moved in quickly, sensing the global business opportunities in world sport[9]. And the politicians, seeing LA's Hollywood-style extravaganza in the opening and closing ceremonies of the Games, sat up and took notice again[10]. The Asian tiger of Korea showed that the momentum could be sustained in 1988, and then in Barcelona 1992 the transformative regional potential of the event (for Catalonia), its power as a national symbol for Spain in general, and its profile in the global consciousness, were all confirmed[11].

The combination of local pride and international posturing has always been the main driving force of the Olympics for those staging the events. The Olympics began in Athens in 1896, the brainchild and dream of a displaced French aristocrat, Baron Pierre De Coubertin. The Baron was really a dreamer who sought for himself and his social class a new role, in a world that had all but collapsed for his generation in defeat in the Franco-Prussian War. He dedicated his life to mediocre philosophising, dabbles in educational thinking, and his one Big Idea — the revival, as he saw it, of the ancient Greek Olympics. He could not persuade his countrymen to commit themselves to getting this off the ground, and so it was with the Greeks themselves that he worked to launch the first internationally-based modern Olympic Games[12].

De Coubertin had got a lot of his ideas from the public schools of England and the ivy-league colleges of the USA, and persuaded groups from those constituencies to get out to Greece. There were around 245 participants and no women, representing only 14 countries. The US topped the list of medal totals, the host country came second, France and Great Britain fourth and fifth. In third place were the athletes of Germany, showing the prowess that would put them at the top of that table for Hitler's Berlin Olympics in 1936, only three Olympics after the country's re-admission following its exclusion after World War I. Greece became so buoyed up by the success of the first Olympics that in the following year its inflated national pride led it into territorial adventures in Crete. In the 30-day Cretan War Greece was crushed at the hands of the German-trained Turks.

Host cities have always been galvanised by the commitment to stage the Olympics. Korea leapt from nineteenth in the 1976 medal table to fourth in its own Games in Seoul in 1988, slipping back to tenth in Atlanta in 1996 (Great

Britain languished at thirty-sixth, a place behind Ethiopia, whose two golds out of three medals outstripped Britain's one gold out of fifteen medals in the ranking). Spain's dramatic improvement as an Olympic nation was planned around Barcelona 1992, when its athletes won 22 medals, 13 gold. Before then, Spain had scarcely featured as a serious sporting power. The Olympics, here, meant a form of rebirth and certainly re-entry onto the world stage, in a post-Franco period of modernism and democracy[13]. Thirteenth in the table in Atlanta, Spain still achieved its second best ever all-round Olympic performance. Australia was tenth in Barcelona, seventh in Atlanta and geared up for further glory in its own Olympics, spurred on by its lavishly funded national initiative, the Australian Institute of Sport[14].

Staging the modern Olympics, or featuring consistently in the medal tables, are ways of saying to the world that the country matters. The Tokyo Olympics of 1964 were a source of international rehabilitation for a humiliated nation. All Olympics are a form of cultural aspirational politics. The early Games were in many ways sideshows to international trade festivals, motivated in France, the US and England by the desire to demonstrate the qualities that made such nations and civilisations great. For De Coubertin, athletics would be a new-found international diplomacy: "Let us export rowers, runners and fencers; there is the free trade of the future"[15]. De Coubertin had formed the Olympics and revived the Games as a way of rebuilding the strength of the youth of nations such as his own. He was frighteningly messianic about this:

> I shall burnish a flabby and cramped youth, its body and its character, by sport, its risks, and even its excesses. I shall enlarge its vision and its hearing by showing it with wide horizons, heavenly, planetary, historical, horizons of universal history which, in engendering mutual respect, will bring about a ferment of international peace.[16]

He also urged that this be for everyone, regardless of money or status. Yet he loathed professionalism, and disapproved of women's sports. De Coubertin was really a mishmash of contradictions, driven to peace but utterly imperialist; a declared republican and egalitarian, but rooted in privilege and its persisting ideals; a romantic anti-industrialist laying the foundations for sport as mass production.

Creating the spectacle

The grossest distortion of De Coubertin's doomed athleticist ideal was to come in the Nazi Olympics of 1936, when the world's most brilliant propaganda machine combined with the century's most horrific political regime to stage the Olympics as mass spectacle for the first time[17]. The Nazi culture machine nurtured Leni Riefenstahl in her film-making of both *Triumph of the Will*, on the Nazis' 1934 Nuremberg rally, and *Olympia*, the film of the 1936 Olympics. In both these films the reality of the Nazi war machine is blurred in the pastoralist and romantic images of a bucolic and traditional old Germany. The individual is subjected to the will of the collective, in apparently innocent Baden Powell-style Boy Scout frolics in the campsite, the sauna or the pool. But look again, beyond the track, at Olympia, and you will find the athletes of fascist nations — Italy as well as Germany, for instance — depicted as the more modern organic community, some athletes from less developed nations distorted as almost sub-human, metamorphosed into exotic animal species. At the beginning of the film in one of the most breathtaking sequences in 1930s cinema, Riefenstahl narrates the travel through time of the Olympic flame and torch, from ancient Olympia in Greece to modern Berlin. A statue from Olympia gradually transforms into a modern discus thrower in this sequence, at one point the body shaped as a human form of the swastika itself[18]. In connecting the Greek ideal to the fascist Aryan present, Riefenstahl reworked Olympic themes and icons — statues, ruins, the performing and competing body — to fit an elitist politics of racist superiority[19]. The Nazis innovated for this Olympic spectacular. The giant Olympic Bell tolled at no further Olympics. The more successful innovation was the torch relay.

Sydney ceremonies

Australian Ric Birch was director of ceremonies for the Sydney Olympics. He has an impressive pedigree, as director of production for David Wolper's LA '84 spectaculars. Remember them? The Rocket Man who flew down into the Coliseum at the opening ceremony? The 84 grand pianos swivelling into view as Gershwin classics played? The dancing cowboys and cowgirls wagon-training it the wrong way across the North American continent? And in the closing ceremony, a giant Extra Terrestrial thanking us for the hundred years in which we — the "family of man" — have managed to pull off such great achievements. This was selective US history at its peak, cultural invent-ory and political bias rolled into one.

Birch also had an executive producer role in Barcelona's ceremonies. He wasn't saying much in the run-in to Sydney's opening. In fact he was saying nothing at all. SOCOG's Media Adviser Steve Cooke closed up on the ceremonies: "Ric's not speaking to anyone. We've had some trouble with the local media". But it's "tipped to be as Australian as possible", Steve confided, with "athletes out on the field, creating 15 thousand more seats". It would certainly include large numbers of children, young people and volunteers, and there had been disputes about importing US and Japanese boys and girls to play in the marching bands. Ten thousand professional, amateur and volunteer supporters were lined up for the act at the opening, 5,000 at the closing of the event.

All such ceremonies try to balance regional (city), national and global interests. Sydney had a go at this with its unsuccessful mascots. Syd the platypus was the city's. Millie the echidna spoke for the millennium. Olly the kookaburra was named after the event itself. So unsuccessful that they were left offstage as the ceremonies played the modern Olympic refrain of national rebirth and international and global cuddling-up, and Olivia Newton-John and Australian former Essex-man John Farnham warbled vacuous lyrics of welcome and hope to the world.

Birch's triumph was hailed in Australia as a masterpiece of showbiz presentation, an unprecedentedly ambitious show of national and historical pride and cosmopolitan sincerity[20]. Here is a reminder of its themes, narrative and my own accompanying commentary, from close to ringside.

Sydney's Welcome to the global audience in the world's most watched television event was like an advertisement for your local riding school. Or outdoor overcoat supplier. 120 riders draped in dry-as-bone Ozzie bush-coats romanticized the taming of the Australian outback. Riders aged 15 to 77 astride their Australian stockhorses kept their cool in front of the 111,000 in the Olympic Stadium. The horse master didn't mince words: "We're breaking world records with this event and its scale will blow the world away". Well it was truly impressive control of real live animals. And sitting fifteen rows back, the emissions from the panting horses' nostrils wafting into the faces of the $1,400 onlookers, it was certainly stirring. The volunteer riders had also learned the words of the Australian national anthem, rousing stuff for starters. There weren't many more live animals to come after that — a couple of stray dogs or dingoes. But there were lots of imagined ones — imagined in a little girl's dream, and realised like a play-school orgy of the fantastic.

Olympic ceremonies share the same preoccupations. The host nation wants to show that it can put on a global show, but must also feature a quota of Olympic-style spirit — youth, universalism, peace and the like. So from Los Angeles 1984 onwards, opening ceremonies in particular have tried to balance these interests. It draws the audience in, for we all become gleeful spectators again, watching vastly sophisticated technologies reduce complex histories to showbiz formulae. For Sydney 2000 the Sydney Symphony Orchestra worked overtime backing a line-up of Australian popular singers, as well as haunting soloists and choirs, in pop classic and middle-of-the-road numbers stressing dreams, heroism and the power of the symbol of the flame. And political messages get slotted in there too. The Governor General of Australia, representative of Great Britain and Northern Ireland's Queen, told the world that the Olympics was "a powerful tool for reconciliation". But it's the cultural spectacle that grabs you the most, that takes you back to the front row of the stalls or the big-top.

The beginning of Sydney's cultural spectacle, after its welcome to the world, echoed the four-year long Olympic arts festival, which had opened with the theme of Aboriginal dreaming, the life-force and spiritual basis of the longest-surviving of human civilizations[21]. Deep Sea Dreaming placed centre-stage the Hero Girl, an innocent Shirley Temple look-alike, or a refugee from the cast of Peter Pan, who descended into the depths of a pool of fish, and so began a bizarre dream-sequence journey guided by the great tribal dancer Djakapurra, the Songman. Hero Girl, suspended at great height, performed somersaults in the sky, chased by several glowing yellow creatures — they turned out to be young swimmers training, bellowed on by legendary Australian swimming coach Laurie Lawrence in horrifying video close-up. She can't keep up, and the giant figure of the Songman waits to save her and guide her safely to salvation. Then followed Awakening, revolving around the uniting of diverse Aboriginal nations, and the appearance of Wandjina, the creation spirit, arching the stadium like a sunrise, and igniting bushfires that preface the third theme, Fire, as a creative not a destructive force. Circus-time this, with all those fire-eaters. This elemental emphasis persisted in the theme of Nature, the Australian landscape and its plants and animals emerging out of the chaos of fire — with just the one swift guest appearance from a kangaroo, then sidelined by the organisers as an undesirable national symbol, after the scathing response to the bicycling kangaroos that had represented Australia in the closing ceremony of the last summer Olympics at Atlanta. The threat of a dark force of modern culture was then represented in a Tin Symphony, which included Ned Kelly types in iron masks (several performing flying feats), dancing cog wheels, and then merry fiddling music ushering in cheerful jigs. At the end of this segment, Hero Girl looked like she was about to be gobbled up by a mechanical dragon — or was it a horse? She survived, though, and after a few British sailors arrived on a contraption resembling a penny-farthing bicycle, and the penal colony roots of western settlement were conveniently overlooked, the dream could continue. Arrivals, the sixth theme, depicted the arrival (all fit and dancing) of groups of immigrants from all over the world, hailing the New Australia of multi-culturalism, celebrated ultimately (an Australian in-joke, I knew instantly from my time promenading the suburban streets of New South Wales) in a move from shanty-town to suburbia, represented in the opening up of gyrating packing-boxes, transformed into jovial domestic gardeners, the lawn-mower their dancing partners. By now, the narrative didn't foreground many ancient civilizations, and I could have sworn that the lawnmower dance was sound-tracked by Some Enchanted Evening. We'd almost got there, and at least the last segmental theme didn't live up to its name. In Eternity, the blue-collar egalitarianism of Australia was celebrated, workers building an enormous bridge on which 1,000 tap dancers beat out an anthem of celebration, Songman and Hero Girl reconciling in the centre of things. Though as the bridge turned into a tower, didn't they seem to get stuck half way up?

Some experienced Australian commentators were nervous at the world's reaction. Would this be too Australian, too parochial? A concentration on the Aboriginal roots of the country, an encomium to the Australian countryside (the bush), and the making of the industrial culture, dominated. Multiculturalism, ethnicity and reconciliation were central to the display, hailing the cultural diversity and cosmopolitanism of the New Australia. Artistic director and producer David Atkins states that Sydney is important because it is about Australians themselves, and no other culture could have attempted what they did: "They couldn't have matched our mixture of youth, naïveté and larrikinism".

'Larrikinism' is the term in Australia for that streetwise even connish wit and cunning that helps you get on in life[22]. It's an illuminating claim, showing how strong that "see what we can do" spirit is in an Australian consciousness still afflicted by a deep-rooted sense of inferiority.

And then, like a magician's trick, fire and water were reconciled. The last lap of the flame was inside a fountain. Far from extinguishing it, this streamlined the flame, a still more dramatic effect when the cauldron burst into flames. Then runner Cathy Freeman emerged to light the flame, rounding off the ceremony's depiction of the history of Australia as an Aboriginal meta-narrative. Kangaroos — well, just one, in there fairly anonymously with all the other animals. Opera House — come on, that's nearly a third of a century old? This was the new Australia, distorting its history and its tensions, offering a vision in which Wendy learns to fly and all, however different, live happily ever after. Fairy tales do come true after all. Well at least Director of Ceremonies Ric Birch, with his latest triumph after an early apprenticeship at Los Angeles 84, probably thinks so. Everything in Sydney 2000 aspired to be bigger and better than before in this juggernaut of nation-posturing. Birch states confidently that the Sydney spectacle will be "the greatest ever" Opening Ceremony. That is until next time, when the likes of Ric and his team will be there in Athens (if the city gets its act together), telling the same story anew and making us all instant classicists and historians.

Sydneypride

Before and throughout the Games, there was an endearing honesty mixed with nervousness in the manner of the hosts of Sydney. Some would say it was generated by the stories of behind-the-scenes bungling and corruption, and nobody really knows how these billion-dollar and unaccountable budgets work. But there's a deeper source of nervousness than this. Australians didn't want to be seen as less competent than the Atlantans last time round in the US. As John Slee, influential leader-writer at the *Sydney Morning Herald*, says, "Australians are truly nervous about cocking up in the eyes of the world"[23]. Ron Wall, veteran Olympics observer and Agence-France Press man in Sydney, adds: "It's all about national spirit, Australians are very patriotic. These are 'Our Games', they say, and they don't like to receive criticism. They have a lot of pride, pride in the accomplishment. They want the Best Games Ever — they will want to say YES IT WAS GREAT"[24]. And there's a lot to balance in going for this. Who was going to open the Games with Samaranch, just after when a Queen on the other side of the world has been retained at the head of the nation — would the Governor General do? How was the sensitive Aboriginal issue be handled, when in the view of Delvene Parkin — former Miss Aboriginal Australia and current lecturer in Leisure and Tourism Studies at the University of Newcastle, New South Wales — Aboriginal cultural forms are used to start things off, but then, essentially, marginalized?[25]

Sydney was trying too hard. Thus the twitchiness. It wanted to be too many things. The Athlete's Games. The Green Games. The Recycling Games. The Public Transport Games. The Friendly Games. As well as The Biggest and the Best Games. You can't win them all, as most of the athletes in the village well knew. Make too many promises and you'll be caught out. No ferries up to Homebush for spectators, for instance, when this was one of the sales pitches in the winning bid in 1993[26]. The IOC top brass would get its own ferry, of course. And the majestic views over the Harbour, the absence of bombs in the Royal Botanical Gardens or Olympic Park, and the transcendence of the Aboriginal issue in the iconic profile and triumph of Cathy Freeman, allowed Samaranch to judge his last summer Olympics as "The Best Olympic Games Ever". He gave the athletes a special mention too, in hailing these as The Athletes' Games. The IOC's and Sydney's preoccupation with environmental issues was truly blown away by the crescendo and climax of the closing agenda[27].

And so the tax-free millions will roll in to the IOC. The television companies — though not so much the biggest stakeholder NBC, facing alarmingly low viewing figures in the USA for its delayed-time edited taped packages of the Games — would go home happy. Sydney was in a differeent world from Brisbane 1982, where the Commonwealth Games opened to a Rolf Harris special, a rendition of *Tie Me Kangaroo Down Sport* delivered from the back of a truck. The reported four billion viewers[28] would remember great moments of athletic prowess and physical beauty, more so still if it was a home-grown champion on the rostrum. It's the most magnificent trivia that the world's yet conspired to produce.

Beyond Sydney 2000

Debate in the aftermath of Sydney 2000 centred on how difficult — even impossible — it would be for any city or host-site to match the Sydney Spectacular. Within a few weeks of the close of the Games IOC officials would be visiting Athens, pronounced by IOC vice-president and Presidential hopeful Dick Pound to be woefully behind schedule — "8 to 9 on a scale of 10", he muttered ominously[29]. These officials would have Sydney hospitality in mind as their nervous Greek hosts sought to give watertight guarantees that Athens could play at this level. Samaranch brought the New South Wales Minister for the Olympics, Michael Knight, into the planning frame for Athens. Meanwhile, Seoul looked at its empty warehouse of an Olympic Stadium and planned a follow-up to its soccer World Cup show of 2002, saying that it could do it again for Asia if Athens fell short. And Sydney thought that it was such a good party — and wondered what would fill Olympic Park on any frequent basis after September 2000 — that everyone would want to come back, and offered itself as a real Olympic history-maker, willing to stage successive summer Olympic events.

As the gloss of Sydney 2000 showed no sign of dimming over, it was increasingly clear beyond the marvellous images of Freeman and others, that some serious evaluation was needed. Beyond the editorial skill of the television professionals, and the limited glimpses of the cocooned press corps, we must continue to put critical questions on the agenda of Olympic research.

First, at the most general level, the Olympics must be studied by looking at the relationship between the rhetoric of Olympism itself, and its modes of representation, and the practices of Olympics. Olympic ceremonials offers a marvellous focus for this sort of analysis. Second, far from the ecstatic celebration of the media event and the assumption of some sated and satisfied global audience, we must analyse the range of publics and constituencies for which the Games can have many and varied meanings. This might be as varied an exercise as to understand the mini-Mardi Gras created by Sydney's gay population, as the torch relay passed through the fashionably gay inner-Western suburbs a couple of days before the Games began, or the way in which groups of sponsors' guests were marched around from elite hotel to event or reception site, like so many schoolchildren in crocodile file and sporting awful track-suit style outfits in the colour or image of the privileged Olympic sponsor. Third, attempts must be made to estimate the real costs of events such as the Olympics, away from the bogus accounting of bodies such as the organizing committee of the Games/event, or the International Olympic Committee itself. These are not all the questions that should follow from Sydney. But if the real impact of the continuing Olympic story is to be understood in its social, cultural and economic terms, they are some of the most enduring and important.

Notes

1   I am grateful to generous hosts and colleagues, especially David Rowe, Deborah Stevenson and Kevin Markwell, for support during my time in the Department of Leisure and Tourism at the University of Newcastle, New South Wales, from July to September 2000; and for their input into the public debate.

2   Clive James wrote at the end of the Games that he was leaving Sydney for the umpteenth time, but never with so much regret. For more vintage James, see note 20 below.

3   For some discussion of the closeness of the sports media to their sources, with examples from the France '98 World (Soccer) Cup, see Sugden and Tomlinson (2000).

4   The Jennings trilogy on the International Olympic Committee and the seedy politics of a corrupt organisation and ethos provides incontrovertible evidence of the problems of the modern Olympic organisation. In Simson and Jennings (1992), the political economy of world sports organisations was revealed to be incestuous and hypocritical. In Jennings (1996), the infiltration of the Olympic organisation by new breeds of fixers and hustlers was exposed. And in Jennings and Sambrook (2000) the capacity of the IOC to cover its tracks, and veil its tarnished image in reformist promises, was shown to be highly effective, in the period between the confirmation of corruption in the Salt Lake City successful bid for the 2002 Winter Games, and the staging of the Sydney spectacular itself.

5   The media images of the stadium and the Sydney skyline and harbourscape were indeed dramatic. It would be churlish not to recognise that. But Ebersol's viewing figures back in the US were dependent on something more prosaic than his eye for the dramatic and the spectacular. In opting not to show live action, and to broadcast edited taped highlights many hours later, NBC got drastically low

figures. Viewers in the vicinity of the Canadian border even started tuning in to live programming from the broadcaster North of the border.

6   The fundamental principles of 'Modern Olympism' are listed on the International Olympic Committee's web site at <http://www.olympic.org/ioc/e/facts/charter/charter_intro_e.html> in a section on The Olympic Charter. Or at least they were during July and August 2000.

7   These snippets of Olympic history are culled from the indispensable Wallechinsky (2000).

8   On the Munich disaster, see Passion Picture's riveting and Oscar-winning documentary One Day in September (inspired by the stunning documentary on Muhammad Ali, *When We Were Kings*), directed by Kevin Macdonald. For a review of the film, see Young (2000).

9   On the money men who moved in on world soccer, and then the Olympics, see Sugden and Tomlinson (1997).

10   On Los Angeles excesses in the ceremonies, see Tomlinson (1999), Chapter 11.

11   On the way in which the Barcelona Games provided a forum for the renegotiation of the relationship between the Spanish state and the Catalan region/nationalists, see Garcia Ferrando and Hargreaves (1997) and Hargreaves (2000).

12   For accounts of the first Olympics, see Tomlinson (1999), Chapter 10, and Mandell (1976). For a brilliant account of De Coubertin and the formation of the IOC and the Games, see MacAloon (1981).

13   Spain's 13 gold successes included its soccer side, defeating Poland with a late winning goal; its men's archers; its Finn class solo sailor; its 2-person 470 sailing race, in both the men's and women's events; the 1,000 metre cycling time trial; women's field hockey and the men's 1500 metres.

14   Australia projected a medals target of 60, with 20 at gold. It almost made it, sparring with the United States for wins in the swimming, and also taking medals in first-time events such as water-polo, recently approved Olympic events such as women's beach volleyball, and areas of its traditional prowess such as women's hockey. The Australian attack on the medal table was a conscious strategy to prepare and enter more women than ever before.

15   See De Coubertin (2000): p. 297.

16   Cited in Tomlinson (1984).

17   On the Nazi Olympics, see Mandell (1971).

18   This 'reading' of the sequence is suggested in McGillivray (2000).

19   Riefenstahl's movie-making and aesthetic and cultural pedigree is reviewed in McFee and Tomlinson (1999).

20   Clive James, perhaps handing this view to the press corps beyond himself, recalled "the opening ceremony that had stunned the world and given Australia confidence in its new position as a mature nation" ("G'night Sydney", *The Independent Tuesday Review*, 3 October 2000: p. 1). He recognised, too, the appropriateness of the tongue-in-cheek, camp pitch and tone of the closing ceremony: "The opening ceremony brought Australia together. The closing ceremony might have tried to show a united world, but it would have mocked the very tragedies that have given Australia its unique life. Better to let your hair down and to camp it up" (p. 7). The complete text of Clive James at the Olympics is available on <www.aussieinlondon.com>.

21   The Olympic Arts festival is reviewed by Stevenson (1998). See too Stevenson (2000), Chapter 7: pp. 157–60.

22   Pilger (1990) talks of the "outrageous, yet sceptical 'larrikin' who rejects all convention and authority" (p. 96), as personified in the *Crocodile Dundee* movie of the 1980s. The word may have derived from the abbreviation Larry for Lawrence, common in Ireland, and is first documented in the 1860s in Melbourne. It equates to the term hoodlum, and refers to street rowdy (OED, 1971: p. 1573). It is interesting that contemporary usage in Australia gives an affectionate ring to the term. The larrikin is to be admired, is savvy and streetwise, not bogged down by deference or status inhibition.

23   John Slee was interviewed in Sydney, Australia, on July 26 2000.

24   Ron Wall was interviewed in Sydney, Australia, on August 10 2000. He was right. On 25 September Australia's Prime Minister, John Howard, appeared on the *Today Show*, Channel 9, interviewed by Steve Liebmann. "How good has this past week been? Does it get any better", Liebmann asked. "No I guess it doesn't. It has been a fantastic opportunity for us to show the world what a wonderful people we are. The Games have been a huge success because the whole of the Australian population's got behind them and it's the friendliness of volunteers, of Australians meeting overseas visitors, as much if not more than anything else that's really been the clinch. I mean our athletes have been superb, wonderful:

the organisation's been good; facilities are excellent; the weather's been fantastic. Turned a bit ordinary this morning but all of those things have come together. But the icing on the cake is the welcome mat that the average Australian has put out to people coming to this country and I've been bowled over by the number of visitors who've said to me — gee you are a friendly people. Now I've got to say that this is the nicest thing that can be said to a Prime Minister of a country that the people he's elected to be Prime Minister of are seen by the rest of the world as friendly and decent". This mix of folksiness, mixed metaphors and populist sentimentality shows a crafty politician trading on the readiness, and sometimes desperateness, to please of the Australian people.

25 Delvene Parkin was interviewed in Newcastle, New South Wales, on August 15 2000.

26 The bidding documents from the early 1990s make fascinating reading, and it cannot be denied that the Sydney vision was for the most part realised. But the waterways defied even SOCOG's determination. Volume 2 of the bid documents anticipated a connection between the movement of visitors and the Harbour waterways: "For Olympic Family and visitors, travel will be minimised by the city's brilliant Games plan. Most sports will be held at Sydney Olympic Park and Darling Harbour, 22 minutes apart by fast public transport and joined by the magic waters of Sydney Harbour" (*Sydney — Share the Spirit Volume 2: Olympic Information*: p. 2, 1992/3). Doesn't this sound like you'll be zooming up the park on the water? Or maybe not? Or maybe it's just meant to.

27 The IOC's adoption of the environment as one of its policy concerns, alongside sport and culture, is traced by Cantelon and Letters (2000). On the convergence of environmentalism with corporate interests, see Lenskyj (1998).

27 Moragas *et al.* (1995), Tomlinson (1996), and Puijk (2000) provide context, close analysis and interpretations of Olympic events and ceremonies, and in so doing offer corrective balances to the excessive hyperbole of IOC media claims.

29 See Duncan Mackay, "Athens warned it may yet lose Olympics", *The Guardian*, Saturday 21 October 2000: p. 12. For a later summary of this spat — in some ways bound up with the positioning of Pound and other candidates in the scramble to succeed IOC president, Samaranch — see Duncan Mackay, "Athens furious at officials' negative campaign", *The Guardian*, Saturday 4 November 2000: p. 8.

References

Cantelon, H. and Letters, M. (2000) 'The making of the IOC environmental policy as the third dimension of the Olympic movement', *International Review for the Sociology of Sport* Vol. 35, No. 3, pp. 294–308.

de Coubertin, P. (2000) *Pierre de Coubertin 1863–1937 — Olympism: Selected writings*. editing director Norbert Müller, Lausanne: International Olympic Committee.

Garcia Ferrando, M. and Hargreaves, J. (1997) 'Public opinion, national integration and national identity in Spain: the case of the Barcelona Olympic games', *Nations and Nationalism* Vol. 3, No. 1, pp. 65–87.

Hargreaves, J. (2000) *Freedom for Catalonia? Catalan nationalism, spanish identity and the Barcelona Olympic games*. Cambridge: Cambridge University Press.

Jennings, A. (1996) *The new lords of the rings: How to buy gold medals*. London: Simon & Schuster.

Jennings, A. and Sambrook, C. (2000) *The great Olympic swindle: When the world wanted its Games back*. London: Simon & Schuster.

Lenskyj, H. (1998) 'Sport and corporate environmentalism: The case of the Sydney 2000 Olympics', *International Review for the Sociology of Sport* Vol. 33, No. 4, pp. 341–54.

MacAloon, J. (1981) *This great symbol: Pierre de Coubertin and the origins of the modern Olympic Games*. Chicago: University of Chicago Press.

Mandell, R. (1971) *The Nazi Olympics*. London: Souvenir Press.

—————— (1976) *The first modern Olympics*. Berkeley: University of California Press.

McGillivray, G. (2000) '"Do not forget that you are mortal" — The suppression of theatricality in the staging of state spectacles', presentation at Performance and Spectacle, Annual Conference of the Australasian Drama Studies Association, Newcastle, New South Wales, 4—7 July.

McFee, G. and Tomlinson, A. (1999) 'Riefenstahl's *Olympia*: Ideology and aesthetics in the shaping of the aryan athletic body', *International Journal of the History of Sport* Vol. 16, No. 1, pp. 86–106.

Moragas, M., Rivenburgh, N.K. and Larson, J.F. (1995) *Television in the Olympics*. London: John Libbey.

OED (1971) *The compact edition of the Oxford English dictionary — Complete text reproduced micrographically* Volume 1 A–O. Oxford: Oxford University Press.

Pilger, J. (1990) *A secret country*. London: Vintage Books.

Puijk, R. (2000) 'A global media event? Coverage of the 1994 Lillehammer Olympic games', *International Review for the Sociology of Sport* Vol. 35, No. 3, pp. 309–30.

Simson, V. and Jennings, A. (1992) *The lords of the rings: Power, money and drugs in the modern Olympics.* London: Simon & Schuster.

Stevenson, D. (1998) 'The art of the Games: Leisure, tourism and the cultural Olympiad', in D. Rowe and G. Lawrence (eds), *Tourism, leisure, sport: Critical persectives.* Rydalmere/New South Wales,:Hodder Education.

Stevenson, D. (2000) *Art and organisation.* St Lucia/Queensland: University of Queensland Press.

Sugden, J. and Tomlinson, A. (1998) 'FIFA and the marketing of world football', in G. Lines, I. McDonald and U. Merkel (eds), *The production and consumption of sports sultures: Leisure, culture and commerce.* Eastbourne: Leisure Studies Association.

———— (2000) 'Sports media cultures at work: Issues of collusion and accountability', presented at Communication Beyond 2000: Technology, Industry and the Citizen in the Age of Globalization, 22nd. General Assembly and Annual Conference of the International Association for Media and Communication Research (Mass Media and Sport Working Group, Sesssion 1 — Media Coverage of Mega Sports Events), Mandarin Singapore, 17–20 July.

Tomlinson, A. (1984) 'De Coubertin and the Modern Olympic Games', in A. Tomlinson and G. Whannel (eds), *Five ring circus — Money, power and politics at the Olympic Games.* London: Pluto Press.

Tomlinson, A. (1996) 'Olympic spectacle: Opening ceremonies and some paradoxes of globalization', *Media Culture & Society* Vol. 18, No. 4, pp. 583–602.

Tomlinson, A. (1999) *The game's up: Essays in the cultural analysis of sport, leisure and popular culture.* Aldershot/UK, Ashgate Publishing.

Wallechinsky, D. (2000) *The complete book of the Olympics* (2000 Edition). South Yarra/Australia: Hardie Grant Books.

Young, C. (2000) 'A reply to Edward Said: One day in September', *International Review for the Sociology of Sport* Vol. 35, No. 3, pp. 398–401.

SPORT AS THEATRICAL EVENT

Rebecca Scollen
Queensland University of Technology, Brisbane

Introduction

This chapter will explain how sport can be understood as a theatrical event. Important to include in this context is the thought that sport and theatre are understood to be professional and to be live performances. A discussion of the common aspects of theatre and sport leads to a consideration of aesthetics considerations of sport and theatre, and a metaphorical analysis of both forms. Throughout, statistics gained from an audience reception study on the Davis Cup (Scollen, 2000a) will be presented in support of the claims under consideration.

With this in mind, some initial description of this research is helpful. The Davis Cup is an annual, international tennis competition, where a number of countries are represented by a national tennis team. In 1999, the semi-final was held in Brisbane (Australia) with Australia and Russia competing in this instance. One hundred spectators (1% of the total audience) participated in a telephone survey where they were asked to answer a number of questions with 'true' or 'false'. 50% of those surveyed were male, 50% female. Ages of respondents ranged from 14 to 80 years. All lived in the host city of Brisbane. Telephone numbers of respondents were accessed via the Davis Cup ticketing database. Names on the database were called at random and those who agreed to take part in the survey did so on a voluntary basis.

What do sport and theatre have in common?

Clearly, a large number of similarities between sport and theatre might be considered: what follows is a discussion of some of them.

First, both theatre and sport are simultaneously process and product (Lowe, 1977: p. 91). When spectators purchase tickets to attend a live theatre or sporting event, the entertainment becomes a product as it is a bought commodity. At the same time, it is a process because it unfolds in front of the viewer and can be altered from one performance to the next due to spectator interaction and the variables in live performance. And this double character of process and product is paralleled in sporting and theatrical performances by transience and permanence (Whiting and Masterson, 1974: p. 32). The presentation of live action ensures the product is an ephemeral one. Yet this transience can be rendered permanent by coaches' and directors' notations of play and by film recordings of live performance. These permanent products are not the same as the process presentation however, as they are interpreted by the coach, director or camera and thus do not necessarily represent the same performance that individual spectators have experienced.

Following on from this then, it is clear that sport like theatre is a temporal and spatial form (Lowe, 1977: p. 100). Performances take place in a designated space at an allocated time and are framed by these conditions. The space is often only used for this purpose, so becomes a special place. Examples of unique spaces include a tennis court (where only tennis is normally played), a theatre venue (where plays are normally performed), and a soccer field (where soccer is usually the only thing presented). For a lot of the time these spaces are empty, except when a performance is to take place or training/rehearsing for that performance occurs (Schechner, 1988: p. 11). Both theatre and sport are performed at allocated times made known to the public. It is rare that a performance of professional actors or athletes would take place spontaneously or without advertisement to induce spectators to attend.

Spectators are included into this realm and thus embody this unique space and time, and commonly disengage with 'real time' and everyday life (Lowe, 1977: p. 109). Time and space in performance are perceived differently to that of reality. A theatre performance may run for two hours with a 15 minute interval; this time is 'real time'. The performance contains 'plot time' or how long it takes for the fabula to unfold, such as three days in July in 1975, or 45 years of a man's life. In conceptual dramas with less focus on the fabula but with demonstrations of the human condition (as explained in the theatrical definition), 'contextual time' helps the spectators to make meaning from the performance. Contextual time may run the same length of time as 'real time' but is highly charged with significance. It can be interpreted differently by individual spectators depending upon their perceptions of the performance and their understanding of the rules and conventions that make that performance. For example, some audience members may interpret a theatrical performance as presenting an infinite time or a universal time, others may see it as a representation of the time spent when young. As the performance progresses spectators may interpret the contextual time differently. Time in these instances adds to the meaning of the activity presented and is understood to be important.

Sporting performance also contains contextual time. Although the match may run for two hours (real time), the contextual time may seem a lot longer or shorter. For example, the first 30 minutes may be interpreted by some spectators as dead time or wasted time as little action takes place on the field so this time seems very long. Alternatively, the final five minutes are seen as the most important few minutes in the history of sport and seem to fly by. Thus within the context of these performances, time for spectators is paralleled to real time but is highly charged with extraneous meanings that make the performances special and something other than ordinary life.

In most cases, the contextual time in sport and theatre is interrupted with real time for an interval or half time break. Here audiences return to real time and real situations such as waiting for the performance to return, purchasing drinks and talking with a friend. This is almost a limbo time where one cannot return fully to their real life (go to work or go home) but at the same time cannot be a part of the performance either.

Further, the rules and boundaries (including time and space) that sport and theatre work within create meaning for spectators. Lowe (1977: p. 111) states, "The confining nature of the field, court, or ring set by prescribed boundaries of play defines limits for the athlete as precise as the stage for the dramatic actor". At first the sporting and theatrical domains are seen as objects; however, once interaction with the domain and athlete or actor takes place, the space becomes charged with representational meaning (Barry, 1970 in Lowe,

1977: p. 97). The idea that the empty stage suddenly springs to life or the football oval awakens to become a place of 'blood, sweat and tears' derives from the knowledge that the ordinary 'public' space is now a meaningful performance arena.

All aspects of the domain take on additional meanings understood by a knowledgeable audience. This means audiences who are aware of the rules, standardised conventions and signs in performance can best understand and appreciate what is being presented to them. For example, the lines on the track and the lights on stage are signs as they stand for something other than themselves (O'Sullivan, *et al.*, 1994: p. 284) and they are a part of the rules and conventions that make the performance meaningful to spectators and performers.

The lines on a running track are simply lines when the track is not in use. However, once a race takes place convention states the lines define the lanes athletes must run in and if crossed will be disqualified from the race. The athletes run toward another line 100 metres away as fast as they can because this line signifies the end of the race and victory for the winner. So too, the lights used on a stage are there to illuminate the performance area, but to audiences aware of theatrical lighting conventions there is recognition of their capacity to signify time, locations, and moods. Performances will be more meaningful and thus more interesting to audiences who are aware of the rules, conventions, and signs in performance to those who are not.

Rules in sport and theatre establish frames for the player to perform in. Frames dictate what the performer has to do and what he or she is not allowed to do, and then within these frames there is freedom for self expression (Schechner, 1988: p. 13). Self expression allows the player to be creative and innovative and in turn stretches the boundaries defined by the 'do' and 'don't' frames. Rules (or conventions) can change over time due to the players input, reaction by spectators to the change, and the social/political climate framing the events. For example, at the 2000 Swimming Olympic Trials in Sydney, an Australian breaststroker created controversy by adding an extra little kick to his breaststroke kick. He had adhered to all of the 'do' rules but he had broken a 'don't' rule. However, he was not disqualified because one of the overarching rules of swimming is that if the judges, who walk along side the pool looking for cheats, do not see the offence then it is not considered to be one. The only reason his extra kick was noticed was due to an underwater camera recording.

This swimmer had practiced the extra kicking motion to ensure it could not be observed from above. In time this kick may be allowed as the rules bend to accommodate innovations such as this one. An obvious example of a past rule changing in breaststroke swimming, is the current allowance for swimmers to place their heads under the water when swimming.

Throughout the ages theatre performers and spectators have pushed to bend the rules of convention, resulting in a variety of styles of performance today. A well known example of change in the theatre is the rule that an actor must present his or her lines out to the audience. Before the late 1800s, actors faced the auditorium or perhaps stood in profile when delivering lines. It was considered against the rules to stand with your back to the audience. However, during the modern era of theatre (Brockett, 1991: p. 31), conventions were altered, due to the innovation and persistence of performers' self expression, and now it is common for actors to position themselves anywhere on the stage and to have their back to the audience when presenting lines.

Another shared characteristic might be identified in terms of contest/conflict. Like play which functions as "... a contest for something ..." (Huizinga, 1955: 13) and where there is always something at stake (Huizinga, 1955: p. 49), sport and theatre also have these characteristics. Schechner (1988: p. 16) believes "... dramas are completed actions involving interpersonal relationships usually pivoting on a conflict situation." Dramas according to Schechner are usually the basis of, or starting point of a theatrical event. The drama can be in the form of a written text, score, scenario, instruction, plan or map (Schechner, 1988: p. 16).

Both sport and theatre are based on a conflict situation and do involve interpersonal relationships. Sport comprises competition where humans (mostly) compete against each other and/ or against 'the elements' (time, weather, ocean, etc.) in an attempt to win. A conflict arises instantly in sport when one realises there can only be one winner and the pride and success of the team is at stake. Competitors play against each other to secure the prize. In Rugby Union Football players work together as a team and so must communicate verbally and non verbally with each other to be effective. They must cooperate and be supportive of each other to be a strong force to defeat the opposing team. Interpersonal relationships are developed between opposing teams as well, as competitors interact with each other physically and sometimes verbally and must shake hands and thank each other for playing at the end of the game. In theatre, interpersonal relationships are established and developed between the actors on stage and the actors and audience members through the sharing of ideas and emotions via dialogue and action.

In a theatrical performance there is also a contest presented. This may not be as obvious as placing a ball between the goal posts more often than the opposition, but it is a major part of the drama (Schechner, 1988: p. 16). Due to the social character of theatre, there is always an argument presented of a political/social/ethical nature. Contrasting points of view, most commonly represented by different characters, are put forward and contested. This is usually via the dialogue but can also be demonstrated via visual signs such as proxemics and kinesics, and symbolically through the use of colour, costume and sound.

In most cases the contest is played out before the audience and at the conclusion it is clear which perspective the playwright or production team wishes to win. *Dead White Males* produced by Sydney Theatre Company in 1996 essentially presents a debate between poststructuralist academia and classicists. The production was clear in its bias against poststructuralism and academics right down to dressing the academic in black (symbol of evil) against Shakespeare who was dressed in white (symbol of good).

Some theatre productions allow the audience to decide which perspective has won. Audiences can leave the theatre and think about the issues presented and decide which viewpoint is the most convincing. Other productions only present one 'way of life' or one side of an argument. This scenario can still be understood as a contest because the discourses which have not been represented are those of the 'other' and are significant in their absence. To present one world view is to infer there are others. An example of this style of theatrical performance can be seen in the production of *The Skin of Our Teeth* produced by Queensland Theatre Company in 2000. The myth of the triumph of man and the discourse of patriarchy was represented seemingly unchallenged. However, an oppositional reading may result in challenging this viewpoint, or a negotiated reading may acknowledge the viewpoint as being acceptable in the past but now it is understood to be out of date.

At the core of a theatrical event is a written text, score, scenario, instruction, plan or map (Schechner, 1988: p. 16). The written text, either scripted by playwright or group devised, is often at the core of theatrical performance. Even those performances that are improvised have some outline of actions to take place or a plan of how a scene will generally run. A sporting performance also has a plan at the centre of proceedings. Players are instructed before competing of the strategies they will apply and the overall 'plan of attack'. Just as in an improvised theatre piece, the sporting participants may have to alter their plan, however, a plan still exists at the basis of the event.

Yet a further shared characteristic could be identified in terms of outcome. The contention that athletes do not know the outcome of their performances like actors do is one which some would claim separates sport from theatre. However, as highlighted earlier, both sport and theatre are framed by rules and stem from a script or plan. Athletes like actors rehearse or train prior to performance so they are aware of how to execute the plan well. They know their personal strengths and weaknesses as a performer and try to become familiar with those of their team mates and opposition. Like actors this process aids athletes in their knowledge of the outcome of performance. The outcome of interviews (Scollen, 2000b) conducted with an Australian professional tennis player and an Australian professional long distance swimmer, has shown that both sportspeople believe they do know the outcome prior to their performance. This is based in their knowledge of the rules of play, their strengths and limitations as an athlete, the ability of their rivals, and past performances. Both acknowledge though that the live aspect of the competition and the unexpected variables that can occur can directly affect and alter the expected outcome.

It does seem that an actor would have a better chance of predicting the outcome of a theatre performance if the event is scripted than an athlete, however the live aspect of performance denies total surety. If an actor forgets his or her lines, or falls ill, or if a spectator becomes enraged and attacks an actor, the 'steadfast' medium of theatre could change abruptly and the outcome appear uncertain. If it is an improvised theatre piece, than knowledge of the outcome is as certain as it is for sportspeople. The actors are aware of their abilities, past performances, the general plan that is in place, so they should feel quite confident of the outcome. However, like the sportsperson they cannot know totally due to the variables in live performance and the absence of a written script.

In recent times, sportspeople have been reprimanded for taking bribes, informing the opposition of their game plans and even deliberately losing games. These cases demonstrate the athletes are very aware of the outcome of a match as they have orchestrated it often without the rest of the team realising. Although this is seen as cheating the performance is still seen as sport.

This 'match fixing' steers the argument into the world of professional wrestling, such as the World Wrestling Federation (Lusetich, 2000). Wrestlers compete against each other to determine the winner, but at the same time are working with each other to complete manoeuvres. Rather than ensure the rules are upheld in a wrestling bout and act as a disinterested third party, the referee works with the wrestlers by reprimanding them and separating them so he can help them prepare for specific moves. The referee takes instruction from the 'director' of the match who sits in the auditorium throughout the bout so he can inform the wrestlers which manoeuvres to execute at what times, and to let them know who is to be the winner based on the director's cues.

This sport is definitely staged and wrestlers are cooperating with each other to perform an outcome determined by the director of the performance. This appears to be far more like theatre than sport. However, professional wrestling also contains all of the aspects of sport as outlined in the definitions section of this chapter. One could claim professional wrestling is the best example of sport as theatrical event.

The point is the issue of whether one knows the outcome of a performance or not should not be the factor which divides sport and theatre, and which proves sport is not a theatrical event. As demonstrated, actors in scripted theatre performances should know the outcome of the performance but this can change due to the nature of live events. The sportsperson anticipates the outcome based on a series of factors just as the actor in an improvised theatre performance does. The professional wrestler knows the outcome of the bout prior to performance but this can change if the director believes it is not entertaining enough for the audience. All this proves is that sport and theatre as forms of cultural expression and entertainment consist of many genres or styles of performance. Actors and athletes in some of these genres have prior knowledge of outcomes, and others do not.

Additionally, sport and theatre performances contain narrative (Fotheringham, 1992) which consists of:

> ... the devices, strategies and conventions governing the organisation of
> a story (fictional and factual) into sequence ... Narrative can be

subdivided ... into plot and narration. Plot is the irreducible substance of a story while narration is the way that substance is related. (O'Sullivan *et al.*, 1994: pp. 194–195)

This means that both sport and theatre are structured and consist of a number of elements in sequence which creates meaning. The plot or story can either be fictional or factual so one can state that the actions on the football field (A passes the ball to B, who sidesteps away from C to score a try) are a part of a story that can be interpreted by the spectator. Narration is the way that story is told. This is particularly relevant to sport where most matches are retold by a commentator while the performance is occurring. The structure of sport and theatre is the same as both have a beginning, a middle and an end. Even if the players do not know what the outcome will be (as mentioned earlier) in terms of who wins or loses, or how popular the performance will be to an audience, they do know that the performance will end.

"Every analysis [of narrative] revolves around the notion of an obstacle ..." (Pavis, 1998: p. 232). As earlier in this chapter, both theatre and sport contain obstacles that the performers must try to negotiate or overcome. Spectators of theatrical or sporting performances interpret the actions of performers and the outcome of performance in terms of the barriers presented.

Frayssinet (in Lowe, 1977: p. 109) refers to sport like theatre as o*euvre*, a French term used to identify the product of artistic activity. Like an artistic product, sport presents a representation of reality and thus creates an illusion, while concurrently is a thing of the real world. This duality focuses on the space-time separation that distinguishes art from real life (Lowe, 1977: p. 109). As already established, sporting performance takes place in specific spaces dedicated for that purpose. Spectators must travel to this space to be a part of the event. Once within the space they are a part of the performance and must adhere to the rules and practices that it dictates. As Schechner (1988: p. 11) puts the point:

Special rules exist, are formulated, and persist because these activities are something apart from everyday life. A special world is created where people can make the rules, rearrange time, assign value to things, and work for pleasure.

Although many of these rules may stem from the values of real life, the frame of performance separates spectators from reality and includes them in the realm of the *oeuvre*.

Time as already discussed, is understood differently in performance to that of 'real' time. It holds additional meanings which are directly related to the performance and one's interpretation of that performance. Often spectators can become oblivious to real time when fully engaged with the performance. Concurrently, sport and theatre are confined by real time as performances are held at specific times and run for a particular duration of time, and so this enables sport and theatre to be something of the real world while creating an illusion.

The emotion performance evokes is derived from the illusion created in the space. Feelings of tension, excitement, fear, empathy or happiness are all derived from the story that unfolds before the viewer. To those who enter into the event they willingly suspend everyday life and so engage with the illusion presented. At times, performances may appear tragic or miraculous, but this does not mean that the tragedy or miracle presented is a real life tragedy or miracle. A match may have a "serious or sombre character with an unhappy ending" (Delbridge, 1991: p. 1852) which is a tragedy by dramatic standards, however, for those looking in from the everyday it is hardly a disaster because it has had no direct affect on reality.

Some would argue that sport is real life because the players are real people who are not pretending to be something other than themselves. They are employed to compete and to play their very best. Theatre actors are real people who are employed to perform in a dedicated space too and yet theatre is understood to be a representation of reality. For participants, sporting or theatrical performance is something of the real world to them as it is what they do to financially survive. For spectators however, it is a representation of reality due to the nature of performance and the understanding that players are performing roles. The contention here is that athletes do perform roles and are presenting something other than themselves when performing.

One role many athletes perform is the role of sports hero. The hero is an idol and an icon who belongs to the time of heroes. The time of heroes according to Archetti (1999: p. 96):

> ... represents in the mind of the adoring public a glorious dream-like time
> during which the daily mediocrity of normal life is suddenly transcended

> ... We need sports heroes because they give us relief from our
> monotonous daily life through their magical performances.

Looking more closely at the world of professional wrestling, there are many
facets of the performance that are aligned with theatre. Each wrestler takes on
a character, presenting a specific viewpoint, and speaks and acts accordingly. The
manner in which he or she speaks and the ideology espoused is not necessarily
reflective of the wrestler outside the ring. Each wrestler wears a costume and
performs for the crowd of spectators looking on. It is not only professional
wrestling that does this but all sports. All sportspeople wear a costume, that is,
something other than what they wear in real life. This can be a uniform,
protective clothing or performance enhancing apparel.

Like the actor or professional wrestler who plays a character, the sportsperson
performs in the role of skilled athlete but also as a role model for others in
society. The fact that they enter a performance space which is understood to be
outside of real life, and perform for others (as well as themselves) within the
framework established for the particular event, immediately acknowledges they
are to be read as a sign (Fischer-Lichte, 1992). In the 1999 Davis Cup Semi-Final
reception study, 53% of those surveyed thought that, once players step onto the
court, they are performing a role like an actor might (Scollen, 2000a). Just over
half of the respondents can see that the athlete when playing is something other
than him or herself. A sportsman can enter the space not as Mark Philippoussis
but as an elite tennis player for example. He then performs a series of actions
utilising the skills required of that activity and in some cases takes on specific
characteristics to impress the audience or to distract his opposition. Players such
as John McEnroe who deliberately become abusive and argumentative whenever
they are losing a point to distract the opposition, demonstrate the actor-like
qualities of sportspeople. To be able to understand that the athlete is representing
something other than him or herself, one needs to clearly understand the notion
of sport as something other than real life.

Although only 53% said sportspeople performed roles like actors do, 84% of
the total number of respondents stated they are disappointed if a player they
admire behaves in an inappropriate manner on or off the court (Scollen, 2000a).
This high percentage supports the above claim that sportspeople are seen to be
role models in society. Many spectators expect them to play and act in specific

ways that are considered suitable in the culture with which they are presented. A number of those who state they are disappointed by poor behaviour or attitude expect the player to be a good role model even when not playing. This percentage of people appear to not see the public, sporting performance as separate to the player's personal, everyday life. One could contend the 47% of respondents who do not believe an athlete performs a role like an actor does consists of these spectators, because they expect the sportsperson to be a good role model and good person at all times.

This unrealistically high expectation and interest in sportspeople's personal lives demonstrates that some spectators believe they are exactly like their sporting persona. This is reminiscent of theatre audiences who believe they know actors based on their stage persona. When treated this way the performers of theatre and sport are understood to be celebrities, and are observed by a section of the community to see what it is they do, what they wear, what they eat and what they think about life.

Steinbeck's three layers of significance model (Martin and Sauter, 1995: p. 56), is useful for understanding the different ways athletes and actors are perceived by audiences. Steinbeck explains to understand a performance phenomenologically one must identify the layer of real significance, the layer of intentional significance, and the layer of alleged significance. To understand the roles of athletes and actors according to Steinbeck's model one must understand them in relation to these three layers, as follows. Firstly, they are perceived as real human beings and as performers. This is the layer of real significance where the audience knows they are people working as an athlete or as an actor. Secondly, they are understood in relation to the fiction or the context surrounding the performance which means they are perceived as characters or role models and this is the layer of intentional significance. Thirdly, the layer of alleged significance sees audiences interpret the performer in relation to his or her symbolic function. For example, the marathon runner may represent courage, determination, and strength as he or she runs very long distance races in a relatively short period of time. An actor in the context of a performance may represent honesty, freedom, and faithfulness or greed, jealousy, and hatred, depending upon the character he or she plays and the position they fulfil within the drama.

Theatre and sport are seen as non-productive activities (Schechner, 1988: p. 11) because they do not produce tangible objects or goods that people need to consume unlike the retail, agricultural and pharmaceutical industries. It is true one can purchase objects derived from performance including specific merchandise like clothing, programs, key rings and toys, however, these are not produced by the performance itself. Sport and theatre do produce an important social service for the public instead. Both forms comment on society, reflect cultures, are outlets for encouraging imagination and for relieving stress. A representative of the World Wrestling Federation states, "Fans love to get release from everyday stress. Let us fight their battles for them — live it out vicariously through us, and I think a lot of people do" (Lusetich 2000: p. 22). Schechner (1988: p. 11) also claims the forms allow society to fantasise. He believes that as theatre and sport stand apart from ordinary life they give an outlet for people to idealise it because in these activities (sport and theatre) people play by the rules (unlike in real life) and to criticise ordinary life by wondering why it cannot be a game too? "Sport has a unique power of fascinating and setting standards for human excellence across boundaries that usually divide: boundaries of cultural traditions, class, sex and age" (Klausen, 1999: p. 174).

In the 1999 Davis Cup survey, 90% of respondents believed that a tennis match teaches or reinforces society's norms or values. Here spectators see the players and their actions reinforcing the social standards of the culture. As McPherson *et al.* (1989: p. 51) note, "Teachers and coaches claim that ideal character and moral traits can be learned by those who participate in sport" [including spectators]. Examples of these traits include sportsmanship, honesty, courage, cooperation and achievement. This sense that sport teaches ethical and moral virtues stems from the performances of players during the event and the ideals they represent through their actions and reactions.

Foster (1988) urges that an event is to be viewed as a reflection of, or comment on, or alternative to, the culture it is presented in. It is a place for examining the concepts of culture. Theatre and sport are cultural events. It has been illustrated that sport reflects and reinforces culture and the social nature of theatre ensures it does the same. Both help spectators of performances and spectators at large (members of society) to analyse and understand the ways culture operates. Particularly in a capitalist society which at least western culture conforms, achievement is paramount to success and happiness. Sport is the epitome of this ideal as spectators observe how to win and how to lose, and what behaviour and thoughts are rewarded and which are punished. Theatre too upholds these structures as at its core is contest and debate as in sport. This ensures audiences observe how characters behave and think, act and react in certain situations to discover which aspects are rewarded and punished, and which ideals are seen to win or lose. McPherson *et al.* (1989: p. 291) claim, "More and more the contests have grown beyond simple games or leisure time diversions. They are intended to be important episodes in the spectators' lives and identities."

Just as 'play' is understood to be a non-productive past time like sport and theatre it also contains some other aspects these two forms have in common. Both are characterised by over motivation which, according to Piaget, is like "… drawing figures with a broom while sweeping a floor" (Calhoun, 1987: p. 44). This means as humans we embellish practices and make a task more difficult and often more time consuming for our enjoyment. Examples for this include athletes jumping a series of hurdles to arrive at the finishing line when they could have run a 100 metre sprint without the added burden of obstacles; a diver who achieves a number of twists, turns and somersaults before he reaches the water rather than simply jumping in; the actor who embellishes her lines with paralinguistic signs and nonverbal gestures rather than stating the words denotatively; and the desire to perform an allegory in a 3 hour performance of *Macbeth* rather than simply informing people in a brief statement that greed and naked ambition are wrong and will be punished.

According to Schechner (1988: p. 9), all objects in theatre and sport have a market value much less than the value assigned to them in the context of the activity. Returning to our running race, the finishing line which all athletes aspire to reach first, is just a line. It holds no practical use (tool), it has no monetary value (jewellery), and it is not a rare artefact (archaeological find) (Schechner, 1988: p. 9) and yet it is the most important object in the world to those involved in the activity; athlete and spectator alike. In a theatre performance an actor may finally attain the sword of Excalibur and so now possesses the power and authority of a king. Both he and the audience place great importance upon the sword as the quest for it has been the focus for the whole activity, yet in reality the sword probably cost $5 to make by the design department.

Throughout this chapter the spectator is constantly referred to when discussing sport as a theatrical event. Addressing the nature of spectatorship, Keenan (in Lowe, 1977: p. 103) states, "The drama is an art form developed with spectators in mind. It is perhaps in the drama that sport reaches its closest affinity with art as process". This emphasis is because the presence of the spectator and his or her reactions at the event complete the process of performance in theatre (Bennett, 1990) and sport (Lowe, 1977). The theory that theatre occurs when A represents X while S looks on (Fischer-Lichte, 1992: p. 13) includes the spectator (S) as an essential part of theatrical performance. One could soundly argue that the spectator does more than simply witness the performance, but instead actively contributes to it by his or her presence. In this way, audiences can affect the performer and his or her performance via their applause, cheers, comments, and physiological actions such as yawns and general restlessness. 52% of those surveyed in the Davis Cup audience study (Scollen, 2000a) believe that as an individual spectator their presence affects the players, and another 42% believe that *as part of a crowd* of spectators they have an affect on the players' performance.

As Maheu asserts:

> In the theater [*sic*] the audience involves itself in the drama being enacted before it, thus becoming, after a fashion, actor as well as spectator, and similarly in the stadium, an intense empathy develops between spectators and performers. (Lowe, 1977: p. 103)

Furthermore, 98% of respondents state the players appreciate spectators cheering and applauding their performances and so feel that the performer expects the spectator to play an active role. 76% of respondents claim that they become emotionally involved when watching a live tennis match, and 89% feel tense when the match is at a critical point. The spectator empathises with the plight of the performer whether in joyous or critical moments of performance. McPherson *et al* (1989: p. 11) supports this claim by stating that spectators experience different mood states while consuming a sport event. Kovich goes further by referring to research in electromyography which has shown that:

> ... observers mimic in a minute way the movement patterns of the performer, thus inducing a form of restrained participation. As the performer feels the art he is creating, so can a perceptive spectator feel this same quality, though not to the same extent. (Lowe, 1977: p. 92)

According to Keenan (Lowe, 1977: p. 103), audiences of sporting and theatrical performances behave similarly as they acknowledge appreciation of skilful performance through applause and their disapproval of poor performance through booing, calling out, or leaving the venue. 100% of those surveyed in the Davis Cup study (Scollen, 2000a) feel comfortable cheering, applauding and calling out at a sporting event. Theatre and sports spectators arrive at perform-ance venues in a similar attitude as they expect to be entertained and to take pleasure in the live experience (Keenan in Lowe, 1977: p. 103). 100% of re-spondents believe a tennis match can be entertaining and engaging (Scollen, 2000a). Like theatre audiences, sports spectators attend live matches to see a high standard of play (95%) and to feel they are a part of the event (85%).

Spectators of sports events could be seen as more active than theatre audiences as fans "… wear team colours or masquerade (paint faces, thematic costumes), cheer and boo, [and] post banners and signs in stadiums …" (McPherson *et al.*, 1989: p. 287). However, this cult behaviour can appear in the theatre at pro-ductions that overtly encourage audiences to participate in performances and attract fans who attend many times to see the same production. For example, productions such as *The Rocky Horror Picture Show* stage musical last per-formed in Australia in 1996, do attract very active audience members. Yet not all sports spectators behave in such dynamic ways, just as many theatre audience members do not. Observation of the Davis Cup audience in 1999, discovered that of the 10 000 people in attendance approximately 10% would fall into the fan category and display fan behaviour as characterised by McPherson *et al.* above.

Aesthetics of sport and theatre

Lowe (1977: pp. 96–98) describes sport as a performing art of the purest kind. This claim derives from Barry's (1970) model which distinguishes four cases of pure and impure art which constitute the artistic conditions of dramatic production. These are:

1. Pure elements in representational relational patterns.
2. Elements seen as representational in representational relational patterns.
3. Pure elements in pure relational patterns.
4. Elements seen as representational in pure relational patterns.

Pure in this context refers to 'as found in nature' and representational means 'as found in art'. Lowe believes sport satisfies two of the four cases (1 and 3), with number three labelled by Barry as the "purest pure form of art" (Lowe, 1977: p. 98). Sport contains pure elements in the form of athletes who are men or women of nature. They perform in pure relational patterns which are the objects that make the sporting domain. Once interaction with the objects takes place they become patterns due to the symbolism ascribed to them. For example, the lines on a soccer field are not just painted lines but are the kick-off line and goalie's box and so the shapes take on a rule bounded pattern. "This pattern becomes a relational pattern due to the prescriptions called sport" (Lowe, 1977: p. 97).

In Lowe's second case, sport can be understood as pure elements (athletes) in representational relational patterns (sport-quasi social activity). The difference here is that the sporting domain and the activity that takes place within it are seen as representational of society's ethical and moral code. The rules that bind the athletes in sport and the ways in which they are rewarded or punished for following or ignoring rules are steeped in society's values.

According to the suggestion made earlier utilising the Steinbeck model, the athlete is understood as something more than simply man/woman or athlete, so one contends that the number of cases prescribed by Barry be extended to three to include: elements seen as representational in representational relational patterns. This means that the athletes are seen as something other than pure natural objects and it acknowledges they perform another role within the sporting and cultural domain.

One important issue here concerns beauty: "Originally the term aesthetics as the Greeks defined it meant anything that had to do with perception by the senses" (Lowe, 1977: p. 3). Today a standard or layman's understanding of aesthetics refers to "the science which deduces from nature and taste the rules and principles of art and pertains to the sense of the beautiful" (Delbridge, 1991: p. 26). Within both accounts, the reference for measuring aesthetic quality is the human form (Lowe, 1977: p. 4). This means that as humans we perceive beauty via our senses and understand beauty in relation to ourselves. As Dobzhansky puts it:

> Let it be clear at the outset that the beauty of nature refers to human feelings about certain natural objects, not to these objects themselves. It

is man who is enthralled by the grandeur of a snow-clad mountain range.
(Lowe, 1977 p. 2)

It is not that the mountain range intends to be beautiful, however, humans may
perceive it in this way due to its great size, power, and steadfastness compared
to the human form. More so, humans are taught what is beautiful as children by
the comments made and the reactions of those around them. Lowe (1977: p. 2)
writes, "We ascribe a consciousness of beauty to those things that we are
culturally indoctrinated to recognize as beautiful."

The aesthetic value of sport is seen in the qualities of "… swiftness, grace,
fluency, rhythm, and perceived vitality" all of which constitute beauty according
to Elliott (in Whiting and Masterson, 1974: p. 112). Lowe (1977: p. 17) adds
other qualities to this list including "… form, balance, tension, poise, variation
and mood." For Lowe (1977: p. 17), these are the specific conditions under
which the perception of the body, both in repose and while in movement, is
appreciated for its intrinsic beauty. These conditions are contingent upon prior
learning and the acquisition of sensitivity by the spectator of sport and theatre.
In a similar vein, 80% of respondents in the Davis Cup survey stated they like
to watch how the players use their bodies to perform on court (Scollen, 2000a).

Lowe goes further to espouse that it is through the beauty of movement that
humans can communicate values of beauty:

By the analysis of the media of movement, a better understanding of
man, his culture, his ideas, and his values can be grasped. Drama, dance,
and sport represent the media of movement which serve this stated
purpose of communication for better understanding. (Lowe, 1977: p. 18)

It is interesting to note that our heroes from popular culture tend to be athletic
and present to society 'the body ideal' (Lowe, 1977). Heroes such as Superman,
Wonder Woman, and Hercules are all seen as powerful, beautiful superhumans
whose bodies represent strength, fitness, sensuality and triumph. Novak urges
"… athletes become [heroic] icons representing mastery over mortality"
(Klausen, 1999: p. 196). Some theorists such as Reid (in Lowe, 1977: p. 112) and
Weiss (in Lowe, 1977: p. 11) argue that athletes do not intend to be beautiful or

to create beauty thus sport cannot be considered artistic or of aesthetic value. Thus, Elliott believes:

> There is no reason why in striving for victory in sport human beings should create or give rise to beauty, any more than that Nature should be beautiful, and we feel very much the same in wonder and gratitude in both cases. (Whiting and Masterson, 1974: p. 112)

Hence if nature does not intend to be beautiful and yet can be perceived aesthetically then nonintentional beauty in sport should be understood the same way.

Although sportspeople may not intend to produce beauty they are able to recognise it and understand it in performance. A famous golfer said:

> What other people may find in poetry or art museums, I find in the flight of a good drive — the white ball sailing up into that blue sky, growing smaller and smaller, then suddenly reaching its apex, curving, falling and finally dropping to the turf to roll some more, just the way I planned it. (Lowe, 1977: p. 21)

Here it is implied that beauty is connected to skill or the successful execution of an action. The ball sailing through the air and landing is not the only reason why a good drive is seen as beautiful, but rather it has moved and landed just as the golfer wished it to. Similarly, 75% of those surveyed in the Davis Cup audience study believe there is beauty in the skilful movements and accurate shots of the players.

Alternatively, there are sportspeople who do think about the way their performance looks to spectators and thus it appears they could be intending to create beauty. An example of this is shown in the comments by Australian tennis player Lleyton Hewitt after a match. Here he talks about when he lunged and tumbled while executing a backhand volley to win a point:

> It looked good, didn't it? I feel fine diving. I did a lot of dives at Wimbledon last year, as well. It's a bit of flair and that's the way I play the game. (Miles, 2000: p. 32)

Skill is a further factor here: spectators must have some understanding of aesthetic qualities to recognise the extreme difficulty of playing, by actor and athlete, and to fully appreciate the artistry of performance (Keenan in Lowe, 1977: p. 20). Keller continues this argument by urging that spectators' "aesthetic gratification occurs through real spontaneous identification with the players" (Whiting and Masterson, 1974: p. 98). This identification comes from an awareness of the skill that is required to perform well. In Keller's example, spectators appreciate the aesthetic value that comes from perfectly played football, as they have played it themselves and have a sound knowledge of the game and strategy. Some more results from the Davis Cup audience study (Scollen, 2000a) suggest similar conclusions, since 100% of those surveyed stated they had an understanding of the rules of tennis and 79% claimed they play tennis themselves either socially or in competition.

For Rivera (in Lowe, 1977: pp. 155–156), the problems imposed on athletes by the rules and ethics of the event give rise to displays of human skill coupled with courage, power, strength and effort in an attempt to problem solve. These qualities can manifest themselves as beauty and the sublime. Theatre too confines the actor and the character with rules, boundaries and situations and thus similar demonstrations of human endurance and effort emerge to create an aesthetic effect. Hein (in Lowe, 1977: p. 23) similarly claims that pleasure is derived from conquest in play and the aesthetic comes from this problem solving.

If the boundaries of the self of both actor and athlete are overcome, and thus typical skill or mental attitude is surpassed the spectator can witness the sublime. Here the viewers see something infinitely greater than themselves. As Elliott suggests, "In a marathon, it is not that the athlete conquers the distance, but that he conquers everything in himself which strives to prevent him from accomplishing his end" (Whiting and Masterson, 1974: p. 114). Such an instance can be described as a virtuoso performance for both actor and athlete (Lowe, 1977: p. 107). Aesthetic creativity shows itself when the actor or athlete sets standards of human action and movement outside the physical realm of a majority of the population (Lowe, 1977: p. 126), and excels within the confines imposed upon him or her in performance (Lowe, 1977: p. 111).

Moreover, discussion on tragedy in performance sees Elliott (in Whiting and Masterson, 1974) urge that the tragedy in sport is more like real life tragedy than that of theatre which is enacted tragedy. Elliott believes in theatre there is "...

nothing at stake as actors imitate an action which might have happened or could happen, and concerns us (spectators) only in an extremely general and uncertain way" (in Whiting and Masterson, 1974: p. 110). However, the tragedy in sport is similar to the enacted tragedy of theatre, as sport is a game already shown to be something other than 'real life'. To lose the game does not affect one's life, salary or health. Players are paid regardless of whether they win or lose. At the end of a sporting performance spectators and players alike leave the playing field and return to their everyday lives. If an actor or athlete was to die or to become seriously injured when performing this could be seen as a tragedy but would hardly be viewed as an aesthetic moment.

Elliott claims that the "... tragic, triumphant and menacing in sport only become aesthetically significant when they are perceived from a disinterested attitude" (Whiting and Masterson, 1974: p. 110). By "disinterested", he means when one is unbiased by personal involvement or advantage (Delbridge, 1991: p. 506). Elliott believes very few sporting spectators view a match in this way and, if they do, he questions whether aesthetes enjoy the dramatic action of the outcome which means nothing to them. Later, however, Elliott (Whiting and Masterson, 1974: p. 111) admits that in certain moments of performance, 'interested' spectators can experience beauty and become fascinated by an aesthetic object and not consider the context of winning or losing in that moment. Thus interested spectators can appreciate aesthetic moments in performance.

The notion of the disinterested spectator appears to derive from the belief that to understand or perceive something it must be done through our thoughts stemmed from the mind, rather than our bodies and our sensory reactions. This belief is strongly influenced by the body-mind dualism theory (Lowe, 1977: p. 107). This idea tends to run contrary to the understanding of aesthetics offered earlier in this section. Here aesthetics involved the identification and experiencing of beauty and the sublime through the senses and as related to the human form. Thus it seems clear that someone who reacts to impulses sent to him/her via performance can have an aesthetic reaction regardless of whether he/she is an interested or disinterested spectator. As long as a movement or an action is perceived aesthetically via senses, the person can experience an aesthetic moment. Concedingly, it is true the more active, knowledgeable audience member who looks beyond the dramatic action to more complex signs will likely appreciate the skill and cleverness of the performance and identify aesthetic qualities more readily than the novice. In the vein, Elliott (in Whiting and Masterson, 1974: p. 110) also offers the idea that sport is a theatrical event by referring to the 'dramatic action' in a sporting performance.

Sport and theatre as metaphor

As Lowe (1977: p. 102) asserts, "... although sport may or may not be seen as a drama, depending on one's particular perspective, many people experience it as though it were". Here, referring to an experiential reality here is not to deny the existence of an objective reality merely that our understanding of reality is through experience (Lakoff and Johnson, 1980). When humans are faced with a new situation they cognitively compare it to past life experiences. In this way their previous experiences are metaphors for understanding new experiences. "Metaphors provide an understanding of one kind of experience in terms of another kind of experience" (Lakoff and Johnson, 1980: p. 154).

Lakoff and Johnson argue that when we use a linguistic metaphor, it indicates that there is an underlying conceptual metaphor in operation. If this idea were accepted, we can see that Lakoff and Johnson are using linguistic metaphors as metaphors for our cognitive patterns of understanding. Indeed, scientific theorems and hypotheses are all metaphors which attempt to explain the world or "reality". As Lakoff and Johnson (1980: p. 3) say:

> ... metaphor is pervasive in everyday life, not just in language but in thought and action. Our ordinary conceptual system, in terms of which we both think and act, is fundamentally metaphorical in nature ... Our concepts structure what we perceive, how we get around in the world, and how we relate to other people. Our conceptual system thus plays a central role in defining our everyday realities.

An example of a linguistic metaphor that serves to indicate an underlying conceptual metaphor, is the phrase "Time is Money". One can say "I don't have the time to give you" just as one might say "I don't have the money to give you". Similarly "I can't *spare* the time", "That *cost* me a lot of time", "I've been *saving* time" and "I *spent* a lot of time on that", all demonstrate that we conceptualise time and money in a similar way. This common understanding is as a valuable resource, to be traded, saved and managed (Lakoff and Johnson, 1980).

So, too, the ways sport and theatre are referred to linguistically identify an underlying conceptual metaphor that binds the two entities as one. That is our experiences of one can be seen as similar to our experiences of the other via the ways we speak about both forms. To illustrate, consider some examples from the media. For example, a member of the Australian public wrote a letter to a national newspaper stating, "Prime Minister to launch new arts direction targetting football loving males. Blimey, I thought getting the ball and scoring a goal was an art" (Bertagnolio, 2000: p. 14). Another brief example from the news media is as follows: "It's been said that football is the theatre of the masses. If that's the case the coaches and players are probably the actors …" (Sheedy, 2000: p. 52). Another comment comes from John Newcombe, Australian Davis Cup Team Captain, who spoke to the media after the Australian team defeated France in the finals, and demonstrates that even sportspeople can see the great similarities between sport and theatre, as here, with the players experienced their sporting performance as a theatrical one.

> Instead of … [the French spectators] being a negative force against us, we were trying to think of it as theatre. We were part of the play. It was fantastic to be out there in front of that noise. (Anonymous, 1999: p. 40)

The author of the following comment, as part of a larger article, is relying on her sporting readership to have an understanding of, and past experience of theatrical performance, otherwise this comment would not make sense. One must understand the concepts of leading ladies, soap opera, melodrama, conflict, characters, and what they mean in theatrical terms to appreciate the point the author is making about women's tennis. To use this terminology in a tennis magazine as if it is sporting terminology, shows the interchangeability of experience of both forms. Thus the underlying conceptual metaphor is sport is theatre:

> The WTA tour has attractive leading ladies, great performances, conflict aplenty, and a soap opera's worth of melodrama. No wonder it's such a

huge hit. … The current cast of characters in women's tennis is reflective
of the times we're living in. (Angle, 2000 p. 50)

Of course, it can operate in the other direction where sport is referred to in one's
discussion of theatre. Thus, an Australian actor who hopes that the popularity of
Rugby League football and the loyalty of its spectators can carry across to theatre
in the future, demonstrates how sporting performance is held as the ideal and is
something that theatre makers should aspire to:

They had 40,000 people there the other night for State of Origin, sitting
there in the rain. I see that and I dream of the day when 40,000 people
in Brisbane will sit out in the rain to watch a theatre production.
(Whiting, 2000: p. 86)

As this comment shows, he understands theatre and sport in a similar way since
he uses a sporting example when talking about theatre. He could have referred
to the large number of people who shop at supermarkets as his example for the
need for greater theatre attendance, however, he has not because he equates the
experience of theatre with the experience of sport.

As final examples of sport and theatre as metaphor, the following comments
highlight the belief that both forms can induce emotion in large audiences via
great skilled performances, and the skills required of performers in theatre and
sport are the same:

The tenor's high C or the sopranic trill can induce an emotion in a large
audience not essentially different from that provided by a perfectly
executed football goal or a brilliant clinching shot in tennis.
(Fotheringham, 1992: p. 3)

And, in the same way, the opera singer Joan Sutherland was described "as a vocal
athlete" (Fotheringham, 1992: p. 3).

Conclusion

This chapter has argued that sport can be understood as a theatrical event. Consideration of the commonalities of sport and theatre, the ways in which both forms are comprehended metaphorically, and the identification of the aesthetic in both, serves to clearly demonstrate that sport can usefully be conceived as a theatrical event. The Davis Cup audience study has statistically supported the theoretical underpinnings of the chapter and serves to indicate what a percentage of sporting spectators experience in performance. No theory of sporting and theatrical forms is offered here; rather, an exploratory review of the relevance of performance theory and associated approaches for thinking about the theoretical dimensions of sports practices and events.

References

Angle, R. (2000) 'The bold and the beautiful', *Australian Tennis Magazine*, March: pp. 50–55.

Anonymous (1999) 'Scud leads Aussies to cup win', *The Chronicle*, Dec. 7: p. 40.

Archetti, E. P. (1999) 'The spectacle of heroic masculinity', in A. M. Klausen (ed) *Olympic Games as performance and public event: The case of the XVII Winter Olympic Games in Norway*. New York: Berghahn Books.

Bertagnolio, R. (2000) 'Firstbyte', *The Australian*, June 22: p. 14.

Bennett, S. (1990) *Theatre audiences: A theory of production and reception*. London: Routledge.

Brockett, O. (1991) *History of the theatre* (6th Ed.). Boston: Allyn and Bacon.

Calhoun, D.W. (1987) *Sport, culture and personality* (2nd Ed.). Champaign, IL: Human Kinetics.

Coghlan, S. (2000) "Sheedy to face AFL tribunal", *The Australian*, June 21st: p. 24.

Delbridge, A. (1991) *The Macquarie dictionary* (2nd Ed). NSW: Macquarie Library Pty. Ltd.

Fischer-Lichte, E. (1992) *Semiotics of theatre*. Bloomington: Indiana University Press.

Foster, S. (1988) *Event arts and art events*. Michigan: UMI.

Fotheringham, R. (1992) *Sport in australian drama*. Cambridge: Cambridge University Press.

Helbo, A., Johansen, J., Pavis, P., and Ubersfeld, A. (1987) *Approaching theatre*. Bloomington: Indiana University Press.

Huizinga, J. (1955) *Homo ludens*. Boston: The Beacon Press.

Klausen, A. (ed.) (1999) *Olympic Games as performance and public event*. New York: Berghahn Books.

Lakoff, G. and Johnson, M. (1980) *Metaphors we live by*. Chicago: University of Chicago Press.

Lusetich, R. (2000) 'Play TV', *The Australian Magazine*, April 29th: pp. 18–25.

Lowe, B. (1977) *The beauty of sport*. New Jersey: Prentice-Hall Inc.

Martin, J. and Sauter, W. (1995) *Understanding theatre: Performance analysis in theory and practice*. Stockholm: Almqvist & Wiksell International.

McPherson, B., Curtis, J., and Loy, J. (1989) *The social significance of sport: An introduction to the sociology of sport*. Champaign, IL: Human Kinetics.

Miles, P. (2000) "Hewitt danger man at Wimbledon", *The Australian*, June 19th: p. 32.

O'Sullivan, T., Hartley, J., Saunders, D., Montgomery, M., and Fiske, J. (1994) *Key concepts in communication and cultural Studies* (2nd Ed.). London: Routledge.

Pavis, P. (1998) *Dictionary of the theatre: Terms, concepts, and analysis*. Toronto: University of Toronto Press.

Schechner, R. (1988) *Performance theory*. New York: Routledge.

Scollen, R. (2000a) An Audience Reception Study of Australian Tennis Spectators (unpublished).

——— (2000b) Australian Professional Sports People Interviewed (unpublished).

Sheedy, K (2000) 'Watching the media actors', *The Weekend Australian*, June 24: p. 52.

Whiting, F. (2000) 'Big dreams for theatre', *The Sunday Mail*, June 4th: p. 86.

Whiting, H., and Masterson, D. (eds) (1974) *Readings in the aesthetics of sport*. London: Lepus Books.

THE PERSISTENCE OF VALUE:
AN OLYMPIC CASE-STUDY

Graham McFee
Chelsea School, University of Brighton

Introduction

For those with a developed interest in the nature of value, the Modern Olympic movement can seem to hold a special place[1], prefiguring modern debates about *globalisation* through the Games' trans-national intent[2] (both morally and economically) — even if only twelve or thirteen[3] teams were at the first Games, in Athens in 1896 — and through presenting a set of trans-historical, trans-national values: *the Olympic Ideal*. For central to such an Ideal (as typically characterised) are the educational potentials of the Games, as "... antidote to the evils of industrial civilisation" (MacAloon, 1981: p. 188); and especially their (assumed) impact on world peace[4]. Thus, De Coubertin[5] claimed in an often-quoted passage:

> I shall burnish a flabby and cramped youth... by sport... I shall enlarge its vision and its hearing by showing it wide horizons... historical horizons of universal history which, in engendering mutual respect, will bring about a ferment of international peace.

And, of course, such a concern is not at all undermined when those values are not actualised in the practice of particular Games. As philosophy teaches us, human frailty in respect of the implementation of values, even Olympic ones, is to be expected — that need do nothing to shake one's faith in the enduring worth and

255

the power of such values (see also below). So a simple account of the Olympic movement has Baron De Coubertin inventing — or, worse, reviving — a set of values that then do (or do not) apply to the activities within successive Games.

But a moment's reflection shows us that the matter is by no means so simple. Indeed, this picture can look down-right simplistic, for a number of familiar reasons. First, in practice, the Games have represented only *indirectly* some of the major principles articulated by De Coubertin at the Congress of 1894. From the beginning, even De Coubertin's frankly *odd* idea of what constituted an amateur[6] was contravened — the cheating British used servants in their team! Second, the *national* (hence locally political) dimension of the Games was apparent even in Athens in 1896: so that, for instance:

> A year after the Olympic Games [of 1896] were staged, Turkey, in response to an increasingly jingoistic and aggressive Greek presence in Crete, declared war.... Greek nationalism, fostered, if not initially created, by the Olympic revival, resulted in a national disaster. (Tomlinson, 1984: p. 96)

Additionally, teams were organised on broadly national lines, in contrast to the super-nationalism, or trans-nationalism, of De Coubertin's dream. But third, and most centrally here, the simple account assumes that what is, and what is not, the *persistence of a value* is (in and of itself) an uncontentious matter. Instead, the values *claimed* for successive Olympic Games are subject to what Alan Tomlinson (1989: p. 7-4) has called "a necessary arrogation": those values were seized, and made anew (or re-made), by each Games, with clear examples[7] here being the Olympic 'traditions' claimed — in the case of David Coleman's claim (in 1984) for the 'tradition' of an opening ceremony at which the host nation (!) displayed its history and culture, a tradition eight years old! How should such changes in sets of 'defining' values be understood?

One temptation must be to treat these Olympic values relativistically: to say that what is truly an Olympic value depends on the time (and perhaps place) of asking. As is well known, naive relativism is self-refuting. Might a more sophisticated version succeed? And, if so, what would it show? In particular, what would it show about the nature of (supposed) globalisation — is it necessarily a kind of value-imperialism? More generally, what is it for values to persist in a changing world?

In exemplification, I will mention briefly a case derived from Leni Riefenstahl's film of the 1936 Olympics, a case of special relevance since, first, the modern Olympics now "... live to so large an extent off television" (Hill, 1992: p. 243: see Whannel, 1992: p. 171 for the amounts) and, second, the mass-communication media are widely recognised as a primary agency for value-globalisation (Giddens, 1989: p. 542 ff.).

Preliminary clarifications?

Let us therefore begin with some preliminary clarifications in respect of the idea of value[8].

(a)   The denial of the coherence of relativism

Given that the charge of relativism is one that must be met here, to count as a relativist, one must accept the following possibility (McFee, 1992: pp. 301–309): that two people be in genuine (and not merely apparent) *disagreement*, and that both be *right* (relative to some culture, time, place or whatever). As this formulation shows, the charge of relativism might be defused either by finding no *real* dispute/disagreement, but only an apparent one (that it was or was not raining *here* made true by two different 'heres' being invoked, say) or by recognising that only one of the assertions can be true (even if we don't know which). Here, the possibility on which two claims 'pass one another by' is the important one. This formulation of relativism also brings out its connection with *truth*.

The relativist is really denying that there are universal truths: for him, any 'truth' might be asserted by one person and denied by another with both right, both speaking 'the truth' (relative to... something). So no truth can be *un-relative*: but what about the truth of relativism? If, consistently, he urges that relativism itself is not universally true, why should we believe him when he claims that it applies *here*? Indeed, what *precisely* would he then be asserting? Presumably, that there are some universal truths (since not all truth-claims behave as relativists assume): but then he is not a relativist — he accepts universal truths. While if he asserts that relativism *is* universally true, he is no relativist either. For *that* is then urged as a universal truth. (Or, at least, a lot of further argument is required to make sense of his position.) And denying *any such thing* as truth must count against the *truth* of relativism as a philosophical thesis[9]. So this position is *self-refuting*[10].

Thus relativism is not the *attractive* doctrine it at first appears, despite its obvious connection with (the virtue of) tolerance for others. But this is progress. For, having recognised such relativism as self-refuting, some other ground for tolerance must be sought.

(b)   The objectivity of value

But is *truth* the issue in respect of value? One might, say, distinguish the factual realm, province of truth, from the evaluative realm. And then my formulation of relativism, with its clear connection to truth, would be beside the point.

Such a position, advocating a separation of questions of value from those of truth, should seem suitably antiquated — and also previously refuted! So here I simply offer some remarks about the objectivity of value. By the term "objective" is meant public, shareable, open to reason — and not (necessarily) 'one right answer'. Indeed, *falsity* is the key notion here, the one that "wears the trousers"[11]. For we can identify cases of *false* value-ascriptions, even when (though) we have more difficulty with true ones. In this respect, the situation resembles that of the duck-rabbit design: some accounts can be dismissed as false (by reference to the features of the design), even though more than one is acceptable. This characteristic is fundamental to the account of objectivity for values offered here[12], for it means that remarks which appear to be contradictory may, on investigation, turn out actually not to be — any more than your claim that the design pictures a duck contradicts my claim that it pictures a rabbit.

Our conclusion, then, is that it would be a mistake to think of moral claims as not in these ways objective. Yet this is precisely what relativism is often thought to be asserting[13].

(c)   The insight of relativism

Two insights behind relativism are, first, recognition that the judgments we make are located historically, so that some can only be made with hindsight — and in two quite different ways. Thus, I may need a kind of historical percipience to assert that in such-and-such a house is presently being born the greatest physicist of the 20th century — suppose both that I am pointing to Einstein's birth-place, at his birth-time, and that Einstein is the greatest physicist of the 20th century: this judgment requires hindsight, because only the passage of time proves it true (or false). In contrast, the judgment that the creator of the theory of relativity is presently being born in the house makes no sense: the expression "theory of relativity" requires later conceptual events even to be meaningful. More than *mere* hindsight is required to assert it. The concepts which make sense of that assertion are only available to us at a certain time and place. Yet when those concepts are in place, the assertion is true; earlier persons could not deny the assertion, since to them it would make no sense. In this way, the judgments 'pass one another by': they are *incommensurable* in the strict sense of being unable to be put into one-to-one correspondence with one another[14]. So what counts as possible now (and hence as true or false) depends in part on the concepts available now — and we should not under-estimate the epistemological significance of this fact for talk of *all* possibilities (or of "a finite totality of possibilities")[15].

The second insight grows from this one since, as Feyerabend (1987: p. 272) notes, the incommensurability it highlights is a difficulty for philosophers, not for scientists. Here he is contrasting the perspective of the philosopher with that of the practitioner: for any contemporary scientist, looking back at the claims of his scientific forebears, may think them wrong (and correctly) while the detachment of the philosopher allows that these forebears' claims are *incommensurable* with those of the contemporary scientist. Applied to our context (as we will see), it will permit us to distinguish a perspective on the arrogation of value which treats it centrally in terms of change from one that treats it in terms of continuity.

(d) Understanding and the concrete

But recognition that we are ineliminably in the fish-bowl (that there is no external perspective) is only worrying if our account of reason or of truth would thereby be undermined: and why should that be? To see one way in which understanding might proceed *without* the demand for determinacy which the relativist and his absolutist opponent both accept, we need a more plausible model of the rational: John Wisdom provides a helpful account of understanding (which he urges is fundamental), one employing concrete cases, since:

> ... at the bar of reason, always the final appeal is to cases. (Wisdom,
> 1965: p. 102)

Adopting such a model brings out two points key for us: first, what counts as, for
instance, *chaste* in a certain context is arguable and often (as Putnam 1992: pp.
104–105 illustrates) arguable with those who disagree — we can still dispute the
applications of concepts learnt from concrete cases. Second, we see clearly the
place of traditions of value-making and value-explaining (with Olympism as one
such, or as participating in one?). For to begin from particular cases is to appeal
to what we know and understand, to *familiar* cases: and these derive from the
history of the concepts in question. In this vein, we recognise:

(i)   traditions as ways of articulating a relevant reason here — that is, of
        clarifying relevance — as what allows us to identify a certain claim as being
        a *reason* in the context of Olympism: as being an *Olympic reason*, as we
        might say.

(ii)   appeals to tradition as ways of *not* explaining[16]: saying that this action or
        event was traditional, or seeing it as part of some tradition, justified it.

That is, the appeal to traditions was part of both value-making and value-
explaining: to count as an *Olympic reason* is to be appropriately related to the
history of Olympism. We recognise that, as Baker and Hacker (1984: p. 4) put it:

> We cannot return the apples from the Tree of the Knowledge of History...
> Though we know the Impressionists were outrageous revolutionaries in
> the theory and practice of painting, we can no longer *see* them as
> outrageous.

But this is still to see the Impressionists as part of an on-going tradition, where
later events shape how *we* can make sense of the past. In plotting an Olympic
tradition, then, we are sketching a narrative within which certain values obtain,
values which serve to *define* our thinking as appropriate by linking it to the
Olympic Ideal. For we can understand *Olympism* only by reference to what has
happened *previously* as Olympism — although some such reference (as with
revolutionaries) proceeds through denial.

In this way, the appeal to traditions and histories is an appeal to practices worth preserving, "having the weight of... something that has flourished" (Scruton, 1980: p. 42[17]): such flourishing gives us reason to esteem them. But the justificatory force of such appeals to tradition is fragile. And Giddens (among others: see Giddens, 1994: p. 6) is noting this fragility in recording the forces that undermine such appeals to the justificatory weight of *tradition*.

In a world of increasing "detraditionalisation" (Giddens, 1994: p. 47), it makes even more sense than previously to appeal to traditions — even if, as in this case, that also involves *inventing* or *creating* such traditions. De Coubertin's original actions involved an appeal to a (supposed) classical tradition: the Greek Olympics (contrast Kidd, 1984) — one message of the opening sequence of Riefenstahl's *Olympia* (as we will see), with its evocation of a classical past and its 'geographical' argument connecting that past to the Berlin Games of 1936.

We have recognised, about value, how its objectivity is consistent both with divergence in specific contexts, and with a characterisation of values through concrete cases rather than formulae. We have recognised, too, the potential of tradition to hold such values in place, and to explain them. These points are rooted in the insights behind relativism, without thereby making us relativists. Where does that leave the arrogation of value?

Arrogation and persistence

Let us grant Tomlinson's thesis (cited earlier) that the history of the Olympic movement is a history of the "necessary arrogation" of the central values: of the Olympic Ideal, as it were. Now we ask: *is arrogation a species of persistence?* Certainly, speaking of the arrogation of certain values implies *some* sense of their persisting through that 're-making': the terms "arrogation" and "persistence" both imply a *kind* of continuity, although "arrogation" also implies some non-continuous aspects. Clearly the sort of persistence of values implied by the arrogation of those values cannot mean that all implications from a previous account of those values would carry-over into the new account: that is tautological, from the very idea of arrogation.

So is the word "arrogation" a way of describing *change*? Certainly, there must be a complex relationship here between what *persists* (enough to give some substance to the claim that it is *the same* value) and what *changes* for this to count as modification rather than replacement.

But now we introduce the question posed earlier: from whose perspective? That of the philosopher or that of the practitioner? For part of the solution here (see below) is to recognise that the practitioners may well see as *persistence* what the philosophers ("for analytical purposes"?) will treat as *change*.

In what sense is the arrogation "necessary" (Tomlinson's expression)? Well, it is not necessary *just* in the sense of responding to changing social and emotional conditions, to a changing social and emotional 'world' (although that is part of it). Rather, in the context of globalisation, we might *now* locate a further key factor — manufactured uncertainty, or the erosion of tradition (or both: see below)

We see that the passage of time is operative in at least two different ways: first, time's passage generates a number of new truths but (as we have seen, and second) there is also the development of new conceptual structures. And either of these might be treated as examples of "necessary arrogation".

Values and Olympism: Case-study part I

Some evidence for our interpretation of the historical character of value is visible, mobilized in propaganda[18]. As Cooper Graham (1986) claims, the Olympic Games of 1936 offered the German government the opportunity to achieve three propaganda aims. First, they could "impress the world with the size and the efficiency of the Games" (p. 4). Second, they "... could impress the world with the accomplishments of German athletes" (Graham, 1986: p. 4). (To a certain degree at least they were successful there, with Germany winning 33 gold medals, 26 silvers and 30 bronzes — far and away the highest total: Wallechinsky, 1992). Third, the Nazis could demonstrate "... that they were full of good will towards the whole world and wanted only to be friends" (Graham, 1986: p. 5). We do not think — and subsequent history has confirmed this — that the last aim reflected the truth. Whatever the success of these first two aims, we believe, as the result of further reflections, that any appearance of good will was some kind of sham. Yet, once a state has in place both sport and some propaganda aims, it becomes easy to imagine how the media might be employed to achieve such aims[19]. If one wanted to impress the world in these two ways and demonstrate good will, how better to do it than by showing a major sporting event to the world? How better to do that than with a suitable media event? Once we see what the propaganda aims might be, we see how the media might well satisfy them.

As Richard Mandell (1971: p. xiii) puts it, "the world drew lessons from the Berlin Olympics", in particular the lesson about good will. "The athletes harmonized at the Olympic village, as planned" (Mandell, 1971: p. xiii), he says. Again, that is in contrast to the remark from the American basketball team at the Barcelona Olympics — in explanation of their not living in the Olympic village — that Custer didn't have lunch with the Indians. On the contrary, in the Berlin Games such an effort for harmonization *was* seen as important. Mandell describes that outcome as being "planned": with the clarity of vision that hindsight can bring, we may see that the planning in this case was not that done fifty years before by Pierre De Coubertin, but rather that done by the National Socialists. No doubt, the 1936 Games were an important event and the world drew lessons from them. But what lessons were those and how did they work? Here is Mandell's version: "... much of the success of the 1936 Olympics was due to the pursuit by the National Socialists [the Nazis] of supremacy in mass pageantry" (Mandell, 1971: p. x). For Mandell, these points come together when he says, "The impression dominant among us as to what took place at the 1936 Games has been largely due to Leni Riefenstahl's film, *Olympia*" (Mandell, 1971: p. xiv). If that is broadly right, Riefenstahl's film deserves close attention since, according to Mandell, it is the source of what everybody, except for those who were there, thought went on at the 1936 Games.

That is to say, we can recognise the moral situation in/through the distorted situation. Thus, we might *learn* about the one situation by studying the other (compare McFee, 2000). So here we have the distortion of what *truly* follows from Olympism. But the claim has the appropriate structure: it should be seen as a *failed* appeal to the Olympic Ideal.

The arrogation of value-formulations

There are two main ways in which there is a mis-match between Olympic ideals/ values and Olympic practice. The first turns on differences between what is *claimed* and what actions are *performed*, explained as we normally explain such matters: in terms of human frailty, weakness of the will, local politics, occasionally conspiracy, and the like. The second — implicit in the idea of the arrogation of value — turns on interpretations of what value *amounts* to.

Before turning to the second point, it is worth saying a little more on the first. For it might seem that the values are necessarily unimportant if they are not in the forefront of practice. But, when we reply by appeal to human frailty here, we might usefully distinguish three cases. Saying a little more about each clarifies our point here.

First, let it be granted that the process for the selection of a host city for the Games has been corrupt, at least in the last few years — with Salt Lake City a clear example (Jennings and Sambrook, 2000: pp. 19–48). Still, did this really disadvantage the athletes/competitors? For, if it did not, perhaps the values of the sporting event itself were not (much) compromised. Surely Salt Lake City would offer good facilities, at least as good as those of its rivals. So that, while money that might have gone into sport is 'diverted' into the capacious pockets of the IOC (let it be granted), no damage was done to the sport itself — the damage was to the context, not to the competition! A similar case might even subsume the re-scheduling of races at the 1988 Games in Seoul to coincide with prime-time television in the USA (Jennings, 1996: p. 72): here (one might think) the sport was not *really* hurt — at least all the competitors were similarly positioned. While this sort of corruption is to be regretted (and, ideally, eliminated), it does not tarnish the Olympic *values* as such but merely their implementation in practice.

A second case, at the other extreme, might be provided by the boxing finals in Seoul: if even half of what Andrew Jennings (1996: pp. 79–92; Jennings and Sambrook, 2000: pp. 205–208, 212–216) describes is correct, these events involved unfair judging — a situation that continues in amateur boxing's world championships (Jennings and Sambrook, 2000: pp. 253–262). Here the corruption operates in the sporting practices themselves. Again, this is corruption to be regretted (and, ideally, eliminated) but now the task is much more pressing: any virtues that accrue to *sporting* contests cannot accrue to these — they are *not* sporting (in the other sense of the word) because not fair. (Notice, too, that this case is of systematic and deliberate lack of fairness, not merely occasional error.)

The issue of drug-taking might provide a third case, somewhat intermediate. In part, and like the first case, this is simply a place where Olympic rhetoric (as when Samaranch says that future Olympics will be clean; and that, "The message is very clear. This is a new fight against doping": quoted Sullivan, 2000: p. 55) does not match the practice — proscribed drugs are taken at the Olympics. An Olympic movement genuine committed to the elimination of such activities would not act as this one has (Jennings, 1996: pp. 232–249; 298–299; Jennings and Sambrook, 2000: pp. 290–306): but, again, that is corrupt practice only. But (and resembling our second case) there is an unfairness here too: some athletes will be punished for drug-taking while, for others, the Prince de Merode will (unfortunately?!) shred the documents necessary to identify their 'B' samples — both in Seoul 1988 (Jennings, 1996: pp. 241–243) and, perhaps, Atlanta 1996 (Mackay, 1996: p. 2)! And, in all cases, these were samples taken towards the end of the Games: that is, likely to be those of finalists, medal-winners and the like. If these athletes *were* guilty (and, afterall, their 'A' samples were ruled positive), they had 'got away with it'. Here too, though, the solution seems to call for a more vigilant, and perhaps differently motivated[20], IOC.

Whatever one makes of the *detail* of such cases, they indicate different obligations which (one might think) have not been met. And some, by running counter to Olympic values, are quite fundamental. But the manner in every case suggests something remediable by a more scrupulous Committee, more consistent in the understanding and application of its own rules, and more attentive to the demands of natural justice. (Compare Jennings and Sambrook 2000: p. 321–322.)

As suggested above, the *second* area of mismatch between Olympic ideals and practice— implicit in the idea of the arrogation of value — turns on interpretations of what value *amounts* to. Some cases turn on the different perspectives on value-change (the perspectives of philosopher or of practitioner). But there are claims on the Olympic Ideal not readily understood in this way. Thus, Avery Brundage (later President of the International Olympic Committee) asserted[21]:

> Certain Jews must now understand that they cannot use these Games as a weapon against the Nazi.

This is the site of (potential?) arrogation. Yet what are we to make of it?

Notice that Brundage was here speaking about a (potential) political abuse of the Games: he was speaking the 'language' of Olympism, even though misinformed about the power situation. This is better regarded as the arrogation of *value-formulations*, rather than of the values themselves[22].

If I could wave a magic wand, I would ban such value-formulations (say, of an Olympic Ideal): they give the illusion of a clarity not possible — they seem to imply that one can always determine, from the formulation, whether or nor a value is being implemented. And this is manifestly not true. One case here concerns codes of professional conduct (see McNamee, 1995): their successive refinement *seems* rooted in the idea that a perfect formulation is possible — that is, a formulation that deals with all conceivable cases. But this implies exactly the kind of complete, 'exact fit' definition, the possibility of which I deny.

For, first, the unrefined code probably deals with all/most actual cases — and a concern with *all possibilities* is unwarranted[23]. But, second, one cannot *in principle* deal with *all* possibilities, since (as we saw: in [c] above) the idea of a finite totality of possibilities makes no sense. Just as we do not know what to make of a bird which explodes or quotes Virginia Woolf (Austin, 1970: p. 88[24]), so there are surely cases where — faced with a value-formulation — we do not know what to say; and nor should we. For these are not cases our concepts confront: they are equivalent to the forever-hidden contradictions in mathematics which (as Wittgenstein notes[25]) are irrelevant to the practice of mathematics.

Of course, there is no magic wand: but the point is clear enough — that value-formulations are always open to arrogation, in changing circumstances. We might well expect it: certainly, we should be unsurprised to find it. And this is a site for contestation, where you urge that this is a legitimate way to 'read' the value-formulation and I deny that it is. The debate between us might be very complicated: for instance, it might turn on the way each understands the changing economic or historical situation. But that debate takes place in an arena circumscribed by our previous value-commitments: by the traditions of value-making (for instance, through art?) and value-explaining we share (to the extent that we do). These are ways of referring to what, elsewhere, we have spoken of as *traditions*.

As is widely recognised, for values in respect of public events such as the Olympic Games, the media represent one side of the public version of such arguments: mass-communication events[26] embody the selection of a collection of value-commitments, and hence play a part in getting us to understand or to adopt[27] a certain conception of value — working by exemplification rather than the offering of (putative) definitions or accounts (in line with ideas from Wisdom, 1965).

Here we reach our first substantial conclusion, summarised by pointing out that the arrogation of value is a species of persistence (for the practitioner) — though what persists is sometimes little more than the value-formulation — but also a species of change, from the philosopher's perspective. And by recognising that arrogations of value are often no more than arrogations of value-formulation. So there are two overlapping explanations: value-arrogation does consist both:

(a)   of treating change as continuity because there is *formulation*-continuity, and

(b)   of treating *as change* what is, from the practitioner's perspective, continuity (or vice versa).

In addition, there is the question of *tradition*: but in our case study we shall see (one aspect of) of the re-invention of tradition: the case of the Olympic flame.

Values and Olympism: Case study part II

Our concrete case here, Riefenstahl's film *Olympia*, must be seen as a presentation[28] (or actualisation) of certain values — not to be confused with either Riefenstahl's own values, those of her (Nazi) sponsors, or those the audience 'get' from the film: rather, we must look to the values *in* the film, while recognising that these constituencies (and their values) had a role in its making and/or reception. For our purposes[29], at least five features of the film are of special relevance:

(a)   Riefenstahl's use of the torch relay as a way of making a connection to the values of (an imaginary) Classical Greece [a path retraced by Hitler's tanks, without the message of 'brotherly love'...?]

(b)   The bucolic atmosphere presented, especially in the 'Olympic village' sequences that open the second part (also a characteristic of her explicitly propaganda film of the 1934 rally, *Triumph of the Will*).

(c)   Relatedly, the friendliness in the Olympic village: but what does 'brotherly love' amount to here? Consider Mandell's remark (quoted earlier) which might suggest that the friendliness was designed, rather than real. (See also *Triumph of the Will* for a picture of friendliness.)

(d)   The portrayal of German triumphs at the Games: but, first, the Germans did do extremely well (as noted earlier) and, second, there were at least five different versions of the film (Downing, 1992: p. 9), each 'featuring' a different country's athletes.

We might recognise some of the traditional rhetoric of the Olympic movement here. Never-the-less, these points are broadly consonant with a film directed at the propaganda aims identified by Cooper Graham (quoted earlier). The final point is not.

(e) A concern with the 'physicality' of athletes including (especially) Jesse Owens: through the 'lingering looks' of Owens (and Metcalfe), Riefenstahl "... had shown too much interest in the black American athletes" (Downing, 1992: p. 44) for Goebbels' liking[30].

Equally, the 'Festival of Beauty' idea involves concern neither with the strong ideological points nor with narrative — for example, the men's diving events have no commentary: we are to enjoy the spectacle, not worry about winners and losers (Downing, 1992: pp. 82–3).

We see here a (partial) *aestheticization* of the event[31] — and perhaps some connections with *art*[32], although that is not an issue I will address in this paper.

The Riefenstahl film *Olympia* offers *one* way to see the Games of 1936, a way embodying certain values which (within the limits of "necessary arrogation") it would not be false to call "Olympic Values": and it offers them to the world — it is a mass-communication/mass-media event. That way of viewing the Games can (although it need not) be passed on to later generations: it can become a *traditional* way of conceptualising what happened then, but also of conceptualising a success/failure of the Olympic Ideal. In this way, its status as a mass-communication event serves to install it as having a scope wider than merely that provided by the sporting occasion itself — indeed, it has a world-wide scope, at least potentially[33].

Globalisation and 'manufactured uncertainty'

Giddens' account of globalisation emphasises the loss of the explanatory force of tradition. For Giddens (1994: p. 5):

A post-traditional social order is not one where tradition disappears — far from it. It is one in which tradition changes status. Traditions have to explain themselves, to become open to interrogation or discourse.

As Giddens urges, we should see "... [u]npredictability, manufactured uncertainty, fragmentation" as "... one side of the coin of a globalising order" (Giddens, 1994: p. 253). So manufactured uncertainty is a problem for empowering understanding (emancipation) in respect of more than just the behaviour of trans-national companies. The activities of trans-national companies have a *kind* of direction, given (one hopes) by their directors; but manufactured uncertainty is not created on purpose, even when it is the result of economically-motivated decisions.

Giddens' point here, though, is that manufactured uncertainty can pose ".. the question of generating active trust" (Giddens, 1994: p. 93) — not merely the rejection of sceptical argument, but more positively a need to replace the appeal to tradition with a critique of tradition.

Manufactured uncertainty might be thought to be solely an epistemological concern, reflecting nothing but our ignorance of the current situation: that, as it were, it does not address conceptual — hence, philosophical — matters. But much turns on both the degree to which we conceive the scope of philosophy in terms of the confronting of logical possibilities and on our understanding of what is (and what is not) logically possible, given a plausible account of logical possibility, one that accepts the range and depth of our conceptual connections (see below).

An over-arching question is, what counts as a new value? Although Riefenstahl's film occasionally implies simple-minded answers — unsurprising in a film with even a partial commitment to propaganda — we may gain insights from its simplification. For instance, at the beginning of the film, the geographical appeal to a Classical pedigree — (apparently[34]) following the torch from Greece to Berlin — may strike us as ludicrous; as the commission of the genetic fallacy at least! But it alerts us to what would need to be done if such a claim were to be sustainable. More realistically, it illustrates how appeal to 'Olympic tradition' now stands in need of justification: it is not itself a justification. And here Riefenstahl's aestheticism (especially in Part Two of

Olympia) might seem rather modern, the mass-communication instantiation of the relevant values.

Consider, also, two factors suggesting that there might be value-imperialism in the Olympics: the first that, realistically, current[35] successful host cities must be (a) first-world, (b) rich, (c) democratic (Hill, 1992: p. 241: p. 247): the other, with which it must combine, the origin of the values at issue as (roughly) Western European thought — for example, through the Baron's *influences*, as well as his influence!

Of course, certain values may have arrived in certain locations under colonialism (hence imperialistically?). But if they are appropriate values for the activities, that is just an irrelevance. Yet to show the values' appropriateness is to make connections from them:

- *to sport* — itself a Western European construction — and especially to the rules and aims of sports;

- *to the social and political system which the values support.*

We have seen that the *origin* of values is not, strictly speaking, relevant: the question is better formulated by asking if there are contexts where these values have a place — and, for *some* at least, the answer must be "yes".

Consider here the idea of amateurism which had, for De Coubertin, two purposes: both to support the educational aim of the Olympics ('athletics for its own sake') and to ensure equality — which has in practice meant that some get sponsorship, while others lack the training-shoes that come with sponsorship; even ignoring the differences in basic facilities in different nation-states! The *values* might seem enduring, even if the ways of actualising them were flawed.

Philosophical intervention

A central unclarity, then, concerns the place of claims for Olympic traditions, given in the media by (for instance) David Coleman — having seen the importance of claiming *tradition*, it is important not to make the claim wildly... and to recognise the various ways in which "arrogations" can take place. We are here disputing with theorists of value and/or Olympism, where this is understood as a *value*-commitment.

In a sense, I am responding both to those who deny that there are *abiding* Olympic values and to those who think that the invention of so-called 'traditions' *automatically* gives them a place in the Olympic Ideal, although not by denying what either group assert. Rather, in line with Ramsey's Maxim[36], my strategy has been to deny a thesis about the persistence of value shared by both my opponents (although merely assumed, rather than stated or argued-for): the thesis that persistence requires constant application of trans-historical value-formulations. My opponents differ as to whether there *is* such constant application, but agree that *if* there were, there would be persistence of value: and if not, not. And hence one side, failing to find such a formulation, infers that there are not abiding/ persisting values. Equally, those that take appeal to (newly created) Olympic traditions to *assure* the persistence of values do so *because* they take such traditions to constitute just these trans-historical value-formulations.

But what this thesis assumes (namely, that for values to persist there must be some trans-historical value-formulation that persists) is neither necessary nor sufficient for such persistence. Formulations may be subject to arrogation; and hence *amount* to something different. Equally, values might be thought to persist (from the *practitioners'* perspective) even though (from the *philosophers'* perspective) there was no trans-historical formulation. My point here is that, given these contexts, value-persistence is contestable, debatable.

Further, my opponents assume that values were *only* mutable under changes in *social* situation: hence one side, finding no such social changes, infers that there *cannot* be value-changes; while the other side, finding the value-changes, infers that there *must* be social changes at work here. But *manufactured uncertainty* blurs the distinction between the social and 'natural' worlds in ways that defeat such simplistic inferences; and we have recognised Giddens' connection of *manufactured uncertainty* with globalisation[37].

Conclusion

A *big* question: what is it for certain values to persist? (What needs to be 'the same' for it to count as *the same value*?) Clearly, using the same words to describe/characterise them will not do — that is a recipe for the arrogation of value-formulations! It is also a big problem for (supposedly) timeless statements of values: for example, a statement of the Olympic Ideal. And the possibility of manufactured uncertainty and of the post-traditional conception of society in globalisation exacerbate such difficulties, by highlighting 'new' forms of change of 'initial conditions'.

I am suggesting that the key lies in finding the explanation of those values within a tradition of value-making and value-understanding: and that, in these terms, the "necessary arrogations" of which Tomlinson spoke really constitute a way of values being maintained or preserved through time. Of course, I am not arguing with those who deny this — so I might easily have called this paper, "The Transmutation of Value". But the dispute between us would be a purely verbal one: we agree about the historical character of value, and about its clear appearance in the history of Olympism.

Notes

1   Of course, this is only true for those who take Olympism to be a set of values, rather than (say) principles of other kinds.
2   See Hill, 1992: p. 122: "The Olympic movement sees itself as universal. To extend is to be more successful...".
3   On the discrepancy, see Mandell 1981: p. 110.
4   Some indicative quotations, taken from MacAloon 1981, since he translates them all, and also since his references are not always complete:

(a) physical activity is to be judged "... from the moral and social point of view" (MacAloon, 1981: p. 119);

(b) the Olympic Movement is "... a potent if indirect factor in securing universal peace" (MacAloon, 1981: p. 261);

(c) Article VIII of the Congress of 1894 justifies the Olympic Games "... from the athletic, moral and international standpoint" (MacAloon, 1981: p. 167);

(d) De Coubertin famously stressed the idea that, for Olympism, "... the important thing... is not winning but taking part. Just as in life, the aim is not to conquer but to struggle well" (MacAloon, 1981: p. 5);

(e) "Healthy democracy, wise and peaceful internationalism, will penetrate the new stadium and preserve within it the cult of disinterestedness and honour which will enable athletics to help in the tasks of moral education and social peace as well as of muscular development" (MacAloon, 1981: pp. 188–189).

5   The full quotation is:

> I shall burnish a flabby and cramped youth, its body and its character, by sport, its risks and even its excesses. I shall enlarge its vision and its hearing by showing it wide horizons, heavenly, planetary, historical horizons of universal history which, in engendering mutual respect, will bring about a ferment of international peace. All this is to be for everyone, with no discrimination on account of birth, caste, wealth, situation or occupation.

It is quoted in many places: for example, Tomlinson, 1984: quote: p. 97. (Tomlinson goes on to comment: "As long as you were amateur or male!").

6   MacAloon (1981: p. 166) calls these "British definitions of amateurism" which "... excluded not only those who played for money, but also those who made their living through manual labour".

7   Another example might be the way in which the organisers of the Los Angeles Games of 1984 adopted the IOC position on sponsorship; and read it as permitting franchising of, say, the torch-relay and the Olympic ring-symbol: see Hill, 1992: pp. 165–168; also Gruneau 1984.

8   Any one of these could take a whole paper, and therefore are merely stated or sketched here.

9   Conceptual relativism is fashionably contrasted with moral or value relativism here: the differences do not strike me as fundamental — moral obligations are denied to be universal in the way that truths are, and with the same self-refuting outcome.

10   Our argumentative strategy against the relativist is simply to say, "relativism is not true-for-me" and, since he accepts no truth *other than* truth-for-me (or someone else), he has no reply. Anyone who, faced with this remark, has a desire to debate — that is, to contest the remark — is not a relativist: but, if a thinker is so easily discomforted, we might worry about the value of his theses. [As recognised (McFee, 1994: p. 3; and contrast McFee, 1992: p. 303), this is a remark Putnam (1988: p. 288) attributes to Alan Garfinkel.]

11   See Austin, 1962: p. 15; also: pp. 70–71 for a discussion of "trouser-words".

12   From discussion of this topic, see Bambrough, 1979. Two further fundamental points: first, the need to compare like with like If a moral sceptic reminds us that

there are those who reject moral claims: "... we can offer him in exchange the Flat Earth Society" (Bambrough, 1979: p. 18). Second, Bambrough rightly insists on the *situatedness* of truths here: that, as he puts it, "Circumstances objectively alter cases" (Bambrough, 1979: p. 33). He makes the point clearly with an example: "the relativity of the fit of clothes to wearer" (Bambrough, 1979: p. 33). But there is nothing relativistic here. Rather, the point is that no abstract specification can be given — in Bambrough's case, what it means for the suit to fit is always for it to fit *you* or to fit *me*: that is all.

13 As I have urged elsewhere (McFee, 1998: pp. 3–18, esp. p. 4), in spite of Hume's claims to the contrary, it is ethical or moral questions where the *specifics* of the activity are most relevant: in particular, in reference to the place of ethical issues/ debates in the field of sport.

14 Thus Kuhn, 1976: pp. 190–191: "In applying the term 'incommensurability' to theories, I'd intended only to insist that there was no common language within which both could be fully expressed and which could therefore be used in a point-by-point comparison between them". Also, with Feyerabend (1987: p. 272), I take incommensurability to be a rare occurrence (see McFee, 1992: p. 306).

15 Such a *fishes'-eye view* conception of truth and understanding is the position dismissed as relativism by his critics when it appears in the writings of Peter Winch (see, for example, Winch, 1987: where he identifies and responds to some such critics); and embraced as relativism (at least sometimes) by Paul Feyerabend. I am not much bothered by what the view is *called*. Instead, my point would be to defend *that* view against the criticism that it is just the trivial, self-refuting relativism.

16 For example, Giddens (1994: p. 6) version of traditions in a pre-globalisation society: "The point about traditions is that you don't really have to justify them: they contain their own truth, a ritual truth, asserted as correct by the believer".

17 As Scruton (1980: p. 42) continues, such practices must "engage the loyalty of their participants" (as Olympism clearly has), and "must point to something durable, something which survives and gives meaning to the acts that emerge from it". [These passages are also quoted by Giddens, 1994: p. 45.]

18 What follows draws on McFee and Tomlinson, 1999: pp. 86–106; see also McFee and Tomlinson, 1995: pp. 229–234.

[19] Compare, for example, the papers in Wenner, 1998.

[20] Jennings, 1996: p. 237 quotes from *Olympic Review* 1981: p. 158: " '... the Olympic Games in Moscow had been the most "pure". Proof of this is the fact that not one case of doping was registered.' Although this comment (attributed to Prince de Merode) was later withdrawn, it indicates a certain attitude to evidence: there was no drug taking because none was found! We know that this is just what sponsors want to hear!" (Jennings and Sambrook, 2000: p. 292).

[21] Quoted in "Chariots for Hire", *Diverse Reports*, Channel Four Television, 1984.

[22] There is an important connection here to the idea of *definiteness* in philosophy: see Baker and Hacker, 1980: pp. 315–384.

[23] I have explored some of these issues in 'A Nasty Accident With One's Flies', my Inaugural Lecture as Professor of Philosophy at the University of Brighton, 7th May 1996.

[24] See also Austin, 1970: p. 84: "Enough is enough: it doesn't mean everything".

[25] See Diamond, 1976: pp. 209ff, 217ff; Wittgenstein, 1978: pp. 213ff, 375 ff.

[26] Thompson, 1988 especially: pp. 364–366 where four characteristics of mass communication (in contrast with 'standard' communication) are identified.

[27] Power relations are here viewed as hegemonic, in terms of the negotiation of power, rather than (solely) its imposition from above (see Hargreaves, 1992: pp. 263–280). For the very idea of negotiation implies at least some power to both sides of the negotiation-relation.

[28] Compare Hart-Davis' remark that Riefenstahl managed "... to record a triumph of propaganda" (Hart-Davis, 1986: p. 242).

[29] Some of the material in this section draws on McFee and Tomlinson, 1999.

[30] A fuller exposition would expand this point, showing both its relation to, and its deviation from, Aryan Ideals of Beauty.

[31] I consider some relations between *aestheticisation* and *fictionalisation* in McFee, 1986 especially: pp. 164–169.

[32] Some discussion of the points here is included in McFee and Tomlinson, 1999.

[33] As Cooper Graham (1986: p. 209) records, "*Olympia* did not get a general showing in England until after the war".

[34] As Downing (1992: pp. 53–54) notes, Riefenstahl had to restage the event for her cameras.

35 For 1984 Games, the only bidding-city (apart from Los Angeles) was Tehran —
     and it dropped out! (Hill, 1992: p. 158). But since then the Games have been
     attractive.

36 The term is Renford Bambrough's: see Bambrough, 1969: p. 10: "... wherever
     there is a violent and persistent philosophical dispute there is likely to be a false
     assumption shared by both parties".

37 Moreover, explicit philosophical conclusions are implicit in thinking that only one
     perspective represented truth, and about the epistemology of finite totalities: these
     are matters fraught with potential to mislead, which have misled some writers!
     In addition, it is a philosophical thesis, contested here, that (crude) relativism and
     absolutism about values exhaust the alternatives. And this idea too is widely and
     uncritically assumed by writers on philosophy, and elsewhere.

References

Austin, J. L. (1962) *Sense and sensibilia.* Oxford: Oxford University Press.

———— (1970) *Philosophical papers* (Second Edition). Oxford: Oxford University
     Press.

Baker, G. and Hacker, P. (1980) *Wittgenstein: Understanding and meaning. Volume 1
     of an analytical commentary on the Philosophical Investigations.* Oxford:
     Blackwell.

Baker G. and Hacker, P. (1984) *Frege: Logical excavations.* Oxford: Blackwell.

Bambrough, R. (1969) *Reason, truth and God.* London: Methuen.

———— (1979) *Moral scepticism and moral knowledge.* London: Routledge, Kegan
     Paul.

Diamond, C. (1976) [ed.] *Wittgenstein's lectures on the foundations of mathematics.*
     Hassocks, Sussex: Harvester Press.

Downing, T. (1992) *Olympia.* London: British Film Institute.

Feyerabend, P. K. (1987) *Farewell to reason.* London: Verso.

Giddens, A. (1989) *Sociology.* Cambridge: Polity Press, 1989

———— (1994) *Beyond left and right: The future of radical politics.* Cambridge:
     Polity Press.

Graham, C. (1986) *Leni Riefenstahl and Olympia.* Metuchen, NJ: Scarecrow Press.

Gruneau, R. (1984) 'Commercialism and the modern Olympics', in A. Tomlinson and G. Whannel (eds) *Five-ring circus: Money, power and politics at the Olympic games*. London: Pluto, pp. 3–15.

Hargreaves, J. (1992) 'Revisiting the hegemony thesis', in J. Sugden and C. Knox (eds) *Leisure in the 1990s: Rolling back the welfare state* (LSA Publication No. 46). Eastbourne: Leisure Studies Association, pp. 263–280.

Hart-Davis, R. (1986) *Hitler's Olympics*. New York: Harper-Row.

Hill, C. (1992) *Olympic politics*. Manchester: Manchester University Press.

Jennings, A. (1996) *The new lords of the rings: Olympic corruption and how to buy gold medals*. London: Simon and Schuster.

Jennings, A. and Sambrook, C. (2000) *The great Olympic swindle: When the world wanted its Games back.* London: Simon and Schuster.

Kidd, B. (1984) 'The myth of the ancient games', in A. Tomlinson and G. Whannel (eds) *Five-ring circus: Money, power and politics at the Olympic games*. London: Pluto, pp. 71–83.

Kuhn, T. S. (1976) 'Theory-change as structure change: comments on the Sneed formalism', *Erkenntnis* Vol. 10: pp. 179–199.

MacAloon, J. (1981) *This great symbol: Pierre de Coubertin and the origins of the modern Olympics*. Chicago: University of Chicago Press.

McFee, G. (1992) 'Goal of the month: fact or fiction?' *Leisure Studies* Vol. 5, No. 2, May: pp. 159–174.

———— (1992) *Understanding dance*. London: Routledge.

———— (1994) *The concept of dance education*. London: Routledge.

———— (1998) 'Are there philosophical issues in respect of sport [other than ethical ones]?', in M. McNamee and J. Parry (eds) *Ethics and sport*. London: Routledge, pp. 3–18.

———— (2000) 'Spoiling: An indirect reflection of sport's moral imperative?', in T. Tännjö and C. Tamburrini (eds) *Values in sport: Elitism, nationalism, gender equality and the scientific manufacture of winners*. London: Routledge, pp. 172–182.

McFee, G. and Tomlinson, A. (1995) 'Notes on bodily culture and sport ideology: the case of Leni Riefenstahl', in C. Pigeassou (ed) *Entre Tradition et Modernite: Le Sport*. Montellier: IRS, pp. 229–234.

———— (1999) 'Rienfenstahl's *Olympia*: Ideology and aesthetics in the shaping of the aryan athletic body', *International Journal of the History of Sport* Vol. 16, No. 2: pp. 86–106.

Mackay, D. (1996) 'Olympic cheats go unnamed', *The Observer*, 17 November: p. 2.

McNamee, M. (1995) 'Theoretical limitations in codes of ethical conduct', in G. McFee, W., Murphy, and G. Whannel (eds) *Leisure cultures: Values, genders, lifestyles* (LSA Publication No. 54). Eastbourne: Leisure Studies Association, pp. 145–157.

Mandell, R. (1971) *The Nazi Olympics*. London: Souvenir Press.

——— (1981) *The first modern Olympics*. New York: University of California Press.

Putnam, H. (1988) *Realism and reason*. Cambridge: Cambridge University Press.

——— (1992) *Renewing philosophy*. Cambridge, MA: Harvard University Press.

Scruton, R. (1980) *The Meaning of conservatism*. London: Macmillan.

Sullivan, R. [with Song, S.] (2000) 'Are drugs winning the Games?', *Time* Vol. 156, No. 11: pp. 54–56.

Thompson, J. B. (1988) 'Mass communication and modern culture: Contribution to a critical theory of ideology' *Sociology* Vol. 22 No 3: pp. 359–383.

Tomlinson, A. (1984) 'De Coubertin and the modern Olympics', in A. Tomlinson and G. Whannel (eds) *Five-ring circus: money, power and politics at the Olympic Games*. London: Pluto, pp. 84–97; reprinted in Tomlinson, 1999: pp. 197–215.

——— (1989) 'Representation, ideology and the Olympic Games: A reading of the opening and closing ceremonies of the 1984 Los Angeles Olympic Games', in R. Jackson and T. McPhail (eds) *The Olympic movement and the mass media: Past, present and future issues*. Calgary: Hurford Enterprises, pp. 7.3–7.11; reprinted in Tomlinson, 1999: pp. 217–231.

——— (1999) *The game's up: Essays in the cultural analysis of sport, leisure and popular culture*. Aldershot: Arena.

Wallechinsky, D. (1992) *The complete book of the Olympics*. London: Aurum Press.

Wenner, L. (1998) [ed.] *MediaSport*. London: Routledge.

Whannel, G. (1992) *Fields in vision: Television sport and cultural transformation*. London: Routledge.

Winch, P. (1987) *Trying to make sense*. Oxford: Blackwell, pp. 194–207.

Wisdom, J. (1965) *Paradox and discovery*. Oxford: Blackwell.

Wittgenstein, L. (1978) *Remarks on the foundations of mathematics* (3rd Edition). Oxford: Blackwell.

Index

A

achievement sport 86, 90
Ackerman, R. 116
Action Man 146
Adidas 50
aestheticism 268, 269, 275
aesthetics 244–250, 268
aggression 26, 28
Ali, Muhammad 223
Allison, L. 4
amateur/ism 12, 15, 101–
    122, 193, 256, 270
Andrews, D. 144, 148,
    149, 164
Angle, R. 252
Archetti, E. 238
Argentina 48–50
Arnold, Thomas 92
arrogation 256, 259, 261–
    262, 263–267, 271, 272
athleticism 146, 149, 192,
    194, 197
Atkinson, P. 113
Austin, J. L. 266, 273, 275
Australian Institute of Sport
    214
Australian Olympic Com-
    mittee (AOC) 73

B

Bachrach. P. and Baratz, M.
    87
Baker, G. and Hacker, P.
    260, 275
Ball, Zoe 124
Bambrough, R. 274, 276

Barbie 145, 146, 148, 161
Barcelona 52
BAYER AG 195
BBC 143, 153
beach volleyball 151, 152,
    156, 157, 158, 159–162,
    163
beauty 249
Beck, U. 97–98
Beckenbauer, Franz 190
Becker, Boris 190, 196
Beckett, A. 67–68
Bennett, S. 243
Berger, P. 86
Bertagnolio, R. 251
Biddiss, M. 8
Birch, Ric 215, 219
Black, T. and Pape, A. 63
Blain, N., Boyle, R. and
    O'Donnell, H. 141
body culture 86, 96
body experience 86
boot money 112
Booth, D. 4, 10
Bose, M. 13
Bouchard, Claude 97
Boulmerka, Hassiba 147
Bourdieu, P. 86–87, 88
Bredemeier, B. 168, 170,
    171, 174, 177, 183
Brennan, S. 152
Breuer, Grit 74
bribes 235
Brimson, D. 124, 125, 137
British Academy of Sport
    89
British Empire 104

Brockett, O. 233
Brohm, J-M. 4
Brown, W. M. 105
Brundage, Avery 265
Burnett, C. 13
Burt, J. 178
Butcher, R.
    and Schneider, A.
    102, 109

C

Calhoun, D. 242
Cantelon, H. and Letters,
    M. 225
Carlos, John 212
Carrington, B. 139
Carter, Jimmy 212
Cashmore, E. 145, 187
Central Council for Recrea-
    tion and Training 198
Chalip, L. 14
Chamberlain, Helen 124
cheat/ing 40, 63, 79, 105,
    108, 171, 172, 174, 232,
    236
Chinese Swimming team
    75
Chu, D. 91
civil society 201, 202
coaches 173, 174, 177,
    178, 181, 182
Coakley, J. 187
Coca-Cola 143
Cockman, M. 169
Coddington, A. 124, 125,
    131
Coe, S. et al. 187

279

Coe, Sebastian *212*
Coleman, David *256, 270*
Collins, M. *94*
Commonwealth Games *220*
community sport *85*
competition *28, 60, 79, 233*
competitive sport *194*
competitiveness *26, 28–30, 29*
Conniff, R. *145, 146, 147, 148, 161*
Cooke, Steve *211, 216*
Coolican, H. *126*
De Coubertin, Pierre *2, 8, 13, 90, 91–92, 92, 93, 94, 144, 192, 198, 213, 214, 223, 255, 261, 263, 270, 272*
Council of Europe *12, 59*
Court of Arbitration in Sport (CAS) *74, 164*
Crook, S., Pakulski, J. and Waters, M. *123, 124, 138*
curriculum structure *180*

D

Daddario, G. *146*
D'Agostino, F. *19*
Daimler-Benz AG *196*
Davies, Jonathan *118*
Davis Cup *229–254*
Dead White Males 234
deep structures *88*
Delbridge, A. *238, 245, 249*
Denham, B. E. *58*
Denk, H. and Hecker, G. *197*

Derr, Silke *74*
detraditionalisation *261*
Diamond, C. *275*
Diem, Carl *198, 199*
Dixon, N. *26, 38–43, 45, 51*
Doll-Tepper, G. *10, 11*
Donnelly, P. *4, 12, 65*
doping *55–82, 97*
Downing, T. *268, 276*
Dream Team *15*
Drewe, S. *167, 168, 171, 172, 173, 174, 175, 176*
drugs *38, 40, 55–82*
Dubin report *67*
duelling *197*
Duncan, M. *146, 151*
Duncan, M. and Messner, M. *157*
Dunning, E. *4*
Dunning, E., Murphy, P. and Williams, J. *125*
Dworkin, R. *15*
Dyson, B. *169*

E

Eady, J. *95*
East Germany *66, 193, 195*
Ebersol, Dick *209*
Edgar, A. and Sedgwick, P. *142*
education *2–3, 47, 72–74, 75, 78, 92, 270*
Eichberg, H. *86, 90, 94, 95*
Einstein, Albert *259*
elite *28–29*
Elliott, R. K. *246, 247, 248–249, 250*
emergent nations *44, 45*
Engels, F. *191*

equal opportunities *133*
equality *11, 270*
ethnography *113, 116, 126*
Ewald, Manfred *66*
excellence *85, 89, 90, 93, 96, 102, 103, 108, 117*
external goods *104–105, 110, 118*

F

fairness / fair play *15, 57, 58, 79, 167, 172, 173, 174, 176, 178*
fan/s *30, 33, 34, 36, 123–140, 171, 241, 244*
feminine/femininity *15, 132, 135, 136, 160*
feminisation *124–126*
Ferrier, Ian *111*
Festina *62*
Feyerabend, P. K. *259, 274*
FIFA *36, 105, 190, 194, 195, 196, 213*
FINA *70, 164*
Fischer-Lichte, E. *239, 243*
fitness sport *86, 94*
Fleming, S. *116*
formalism *19*
Foster, S. *241*
Fotheringham, R. *236, 252*
Foucault, M. *157*
foul *174, 175*
Freeman, Cathy *208, 219, 220*
Fürstenberg, F. *190*

G

Garcia Ferrando, M. and Hargreaves, J. *223*

Gardiner, E. N. *103–104*
gaze *149–159, 160, 163*
German Athletic Federation (DLV) *74*
Germany *44, 187–206*
Gibson, J. H. *117*
Giddens, A. *257, 261, 268, 269, 271, 274*
globalisation *256, 257, 262, 268–270, 271*
Gomberg, P. *26, 30, 31, 38, 39, 42, 52*
Gonçalves, G. et al. *172, 175, 176, 178*
Gough, R. *183*
Graham, C. *262, 268, 275*
Graham, G. *181*
Gramsci, A. *201–203*
Greenberg, C. *5*
Groves, S. and Laws, C. *168, 169, 171, 173, 176*
Gruneau, R. *96, 273*
Gunnell, Sally *151, 153, 162*
Guttmann, A. *52*
gymnastics *152, 158, 159–162*

H

Haan, N. *170*
Hall, S. *123, 132*
Hammersley, M. *113*
Hampshire, S. *7*
Hargreaves, J. *17, 18, 159, 199, 201, 223, 275*
Hargreaves, J. A. *137*
Harris, Iestyn *118*
Hart-Davis, R. *275*
Harvie, S. *13*
hegemony *150, 201–203*
Hellison, D. *179, 180*

hero/es *32, 35, 36*
Herodotus *103*
Hewitt, Lleyton *247–249*
Hill, C. *257, 270, 272, 273, 276*
Hill, Grant *158*
Hill, M. *87*
Hillsborough *124*
Hitler *187, 199, 203, 267*
Hitler Youth *33*
Hoberman, J. *2, 8, 11, 61, 62, 69, 70, 97*
Hoeppner, Manfred *66*
Hoggart, S. *124*
Hollander, W. *13*
Holmes, Kelly *151, 152*
Holt, R. *104*
hooligans/ism *30, 40, 51*
Horne, J. *8*
Houlihan, B. *59, 60, 67, 69, 177, 178, 181, 187*
Howard, John *224*
Huizinga, J. *233*

I

identification *15*
impartiality *42*
Impoco, J. *148*
incommensurability *259, 274*
individualism *27*
informed consent *116*
injury *161*
insider role *114, 116*
institutionalisation *105*
instrumental rationality *98*
integrity *108*
internal goods *104–105, 107, 110*
International Amateur Athletic Federation (IAAF) *67, 74*

International Anti-Doping Arrangement (IADA) *71, 75*
International Drugs in Sport Summit *76, 77, 78*
International Olympic Committee (IOC) *1, 8–9, 10, 12, 64, 65, 66, 67, 69, 73, 75, 77, 78, 148, 203, 207, 208–209, 210, 212, 220, 221, 222, 223, 264, 265, 273*
International Organisation for Standardisation (IS *71*
International Rugby Board *111*
International Swimming Federation (FINA) *70, 164*
internationalism *17*
Interntional Amateur Athletics Federation (IAAF) *105*
IOC Medical Code *59*
IOC Medical Commission *57, 70*
Ireland, Northern *13*
Italian Olympic Federation (CONI) *67*

J

Jackson, S. J. *58*
Jahn, Friedrich Ludwig *189*
James, Clive *208, 222, 224*
Jennings, A. *1, 57, 64, 68, 80, 222, 264, 265, 275*
jingoism *38, 41*
Jobling, I. *9, 10*

Johann and Junker *188*
Johansson, Ingemar "Ingo"
35
Johnson, Ben *58, 73*
Joiner, Florence Griffith
58
Jones, C. *183*
justice *15*

K

Kane, M. and Greendorfer,
S. *146*
Kane, Pat *207*
Katwala, S. *1*
Keating, J. W. *107*
Kidd, B. *2, 8, 261*
Kimmage, Paul *56, 61*
Klausen, A. *241, 246*
Knight, Michael *209, 221*
Koehn, D. *110*
König, E. *61, 63*
Korbut, Olga *161*
Krabbe, Katrin *74*
Krüger, A. *198, 200*
Kuhn, A. *150*
Kuhn, T. S. *274*

L

La Costa, L. *12*
ladette culture *123–140*
Lakoff, G. and Johnson, M.
250
Larfoui, Mustapha *70*
larrikinism *218, 224*
Lasch, C. *25, 26*
Leavy, J. *162*
Lee, M. *167, 168, 169,
170–171, 172, 175*
Lenskyj, H. *156, 225*
Lentell, B. *95*

Lewis, Denise *151, 152*
Lindsey, E. *125, 136*
Lines, G. *142, 163*
lived experience *125,
126–140, 138*
Ljungvist, A. *57*
Lombardi, V. *3*
Lowe, B. *230, 231, 237,
242, 243, 244, 245, 246,
248, 249, 250*
Lucas, J. *91*
Luhmann, Niklas *188*
Lukes, S. *87–88, 95, 96*
Lusetich, R. *236, 241*
Lyotard, J.-F. *6*

M

Maanika, Kaarlo *66*
MacAloon, J. *14, 91, 223,
255, 272, 273*
Macbeth *242*
MacIntyre, A. *38, 104,
105, 106, 107*
Mackay, D. *225, 265*
Major, John *88*
male dominance *162*
Mandela, N. *3*
Mandell, R. *104, 223, 224,
263, 267, 272*
Maradona, Diego *35*
Martin, B. *183*
Martin, J. and Sauter, W.
240
Marx, K. *26, 191, 202*
Marxist *28, 87, 200*
match fixing *236*
McCaffrey, General Barry
69
McColgan, Liz *151, 152*
McConachie-Smith, J. *183*

McDonald, I. *88, 95*
McDonald's *143*
McEnroe, John *239*
McFee, G. *6, 15, 224, 257,
263, 273, 274, 275*
McGillivray, G. *224*
McGuire, Mark *58*
McIntosh, P. *92*
McNamee, M. *110, 266*
McPeak, Holly *160*
McPherson, B. *241, 242,
243, 244*
media *16, 141–166, 177,
209, 266*
Meier, K. *20*
Mendoza, J. and
Andersen, R. *71*
de Merode, Prince
Alexandre *57, 70, 265,
275*
metaphor *250–252*
Metheny, E. *92*
methodology *113–117,
126, 163*
Mikosza, J. and Phillips, M.
147
Milburn, P. *56*
Miles, P. *247*
Miller, S. *177, 178, 179,
180*
Mingxia, Fu *158*
Moceanu, Dominique *161,
162*
modernity *138*
Moore , S. *123, 125, 131–
132, 136, 137*
Moorhouse, H. F. *125*
Moragas, M. *225*
moral development *168*
moral education *167–186*

Morgan, W. J. *20, 43, 44, 45, 102, 106, 107, 108, 109, 110, 117*
muscular christianity *197*
Muslim athletes *147*

N

narrative *236–237*
Nathanson, S. *39, 41*
National Curriculum *183*
National Curriculum for Physical Education *180*
national identity *32, 43*
National Lottery *83, 89*
nationalism *25–53*
Nazi *33, 187, 198, 199, 203, 224, 262, 263, 265, 267*
NBC *148, 149, 152, 209, 220, 222*
neo-Olympism *85–100*
Newcombe, John *251*
Norris, C. *116*

O

objectivity *258*
Ogle, S. *13*
Olympia 215, 261, 263, 267–268, 270, 275
Olympic Ceremonies *9–10, 215–219*
Olympic Charter *8, 9*
Olympic Games *30, 64, 65, 93, 141–166, 193, 194, 199, 255–278, 266*
   Amsterdam, 1906 *198*
   Athens, 1896 *213, 256*
   Athens, 2004 *221*

Atlanta, 1996 *38, 74, 141, 143, 145, 148, 149, 149–159, 150, 157, 211, 213, 214, 265*
Barcelona, 1992 *15, 145, 154, 209, 213, 214*
Berlin, 1936 *187– 206, 188, 195, 203, 213, 215, 261, 262*
Calgary, 1988 (Winter) *12*
Los Angeles, 1932 *199*
Los Angeles, 1984 *67, 212–213, 273, 276*
Melbourne, 1956 *211*
Mexico City, 1968 *212*
Montreal, 1976 *212*
Moscow, 1980 *67, 212, 275*
Munich, 1972 *161, 212*
Seoul, 1988 *58, 213, 264, 265*
Stockholm, 1912 *198*
Sydney, 2000 *1, 12, 56, 57, 71, 84, 207– 227, 215–219*
Tokyo, 1964 *214*
Olympic Games 2004 bid *195*
Olympic Games planned for 1916 *189, 193*
Olympic Ideal *15, 255, 260, 261, 263, 265, 266, 268, 272*

Olympic Movement Anti-Doping Code *57, 60*
Olympic torch *10, 143, 215, 219, 269, 273*
Olympism *64, 90, 91–95, 94, 96, 223, 260, 262– 263, 265, 267–268, 270, 272*
O'Sullivan, Sonia *156*
O'Sullivan, T. *232, 237*
Ottey, Merlene *152*
Ovett, Steve *212*
Owens, Jesse *187, 268*

P

Paddick, R. *11*
Parkin, Delvene *220*
participant-observation *16, 127*
particularist *25, 37*
Paterson, Floyd *35*
patriarchy *123, 141–166, 150*
patriotism *31, 38–39, 42, 96*
Pavis, P. *237*
Philippoussis, Mark *239*
Physical Education *167– 186, 194*
Pilger, J. *224*
Pilz, G. *171, 173, 174, 175, 176, 177, 178*
Pink Dandelion, B. *113, 114, 115, 116*
Pleket, H. W. *103–104*
Podkopayeva, Lilia *154*
policy *86–88*
Pollack, J. *148, 149*
postmodernism *123–140*
Pound, Dick *70, 71, 210, 221*

poverty *47, 49*
power *86–88*
professional *28, 29, 63,*
   106, 107, 109–111, 117,
   120, 142
professional wrestling
   236, 239, 241
professionalisation *111–*
   113
Prokop, U. *200*
Prolympism *12, 65, 66*
Pryce, K. *116*
public school *92, 197, 213*
Pugh, Vernon *111*
Puijk, R. *225*
Putnam, H. *260, 273*

Q

Quinn Patton, M. *127*

R

Ramsey's Maxim *271*
Reagan, Ronald *212*
Real, M. *144*
reasoning *7, 170*
Redhead, S. *124, 125, 131*
Reece, Gabrielle *159, 160*
Rees, C. *168, 176, 177*
referee *173*
relativism *257–258, 258–*
   259, 273, 276
Riefenstahl, Leni *215,*
   224, 257, 261, 263,
   267–268, 275
Rigauer, B. *4, 200*
Rittner, Karin *200*
ritual/s *34, 48, 105, 191*
The Rocky Horror Picture
   Show 244

Rorty, R. *17*
Rowe, D. *150*
Rugby League *101, 252*
Rugby Union *101–122,*
   233
rule/s *4, 174, 175, 232,*
   237, 245
Rütten, A. *201*

S

Sage, G. *201*
Salazar, Alberto *72, 74*
Salt Lake City *210, 264*
Samaranch, Juan Antonio
   9, 57, 68, 69, 70, 207,
   208, 212, 220, 221, 264
Sambrook, C. *1, 80, 222,*
   264, 265, 275
Sansone, D. *102*
Schechner, R. *230, 232,*
   234, 237, 240, 241, 242
Schiffer, Claudia *190*
Schilly, Otto *190*
Schmitt, P. *76*
Schröder, Gerhard *190,*
   195, 196
Scollen, R. *229, 235, 239,*
   243, 244, 246, 248
Scraton, S. *123, 124, 132,*
   136, 138
Scruton, R. *261, 274*
Segrave, J. O. *9, 65, 91,*
   92
Senn, A. *64*
sexual identity *136*
Sheedy, K. *251*
Shields, D. *168, 170, 174,*
   177, 183
Silver, M. *159, 160*

Simpson, Tom *56*
Simson, V. and Jennings, A.
   64, 222
Skerrett, Kelvin *119*
Skillen, T. *2*
The Skin of Our Teeth 234
Skulberg, Per Kristian *69*
Slee, John *224*
Smith, Michelle *151, 154–*
   155, 164
Smith, Tommie *212*
Social Democratic Party
   (SPD) *192, 199*
social exclusion *85*
sociological imagination
   113–114
South Africa *13, 57, 195*
sponsorship *270, 273*
Sport England *13, 84, 85*
Sport for All *4, 5, 12, 88,*
   94, 95, 194
Sport: Raising the Game
   88
Sports Council *73, 83, 88,*
   89, 198
sportsmanship *167, 178,*
   241
Sproat, Iain *88*
Steinbeck *240, 245*
Stevenson, D. *224*
Strugg, Kerrie *153, 154,*
   156, 162
struggle *87*
subjectivism/ity *18*
Sugden, J. *13*
Sugden, J. and Bairner, A.
   201
Sugden, J. and
   Tomlinson, A. *222*

Sullivan, R. *264*
Sutherland, Joan *252*
Sweden *46–47*
Swoopes, Sheryl *158*
symbols/symbolism *34, 35, 191, 273*

T

Talbot, M. *95*
Tamburrini, C. *51, 60, 63*
Tännsjö, T. *26, 30, 32, 33, 34, 35*
Tarasti, Lauri *74*
Taylor, Lord Justice *124*
theatrical event *229–254*
Theodoulides, A. and Armour, K. *180*
theory of relativity *259*
Thompson, Daley *212*
Thompson, J. *141*
Thompson, J. B. *275*
time *231, 238, 259*
Tomlinson, A. *92, 223, 224, 225, 256, 261, 262, 272, 273, 275*
Tomlinson, A. and Whannel, G. *144*
Tour de France *56, 57, 61, 62*
Tout, Mark *73*
tradition/s *260, 261, 266, 268, 269, 270, 271, 274*
Triumph of the Will *215, 267*
trouser-words *273*
truth *6, 17–18, 257–258*
Tulu, Derartu *147*
Turnen *189, 190, 191, 192*
TVM *62*

U

UK Sport *89*
UNESCO *10, 11*
universalism *25, 39*

V

Vallerand, R. *169*
value-formulation *263–267, 271*
value/s *3, 75, 107, 117, 162, 238, 255–278*
van Vucht Tijssen, L. *124, 132*
van Zoonen, L. *141, 150*
Vanstone, Amanda *70*
Verbruggen, Hein *70, 72*
Vinnais, G. *200*
violence *29, 38–43*
Viren, Lasse *66*
virtue/s *172, 173, 241*
Voy, R. *80*

W

Waddington, I. *62, 77, 80*
Wadler, G. *59, 60, 72*
Waldmeir, P. *13*
Wall, Ron *224*
Wallechinsky, D. *223, 262*
Walsh, D. and Follain, J. *67*
Watford Football Club *126–140*
Weaver, C. *123, 131*
Weidman, L. *146, 147*
welfare *27, 42*
Wenner, L. *275*
West Ham Football Club *138*

Whannel, G. *124, 257*
Whiting, F. *252*
Whiting, H. and Masterson, D. *230, 246, 247, 248, 250*
whole child *182*
Wigmore, S. and Tuxill, C. *176*
Williams, A. *183*
Williams, G. *113*
Williamson, Alison *156*
Winch, P. *274*
Wisdom, J. *259–260, 266*
Wittgenstein, L. *266, 275*
Woodhouse, J. *125*
Woolf, Virginia *19, 266*
World Anti-Doping Agency (WADA) *68–71, 74, 75, 77, 78, 80*
World Conference on Doping in Sport *68*
World Cup (soccer) *36, 44, 46, 49, 124, 155, 190, 194, 195, 196, 221*
World Tennis Association (WTA) *251*
World Wrestling Federation *236, 241*
Wright Mills, C. *86*

Y

Yesalis, C. and Cowart, V. *80*
Young, C. *223*
Young, D. C. *103*
Yuan, Yuan *75*

Z

Zakus, D. H. *64*